The *ESSENTIAL* Guide to

GREAT SAND DUNES

NATIONAL PARK

& PRESERVE

Charlie and Diane Winger

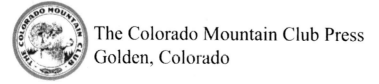

The Colorado Mountain Club Press
Golden, Colorado

Published by The Colorado Mountain Club Press. Founded in 1912, the Colorado Mountain Club is the largest outdoor recreation, education and conservation organization in the Rocky Mountains. Look for our books at your favorite book seller or contact us at: 710 10th Street, Suite 200, Golden, CO 80401, (303) 996-2743, Email address: *cmcpress@cmc.org*, Website: *http://www.cmc.org/cmc*

Managing Editor for CMC Press: *Terry Root.*
Graphics Design and Maps: *Terry Root and Steve Meyers.*
Proofing: *Joyce Carson and Linda Grey.*
Front cover photo: *by Charlie and Diane Winger.*
Front cover inset photo and title page photo: *by Aaron Locander.*
Front cover photo of Great Sand Dunes Tiger Beetle: *by Phyllis M. Pineda.*
Back cover photos: *by Charlie and Diane Winger.*
For a complete list of credits for photographs in this book see page 238.
Copyright 2003 by Colorado Mountain Club Press.
Manufactured in China

The Essential Guide to Great Sand Dunes National Park and Preserve
by Charlie and Diane Winger
Library of Congress Control Number: 2003104695
ISBN # 0-9724413-1-X

We gratefully acknowledge the financial support of the people of Colorado through the Scientific and Cultural Facilities District of greater metropolitan Denver, for our publishing activities.

SCFD
Scientific & Cultural Facilities District
Making It Possible.

WARNING! Although there has been a major effort to make the descriptions in this book as accurate as possible, some discrepancies may exist between the text and the lay of the land. In addition, there may be differences in the way certain individuals interpret the descriptions beyond that intended. Therefore, common sense and care should be taken when following any of the routes or directions described in this book. This book is not intended to be instructional in nature but rather a guide for visitors to Great Sand Dunes National Park and Preserve who already have the requisite training, experience and knowledge. Proper clothing and equipment are essential. Failure to have the necessary knowledge, equipment and conditioning may subject visitors to Great Sand Dunes National Park and Preserve to physical danger, injury or death. Some routes described in this book have changed and others will change; hazards described may have expanded and new hazards may have formed since the book's publication. Each user is responsible and liable for all costs which may be incurred if a rescue is necessary. The State of Colorado assumes the cost of rescuing anyone with a valid Colorado fishing license, hunting license or hiking certificate.

A NOTE TO OUR READERS: PARK OR MONUMENT?

In 2000, the Great Sand Dunes National Park and Preserve Act was passed by Congress, authorizing expansion of the existing National Monument into a National Park and Preserve, almost four times its original size. Roughly 42,000 acres of National Forest Wilderness Area were immediately transferred to NPS management, and renamed the Great Sand Dunes National Preserve.

The final hurdle before the "Monument" becomes a "Park" is the purchase of the Baca Ranch — nearly 100,000 acres of land lying west and northwest of the Dunes. Much of the former ranch is expected to lie at the center of the proposed Baca National Wildlife Refuge. A portion will also be transferred to the Park and Preserve for expansion of those units. The inclusion of this land makes it possible for a single entity to manage and protect an entire natural system.

As of date of publication of *The Essential Guide to Great Sand Dunes National Park and Preserve* (summer of 2003), the final transfer of the Baca Ranch had not yet been completed. According to congressional sources, it is expected that federal funding will be secured in 2003, with final dedication of our nation's newest National Park likely by the end of the year.

The mission of Great Sand Dunes National Park and Preserve is to preserve and protect the Great Sand Dunes and their associated geologic, biologic, and cultural resources, watersheds, and wilderness values; to promote scientific knowledge; to provide opportunities for visitor understanding, enjoyment, and stewardship; and to ensure the perpetuation of the entire ecosystem for the enjoyment of future generations.

Surge flow along Medano Creek

We extend our thanks to many people associated with Great Sand Dunes for taking the time to meet with us, share their knowledge and love of this wonderful place, and review several of the chapters. They were a tremendous help with this book. Thank you to these staff members at Great Sand Dunes National Park and Preserve:

Steve Chaney, Superintendent
Jim Bowman, Chief Ranger
Fred Bunch, Chief of Resource Management
Kris Illenberger, Western National Parks Association
Libbie Landreth, Interpretive Ranger
Patrick Myers, Interpretive Ranger
Phyllis Pineda, Biologist
Carol Sperling, Chief of Interpretation
Andrew Valdez, Geologist

We especially wish to acknowledge the patience, enthusiasm, and help *beyond the call of duty* that we received from three rangers in particular. We bombarded Libbie, Patrick, and Andrew with questions every time we saw them, and emailed questions to them in between visits. They always took time to talk with us, to track down pictures we requested, to dig up literature, and much more. We also thank these scientists for taking the time to talk with us:

Hobey Dixon, President, *Friends of the Dunes*; Professor of Biology, retired
Pegi Jodri, Archaeologist
Marilyn Martorano, Archaeologist

Finally, we wish to thank the following people for their insightful help in editing this book, accompanying us on research trips, and other assistance:

Dan Bereck
Dave Cooper
Burt Falk
Ginni Greer
Randy Murphy
George Vandersluis
Horace Winger
Laura Zaruba
CMC Press volunteers
Board members of *Friends of the Dunes*

Dedicated to:
Vern Lunsford
Friend, Mountaineer
1953-2003

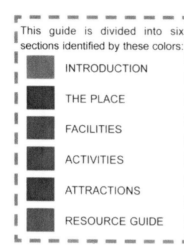

This guide is divided into six sections identified by these colors:

INTRODUCTION

THE PLACE

FACILITIES

ACTIVITIES

ATTRACTIONS

RESOURCE GUIDE

TABLE OF CONTENTS

14 . . . . . .Map of Great Sand Dunes National Park and Preserve

16 . . . . Foreword: From Pronghorns to Pikas
by Patrick Myers, Interpretive Ranger, National Park Service

18 . . . . .Sandy, the Great Sand Dunes Tiger Beetle

INTRODUCTION

21 . . . . .USING THIS GUIDE

22 . . . . .Book Organization

22 . . . . .The Place
22 . . . . .Facilities
23 . . . . .Activities
25 . . . . .Attractions
25 . . . . .Resource Guide

26 . . . . Safety Considerations

26 . . . . .Heat
26 . . . . .Sun
26 . . . . .Eye Protection
27 . . . . .Wind
27 . . . . .Lightning
27 . . . . .Altitude
27 . . . . .Exertion
28 . . . . .Dehydration
28 . . . . .Safe Drinking Water
28 . . . . .Clothing
29 . . . . .Footware
29 . . . . .Pets
29 . . . . .Wildlife Encounters

30 . . . . Backcountry Ethics

32 . . . . .FRIENDS OF THE DUNES

THE PLACE

LOCATION 35
How to Get There 35
Climate and Weather 36

NATURAL HISTORY 38
Eolian Geology - It's All About the Wind 39
Unique Dunes 40
Not All Dunes Are Alike 41
Movement of Dunes 43
Minerals 44
Lightning on the Dunes 45
Water 46
Plants 48
Fire! 51
Animals 52
Birds 53
Fish 54
Insects 55

CULTURAL HISTORY 56
First People 57
Native Americans 58
Culturally Peeled Trees & Wickiups 59
Spanish Conquistadors 60
Zebulon Pike's Expedition .60
Permanent Settlers 62
The Railroads 63
The Toll Road to Montville 64
The Frenchman, Ulysses Herard 65
Preserving a Natural Wonder 66
Great Sand Dunes National Monument 66
Creating a National Park and Preserve 67
Origin of Place Names 68

FACILITIES

71 . . . . .PARK FACILITIES

72 . . . . .Visitor Center

73 . . . . .Map of Park Facilities

74 . . . . .Services Within the Park

74 . . . . .Restrooms
74 . . . . .Drinking Water and Beverages
74 . . . . .Showers
74 . . . . .Telephones
75 . . . . .Picnic Areas
76 . . . . .Campground

77 . . . . .Emergencies

78 . . . . .LOCAL FACILITIES

79 . . . . .Services Outside the Park

79 . . . . .Showers
79 . . . . .Laundry
79 . . . . .Internet
79 . . . . .Public Transportation
79 . . . . .Rental Vehicles

80 . . . . .Campgrounds

80 .Campgrounds Outside the Park
81 . . . . .Campgrounds Near Alamosa
81 . . . . .Campgrounds Near Blanca/Fort Garland
81 .Campgrounds Near Hooper/Crestone

82 . . . . .Lodging

82 . . . . .Lodging Outside the Park
83 . . . . .Lodging in Alamosa
84 . . . . .Lodging in Blanca/Fort Garland
84 .Lodging in Moffat/Crestone Area

85 . . . . .Restaurants and Groceries

85 . . . . .Restaurants & Groceries Outside the Park
86 . . . . .Restaurants & Groceries in Alamosa
87 . . . . .Map of Alamosa
88 . . . . .Restaurants & Groceries in Blanca/Fort Garland
89 . . . . .Restaurants & Groceries in Crestone

ACTIVITIES

THINGS TO DO 91

Backcountry and Wilderness Camping 92

Camping in the Dunes 93
Designated Backcountry Sites 94
Wilderness Camping and Backpacking 98
Medano Pass Road Corridor Camping 99

Birdwatching 100

Wildlife Refuges 101

Driving 4WD Roads 103

Map of Medano Pass Primitive Road 105
Other Types of Vehicles 106

Dune Skiing, Boarding, Sledding, Rolling 107

Horseback Riding and Pack Animals 108

Places to Ride 108
Parking Trailers 109
Camping With Horses 109
Encountering Horses on the Trail 109
General Guidelines for Pack Animals 110

Hunting and Fishing 111

Hunting in the Preserve 111
Fishing in the Park and Preserve 111

Mountain Biking 112

Medano Pass Primitive Road 112
San Luis Lakes State Park 113
Zapata Falls Recreation Area 113
The Rainbow Trail 114

Park Organized Activities 115

For Kids 115

Photography 116

Tips for Photographing at the Dunes 117

Watching Wildlife 118

120 . . . . .HIKING

122 . . . . Hikes in the Park: From Visitor Center

122 . . . . .Visitor Center Interpretive Trail
123 . . . . .Montville-Visitor Center Trail
124 . . . . Revelation Point (Little Baldy)
127 . . . . .Carbonate Mountain Via Revelation Point

130 . . . . .Hikes in the Park: From Dunes Parking Lot

130 . . . . .Exploring the Dunes
133 . . . . .Escape Dunes/Ghost Forest to Castle Creek

136 . . .Hikes in the Park: From Piñon Flats Campground

136 . . . . .Dunes Trail/Piñon Flats Trail
136 . . . .Sand Ramp Trail to Point of No Return and/or Dunes Overlook

140 . . . . .Hikes in the Park: From Point of No Return

140 . . . . .Sand Pit Trail
141 . . . . .Sand Ramp Trail to Sand Creek Trailhead

145 . . . . . .Hikes in the Park: From Sand Creek Trailhead

145 . . . . .Sand Ramp Trail to Sand Creek Campsite

148 . . . . . . .Hikes in the Park: From Montville Trailhead

148 . . . . .Montville Nature Trail
149 . . . . .Wellington Ditch Trail
150 . . . . .Mosca Pass Trail
152 . . . . .Mosca Pass to Carbonate Summit

154 . . . . Eastern Access Hikes: The 3Ms

155 . . . . Eastern Access Hikes: From Mosca Pass

156 . . . . Eastern Access Hikes: From Medano Pass

157 . . . . .Medano Lake Trail
158 . . . . .Mount Herard Trail

159 . . . . Eastern Access Hikes: From Music Pass TH

160 . . . . .Music Pass Trail
161 . . . . .Lower Sand Creek Lake Trail
162 . . . . .Upper Sand Creek Lake Trail

HIKING (continued)

Eastern Access Hikes: From Music Pass Road 163

Rainbow Trail to Crystal Falls 164
Rainbow Trail /Marble Mountain Trail to Marble Cave 165
Rainbow Trail /Marble Mountain Trail to Marble Mountain 169
Rainbow Tr. /Marble Mountain Direct Tr. to Marble Mountain 170

Western Access Hikes 172

Cottonwood Creek Trail 172
Cottonwood Lake Trail 173
Sand Creek Trail 174
Little Sand Creek Lakes Trail 175

Hikes in Zapata Falls Recreation Area 176

Zapata Falls Trail 177
South Zapata Lake Trail 178

CLIMBING 182

Climbs in the Park and Preserve 184

Milwaukee Peak 185
Pico Asilado 186
Tijeras Peak 187
Cleveland Peak & Unnamed Peaks 187

Climbs South of the Park and Preserve 188

Blanca Peak 188
Ellingwood Point 189
Little Bear Peak 190

Climbs North of the Park and Preserve 192

Crestone Needle & Crestone Peak 192
Kit Carson Peak 193
Kit Carson Peak: The Prow 194

ATTRACTIONS

VALLEY ATTRACTIONS 199

Near the Park 199

San Luis Lakes State Park 200

How to Get There 201
Camping 201

VALLEY ADVENTURES (continued)

202 ....Medano-Zapata Ranch

203 ....Attractions in Alamosa

204 ....Alamosa National Wildlife Refuge

205 ....Colorado Alligator Farm

206 ....Attractions Near Fort Garland/Blanca

207 ....Attractions Near Crestone/Moffat

207 ....Hot Springs

208 ....VALLEY EVENTS

208 ....Ongoing Events

210 ....Calendar of Events

RESOURCE GUIDE

217 ....INFORMATION CHARTS
217 ....Mileage Guide to Medano Pass Primitive Road
218 ....Hikes By Destination
219 ....Hikes By Difficulty
220 ....Hikes By Distance
221 ....Hikes By Duration

222 ....Additional Reading

224 ....Organizations

225 ....Equipment List

226 ....GPS Use

227 ....Suggested Trail Snacks

228 ....INDEX
238 ....Meet the Authors

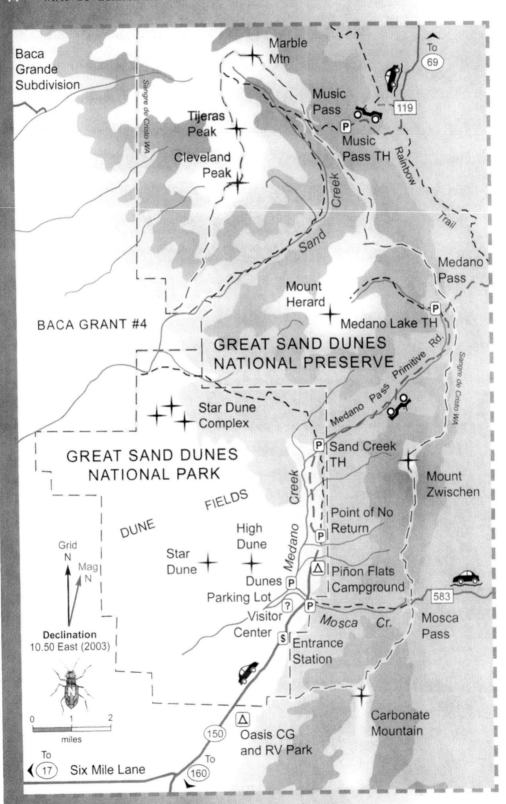

SYMBOLS USED ON MAPS IN THIS GUIDE:

—(150)—	Paved road (State or Federal HWY)
—[580]—	Paved road (County or FSR)
————	Paved or graded gravel road
– – – – –	Unpaved, ungraded road
— — — —	Primary trail
· · · · · · · · · ·	Secondary trail or bushwack
— – — – —	Land management boundary
∼∼∼	Stream or river
∼ – ∼ –	Intermittent stream or river
▬	Lake, pond or tarn
‿⁀	Mountain pass
✛	Mountain summit
P	Parking lot or trailhead
?	Visitor center
$	Entrance station
🛆	Picnic area
△	Developed campsite
▲	Basecamp
📷	Point of interest
⬭	City or townsite
⬙	Piped water
WC	Restroom
C	Road crossing stream
♿	Wheelchair accessible

MAP LEGEND

ELEVATION TINTS:

The maps in this guide are tinted by the colors shown below, to indicate the approximate elevation above sea level in feet. Tinted contour intervals are 1,500 feet apart and range from a low of 7,500' above sea level to a maximum of over 14,000'.

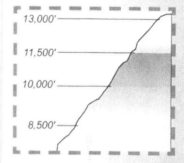

ABBREVIATIONS USED:

The maps in this guide use the following abbreviations:

CO (Colorado highway)
CR (County road)
FSR (Forest Service road)
FST (Forest Service trail)
Rd. (road)
Cr. (creek)
CG (campground)

USGS 7.5 MIN. QUADS:

FROM
PRONGHORNS TO PIKAS

The Great Sand Dunes with the Sangre de Cristo Mountains behind

by Patrick Myers
Interpretive Ranger, National Park Service

Mountain bighorn sheep walking on sand dunes? Tall, long-legged silver and red cranes spreading their giant wings as they land in wetlands beside Kangaroo rats digging in the sandy shore? Thickly furred marmots sauntering across the chilly tundra, gazing down at a sea of warm sand below?

Nowhere else in North America do alpine tundra, tall forests of evergreen and aspen, massive desert dunes, spacious grasslands, and verdant wetlands meet so dramatically in one park of unparalleled natural diversity. The newly expanded Great Sand Dunes National Monument and Preserve protects the whole geological and biological system of the Great Sand Dunes, from alpine snowfields where the park's streams begin their journey, to wetlands west of the dunes where these waters collect into lush pools teeming with life. On that journey from snowfields to sand dunes, these streams pass by a stunning variety of wildlife — wolverines to wood ducks, and elk to egrets.

Medano Creek and Sand Creek start in the spring as snowfields on 13,000' peaks, melting into alpine lakes situated at timberline. Bighorn sheep and elk graze on grassy slopes near the frigid waters. Snow buttercups and pasqueflowers push through the warming snow. Pikas (small short-eared members of the rabbit family), marmots (resembling a large woodchuck with a heavy fur coat), and ptarmigan (chicken-like bird which only lives above timberline) search among the rock and snow for new green shoots, while a large menacing wolverine watches with interest.

As the icy water cascades from the lakes, it enters shady ancient forests of pine, spruce and fir. Golden eagles and peregrine falcons nest in cliffs among the trees. Black bears forage along the stream's edges, hoping to capture a cutthroat trout, while beavers gnaw aspens to strengthen their new dams. On the damp, sun-dappled forest floor grow a plethora of flowers including blue chiming bells, golden banner, and delicate pink fairy slippers. As mule deer graze in nearby meadows, a mountain lion slowly slinks forward before bursting into the air, claws spread in anticipation of food for herself and her cubs.

Ponderosa and pinyon pines grow in fragrant stands on the lower slopes of the Sangre de Cristo Mountains. From there the streams suddenly crash into the massive dunes, cutting the eastern and northern edges of the dunefield, recycling sand from east back to west. The water begins to gather into regular pulses or surges as it flows around the dunes. Aspens give way to cottonwood groves lining the waterway, providing shelter for brilliant red and yellow western tanagers, hummingbirds, and mountain bluebirds. Bobcats, foxes and coyotes prowl the creeks. In the dunes, six species of insects found nowhere else in the world, including the metallic green and ivory Great Sand Dunes tiger beetle, survive extremes of heat and cold, while feasting on hot-sand-fried bugs. Kangaroo rats leap five feet in the air to avoid the various predators that venture into the dunes at night.

At the western edge of the dunes, the visible streams begin to wane and disappear into the sand. The sand is now free again to blow eastward back into the dunefield, and recycling is complete. The high dunes give way to low dunes and grasslands. With no obstacles in their path, pronghorn can run at speeds of over 50 miles per hour across the wide-open expanse. Badgers, weasels, prairie dogs and Black-tailed jackrabbits dig the earth to make homes beneath the sod. On the hot mid-day surface of the sandy grasslands, tiny dinosaur-like short-horned lizards do bobbing pushups to cool off and impress potential mates.

The stream water, seemingly gone, resurfaces as springs and wetlands among the grassy sandhills on the west side of Great Sand Dunes. Avocets, sandhill cranes, and the rare white-faced ibis call and feed among lush cattails and rushes. Amphibians find an oasis too: yellow and black tiger salamanders snap at moths while leopard frogs and spadefoot toads croak and joust in a noisy romantic display.

Medano and Sand Creeks' journeys through so many of North America's ecosystems — tundra, subalpine evergreen and aspen forest, ponderosa pine groves, pinyon-juniper woodlands, cottowood riparian areas, dunes, grasslands and wetlands — now take place within an area managed by the National Park Service, protected for all future generations to enjoy and study. At Great Sand Dunes National Monument and Preserve, the opportunity to see wildlife from these starkly contrasting ecosystems — sometimes in a single view — is yet another reason why this unique park is one of national and international significance.

Re-printed courtesy of NPS

SANDY

THE GREAT SAND DUNES TIGER BEETLE

WHOA THERE! Watch where you're walking: you almost stepped on me! Hey, I'm **Sandy** and I'm a Tiger Beetle. And not just any old Tiger, but a *Great Sand Dunes* **Tiger Beetle!** I'm found nowhere else on earth. Because I'm so special, I've been picked as the *unofficial* symbol of this special place, the Great Sand Dunes. And I'm also your **official guide** for this book. Look for me to pop up every once in a while, as you explore the pages of this guide, with tips and advice. As you might imagine, I know this place pretty well, so folks often ask me a lot of questions. Hey, that's cool, that's what I'm here for! I'll share with you some of the most frequently asked ones:

Q: Can I walk out onto the dunes?
A: Absolutely! When you drive into the Park, look for the first left turn after passing the Visitor Center. Turn toward the dunes, and drive to the Dunes · Parking Lot. This is the quickest access point to hike out onto the dunes.

Q: Can I take my dog onto the dunes?
A: Yes, but you must keep your dog on a leash at all times, and you'll need to clean up after them if they *do their thing* while on the dunes. Remember that the sand can become extremely hot on a sunny day, so take care that your doggie's feet don't get burned out there. And don't forget to bring along plenty of water for your pooch and for yourself.

Q: How tall are the dunes? What is the elevation of the tallest dune?

A: The tallest dune visible from the Visitor Center is named **High Dune**, and rises about 650' above the valley floor to an elevation of 8,691' (this can vary slightly over time). Another prominent dune you may have noticed further west from High Dune, as you drove into the Park, is called **Star Dune**, and it rises about 750' above the valley floor. However, because the valley floor isn't perfectly flat, Star Dune's elevation is 8,617' — a bit lower than High Dune.

Q: How long does it take to hike to the top of High Dune?
A: If you are an athlete *in training*, and you're trying to go as fast as possible, you can hike from the Dunes Parking Lot to the top of High Dune in under an hour. However if you prefer to enjoy the views, or are not in tip-top, aerobic shape, you should allow two to three hours round trip. Be sure to carry plenty of water and wear shoes that will protect your feet from hot sand.

Q: Where did all that sand come from?
A: It's a long story, but glaciers, water and wind have all contributed to break down rocks in the surrounding **San Juan Mountains** and **Sangre de Cristo Mountains** into sand particles. After that, a unique combination of prevailing winds blowing sand into an *elbow* of the Sangre de Cristos (where they become *trapped* by the high peaks), reverse-direction winds, and creeks cutting down the edges of the dunes, then depositing sand downstream for recycling onto the dunes, have created a remarkably stable mass of sand.

Q: Can I camp out on the dunes?
A: What a great idea! You certainly may. Just stop by the Visitor Center and ask for a free backcountry camping permit. The staff person will let you know where you can leave your car overnight and a few simple rules for choosing a spot to camp.

Q: Can I use a sled, boogie board, skis, snowboard, etc. to slide down the dunes?
A: A great thing about sand dunes is that the ski tracks, footprints, paw prints and other marks or grooves you make in the sand today will disappear as soon as the wind blows — and the wind often blows around here. You can run, jump, slide, cartwheel or roll down the sand slopes to your heart's content.

Q: What's so special about this place, other than all that sand?
A: Diversity. Starry nights. Quiet. With a range in elevation from the floor of the San Luis Valley at around 8,000', to the heights of the nearby **Fourteeners** (peaks over 14,000') in the Sangre de Cristo Mountains, the diversity in plants, animals, weather and geology is hard to match anywhere in the world. The clean, crisp air and frequent clear skies offer views of a fantastic dome of stars that you'll never see near a large town or city. And the physical distance from highways and towns will provide an opportunity to experience a natural silence — another pleasure often lost to city-dwellers.

Sandy, served up as the guest of honor by the Friends of the Dunes organization at the dedication ceremony for the Park in 2002

INTRODUCTION

Using This Guide
Book 22
    Organization
Safety 26
    Considerations
Backcountry 30
    Ethics
Friends of the Dunes

Ranger at the Sand Pit Trail

Friends of the Dunes BBQ

Dawn at Great Sand Dunes National Park and Preserve

USING THIS GUIDE

A family investigates animal displays on the Visitor Center patio

Along with the National Park Service and *Sandy, the Great Sand Dunes Tiger Beetle*, the authors wish to welcome you to the **Great Sand Dunes National Park and Preserve**! Our goal with this guide has been to provide a definitive resource that *any* visitor to the Park and Preserve can use. Whether you are a hiker, climber, backpacker, equestrian, mountain biker, camper, photographer, 4WD enthusiast, birdwatcher, or dunes snowboarder, you'll find the information you need in this guide to pursue your adventures in the Park and Preserve. Even if you need to limit your explorations to just a stop at the Visitor Center, our chapters on the fascinating natural and human history of this unique place will help you undertand why our nation has choosen to protect it as one of our crown jewels.

Beyond the boundaries of the Park and Preserve are other opportunities to experience the magic of this special corner of the Colorado Rockies. Use this guide to explore the rich heritage and culture of the San Luis Valley or to climb to the heights of the Sangre de Cristo Mountains for an eagle's eye view of this recreational paradise.

Be sure to read the next section which explains how this guide is organized. It will help you to navigate all the resources in this book. We hope you like what you see here and enjoy the great places we lead you to. *Have fun and be safe!*

AUTHORS' FAVORITE PICNIC SPOT:

Head to the "back" picnic sites (farthest from the entrance) at the **Mosca Creek Picnic Area** (page 75). You can cool off in the shade of numerous trees, and wade in the waters of Mosca Creek!

AUTHORS' FAVORITE HIKE:

The **Wellington Ditch Trail** (page 149) offers outstanding views of the dunes, with a bonus "sighting" of the remains of the old Wellington family cabin!

Book Organization

The information in this guide is organized for your convenience into **color-coded sections**. Colored tabs in the upper corner of each page help you quickly turn to the section that you are interested in. Each section then is divided into **chapters**, with headings such as *natural history, local facilities* or *hiking*.

THE PLACE

This section provides essential information about how to get to the Park and Preserve, as well as basic climate data on this location in south-central Colorado. The map on page 35 shows the major roads leading to the area. **Federal highways**, indicated on all maps as "US" *(US 285)*, and **Colorado state highways**, shown as "CO" *(CO 19)*, are paved roads and open year-round. Local roads are indicated as **county roads**, "CR" *(CR 580)*, or as **Forest Service roads**, "FSR" *(FSR 119)*. These roads may be paved, but more likely are gravel or dirt, and many may not be plowed on a regular basis, or may even be officially closed during the winter season. Some require 4WD to be passable, and others may seasonally be too muddy for passenger vehicles. Jeeping on the backroads of Colorado is not for the timid or unprepared. Respect the limits of your vehicle; and for some of the truly difficult roads mentioned in this guide, such as the Medano Pass Primitive Road, consider using an outfitter rather than your own vehicle. Always inquire locally with the proper land management agency if in doubt about driving on these roads.

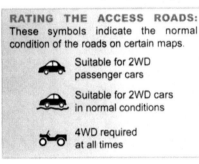

RATING THE ACCESS ROADS:
These symbols indicate the normal condition of the roads on certain maps.

Suitable for 2WD passenger cars

Suitable for 2WD cars in normal conditions

4WD required at all times

In this section, you'll also learn fascinating things about how the dunes have been formed and about the unique plants and animals that inhabit the dunes and the surrounding Sangre de Cristo Mountains. The Park and Preserve encompasses such a huge elevation gradient, from desert and scrub lands to alpine tundra, that visitors come away astonished at the natural diversity of species, including some found nowhere else on earth. Equally interesting is the cultural history of the Park and Preserve, and the San Luis Valley. The brief history in this section hardly does justice to the amazing capacity of native peoples, and later Hispanic and Anglo settlers, to survive, and even thrive, in such a harsh and unforgiving landscape.

FACILITIES

Turn to this section for complete information about needed services and facilities, both within the Park and Preserve and in the small, nearby communities of the San Luis Valley. You'll find everthing from campgrounds to hotels, basic groceries to fine dining. The Park and Preserve itself has much of what you would expect of developed facilities: a visitor center, a campground and several scenic picnic areas. But for most modern conveniences, you'll want to drive some distance out into the communities of the San Luis Valley. The town of **Alamosa** is the economic heart of the valley, with virtually everything you'll need and a warm, small-town feel. A map on page 87 locates most services and facilities in town.

We indicate the relative prices for restaurants in the valley, but keep in mind that none of the restaurants listed would be considered *expensive*. Prices are subject to change and may do so seasonally. We also indicate that some establishments may close entirely during certain slow times of the year. And in a good sense, *slower* describes the way

> **RATING THE RESTAURANTS:**
> These symbols appear in descriptions for restaurants indicating relative affordability:
> $ — under $10
> $$ — $10 to $20
> $$$ — $20 to $30

of life in these small communities — traveling against the fast pace of modern society. Hopefully, visitors will be relaxed and refreshed by a visit to this beautiful valley.

> **MAKING CONTACT:**
> These symbols appear in descriptions for services and facilities:
>
> Mailing address
>
> Phone or fax
>
> Email or website

You'll find **contact information** — mail addresses, phone numbers and email addresses — throughout this section. These things change often but are current as of 2003. We'll continue to update and refine these in future editions of this guide. If you find inaccuracies or omissions, please contact us at *cmcpress@cmc.org* or write us at 710 10th Street # 200, Golden, CO 80401.

ACTIVITIES

The range of fun things to do at the Park and Preserve is enormous; and this section is the largest in the book. It would be a shame if all that visitors to the Park and Preserve did was get out of their vehicles to snap a few pictures. Check out this section for dozens of fun activities, and you are sure to find something that matches your interests. For easier, less-taxing activities, there are **photography**, **wildlife watching** and **picnics**. Looking for something a little wild and crazy? Grab your snowboard and head out on the slopes — *sand slopes* that is — for some summertime shredding. For those seeking solitude, the backcountry beckons with **backpacking**, **hiking** and **climbing**.

Mountain biking is excellent at nearby Zapata Falls Recreation Area, with trails designed specifically for the enthusiast. While biking opportunities are somewhat limited in the Park and Preserve, we still have come up with some possible rides of varying difficulty. Each description of a ride includes an **information box** that lists the one-way distance of the suggested ride and approximate elevation gain. Most of these rides can be shortened by altering the turn-around point. These rides are rated as *easy, moderate* and *difficult*, depending on the level of fitness required or needed expertise. A beginning rider can handle the easy rides, but for moderate or difficult rides, riders should be experienced in single-track riding on steep courses. All levels need safety equipment, including helmets. The ride on the Medano Pass Primitive Road requires extra precaution since motor vehicles share the road.

> **RATING THE BIKING TRAILS:**
> These symbols appear in information boxes next to each biking description and indicate the relative trail difficulty.
>
> Easy bike ride, short distance, easy grade, good riding surface
>
> Moderate bike ride, medium distance and grade, bumpy riding surface
>
> Difficult bike ride, long distance, steep grade, poor riding surface

We describe **30 trails** in the Park and Preserve and the surrounding public lands for hikers, as well as backpackers and climbers. Even if you have never walked a trail, you will find nature walks and short, easy strolls to magnificent vista points that anyone can enjoy, including families with young children or seniors. There are even wheelchair accessible excursions (and you'll want to check out the specially designed *dunes-capable* wheelchair on display at the Visitor Center.)

Experienced hikers will find hikes in the Park of varying difficulty, mostly with minimal elevation gain and in sand. However, hikes in and around the Preserve are mostly on rocky trails with steep elevation gains. Beside each hike description, you will find an **information box** with the one-way hiking distance and approximate elevation gain to the furthest described destination. Some hikes have alternate destinations for a shorter hike. Many trails can be linked for a longer hike or to provide an alternate return route. Hikes are rated as *easy, moderate* or *difficult,* depending on the fitness level required or the amount of difficulty you may encounter. While even beginner hikers may be able to handle any of the easy hikes described here, moderate or difficult hikes require experienced hikers who are properly equipped. Hikes at all levels will be difficult, and even dangerous, for people not yet acclimated to elevations in the Park and Preserve that start at 8,000 feet above sea level and run to over 13,000 feet on mountain summits.

RATING THE HIKING TRAILS: These symbols appear in information boxes next to each hike description and indicate the relative trail difficulty.

 Easy hike - short distance, minimal grade, good walking surface

 Moderate hike - medium distance and grade, rougher walking surface

 Difficult hike - long distance, steep grade, rough walking or off-trail

 Climbing - very steep grade with scrambling or roped ascents

Included with each hike desciption is a **trail map**. While the effort has been made to make these maps as informative and useful as possible, they should not serve as your sole guide in the field. You'll want to bring along more detailed maps such as **USGS 7.5 min. Quads** (listed on page 15) or the appropriate National Forest map. The USGS Quads are, in many cases, somewhat old and may not show man-made features, like trails and roads, accurately; although they are extremely useful for their topographic detail. There are a couple of excellent commercial maps that cover the southern Sangre de Cristo area — these are listed in the *Resource Guide* section in the back of this book (page 222.) Symbols used for all the maps in this book are shown on page 15.

Finally, for the hard-core, we include some **suggested climbs** for mountaineers within the Preserve, as well as in the surrounding National Forests and wilderness areas. For the experienced, there are some of the finest climbing challenges in the Colorado Rockies here, including several of the famous **Fourteeners** (peaks above 14,000' (4268m).) Most of these are classified as scrambles and NOT for the casual hiker. We offer no ratings on these climbs, to stress that fact that these are only for experienced climbers familiar with all the difficulties and risks of climbing in the Colorado mountains. However, an **information box** lists the one-way distance and approximate elevation gain from the suggested base camp. A **route map** accompanies the description of each; but climbers will want to have an appropriate field map, such as a USGS 7.5 min Quad for more practical use. The final climb listed, *The Prow* on Kit Carson Peak, is a technical climb for experienced alpine, rock climbers only. For any climb, you need training and experience — check in the *Resource Guide* in the back of the book for information about organizations that offer this (page 224.)

ATTRACTIONS

What do alligators, bison, chocolate, hot springs, stagecoaches, steam locomotives, UFOs and whooping cranes have in common? They all come together in the splendid isolation of the San Luis Valley. We won't explain what all these diverse things are doing in the valley — we'll let you turn to this section in the guide to find out. But there are plenty of interesting and fun things to do beyond the National Park and Preserve. Explore history of the 1880s at old **Fort Garland** or take a tour with the Nature Conservancy on a working ranch. Visit **San Luis Lakes State Park** for a relaxing day at the beach or drive a **Colorado Historic Scenic Highway** through some of the oldest established towns in Colorado.

All of the attractions in this section can be enjoyed in conjunction with a trip to the Great Sand Dunes National Park and Preserve. Most are within 50 miles from the Park entrance. In the descriptions, we alert you that some attractions are only open seasonally. We also provide a **calendar of year-round events**, listing annual festivals, events and special attractions that might interest you. These home-grown affairs are a great way to get a genuine taste of life in the valley.

RESOURCE GUIDE

The final section in this guide pulls together lots of supplemental information about the Park and Preserve, plus provides you with recommended resources for discovering more. You'll find several handy charts that categorize all the hikes described within this book. You'll be able to zero in on hikes of certain lengths or all the hikes to a specific destination, if you so desire. We also include an extensive list of other books and publications about this area and on related topics. If you feel you need training or more experience for some of the activites in this books, such as hiking, climbing or backpacking, join one of the oganizations listed in this section. And of course, you'll find an extensive index to help you navigate this guide.

Heading out to the dunes in late afternoon

Safety Considerations

Visiting your Great Sand Dunes National Park and Preserve can be an enriching and fun experience, but not without some potential hazards. Before setting out onto the dunes or into the surrounding mountains, familiarize yourself with these hazards and be prepared with the best ways to avoid them.

HEAT

The unprepared Park visitor is potentially at risk from **heat exhaustion** or **heat stroke**. While normal summer temperatures generally hover around the mid-80° F readings (29° C), they can soar into the low 90s (33° C) at times. Combine these daytime-high readings with the reflective nature of the sand, and your body heat saturation level can be substantial. Be wise; wear a wide brimmed hat and drink plenty of water and other non-diuretic fluids.

SUN

There are two types of **ultraviolet rays** (UVRs) radiating from the sun. They are UVB and UVA. If you desire *old* looking skin (or dismiss the risk of skin cancer) hang around out of doors without adequate sunscreen protection. Otherwise, apply sunscreen to all exposed skin areas, one hour prior to sun exposure. This gives the sunscreen time to penetrate the deeper skin layers. Be aware that reapplying sunscreen does not extend the total amount of time that you can safely be exposed to the sun's rays. Sunscreen which is rated **SPF 30** is the suggested standard for extended outdoor exposure. Look for sunscreens that block both UVA and UVB rays.

Studies have shown that about 30% of the total daily UV flux hits the earth between 11 AM and 1 PM, so if possible, activities should be planned to avoid this peak exposure time. A useful rule of thumb is that if your shadow is shorter than you, the risk of sunburn is substantial.

At higher altitudes, like in the Park and Preserve, UVRs are approximately 50 to 60 percent stronger than at sea level. Therefore, sunburn can occur more quickly and severely at altitude, especially in sandy terrain where the sunlight is reflected back up by the sand. Also, UVRs can penetrate cloud cover, so that even on cool, overcast days, you can be at risk.

EYE PROTECTION

The sun's rays are damaging to your eyes, as well as your skin. The eye can become permanently damaged as a direct result of any source of bright light, such as the sun. In hiking out on the dunes, not only do you have direct sun encroachment on the eye, the reflective nature of the sand on the dunes exacerbates the intensity of these rays. High altitude mountain climbers have long been aware of one danger associated with climbing on snow — snow blindness. We've never heard the term *sand-dune blindness*, but you don't want to be unfortunate enough to experience it! Wear proper eyewear that protects against both UVA and UVB rays. Dark lenses with side shields are quite appropriate (and trendy).

Contact lens wearers need to be aware that the wind carries all manner of fine silt and sand through the air. This may prove to be harmful to your eyes and cause irritation when wearing contact lenses. Consider bringing along some ski goggles to keep the fine sand out of your eyes when the wind blows.

WIND

Can it be windy in the Park? You bet! Without those winds, we would not have those beautiful sand dunes that you've come to visit. Visitors to the Park can expect wind at any time of the year, with March through June usually being the windiest months. Wind speeds will vary along with other atmospheric conditions, but gusts in excess of 50 mph (80 km) are possible. Thanks to the wind, the dawning of each new day can erase all traces of man's presence on the dunes.

LIGHTNING

Deadly lightning is always a threat when thunderstorms are present. Afternoon thunderstorms are fairly common during the summer, especially on the high peaks of the Preserve. These storms are quick moving and brief, but can be very violent. Lightning normally strikes the highest features in the vicinity — that could be YOU, if you are out on the dunes during thunderstorm activity! Head down from the dunes immediately when you see a thunderstorm starting to materialize. Observe this exciting phenomenon from the safety of the Park Visitor Center or your vehicle. *Live better electrically* is fine for your home, but not for your body!

ALTITUDE

You must recognize that you are at altitude when you visit the Park and Preserve; your body recognizes it. The Park Visitor Center is located at an elevation of 8,175' (2492m) and the highest point in the Park and Preserve is the summit of Tijeras Peak at 13,604' (4148m). **Acute Mountain Sickness** (AMS), a mild form of altitude sickness, is caused by a lack of oxygen when traveling to higher elevations. This usually occurs in individuals exposed to an altitude over 7,000 feet (2,100 m), who have not had a chance to acclimate to the altitude before engaging in physical activities.

Driving to Colorado from Florida or other lowland states, and then deciding you're going to set a new speed record for climbing up **Star Dune**, is a perfect recipe for getting AMS. The symptoms of AMS include, but are not limited to, headache, nausea, vomiting and shortness of breath.

Drinking plenty of fluids and ascending at a reasonable rate will help to offset the potential of being afflicted with AMS. If you do get AMS, the best advice is to descend immediately to a lower altitude.

EXERTION

Don't overdo it! A general rule of thumb, when hiking or climbing, is that if you can't talk to your hiking partner (or yourself), you're working too hard. If you can sing a song while you hike, you're not working hard enough!

Determining your **age-predicted maximum heart rate** will also help you from over-exerting yourself. It is generally accepted that you will derive the most benefit when you are exercising at 60-90% of your maximum exercise heart rate. Take into consideration your overall physical condition and past medical history when attempting physical exercise at elevation.

Calculate the **beats per minute** and write it down on your palm for monitoring your heart beat while hiking:

220 - (your age) = (age-predicted maximum heart rate) X .90 = (beats per minute)

DEHYDRATION

Your body consists of about two-thirds water. The effects of sun, wind and exercise in the Park's high-desert climate rob your body of its proper level of fluid. You will be dehydrated long before you become thirsty. Fluid losses of up to 5% are considered mild, up to 10% are considered moderate and up to 15% are considered severe. *Drink, drink, drink!*

Water and sports drinks will help you recover your normal fluid and electrolyte level much faster than caffeine-based beverages like coffee, tea and colas. Coffee and colas act as diuretics and can cause you to lose fluid. Alcohol has an even greater negative effect on your body's fluid level.

SAFE DRINKING WATER

Treat any water taken from unprotected sources before you drink it, and practice proper hygiene. You are at risk from **Giardia** contamination anytime you drink from untreated water sources in the Park and Preserve. Giardia is a microscopic organism. Once it has inhabited the digestive system, it can cause diarrhea. Giardia is mainly spread by the activity of animals in the watershed area of the water supply, or by the introduction of sewage into the water supply.

Giardia has become so common, even in wilderness areas, that water should always be treated chemically with pills which are specifically designed for water purification, by filtering the water with an approved water filter, or by boiling untreated water for several minutes before using. Adding a little flavored *Gatoraide* to boiled or treated water makes it taste so much better.

CLOTHING

The Lawrence of Arabia look is in

If you are out in the sun a lot at altitude, without the proper protective clothing, you'll soon get the sunburn of your life, and a painful lesson to boot! We like long, lightweight pants, a long-sleeved, lightweight shirt and one of those *foreign legion* hats that have a protective cover draping the back and sides. That *Lawrence of Arabia* look will fit right in, when out on the dunes!

A useful rule of thumb is to hold a shirt up to a strong light source such as a light bulb. If you can see images through it, it probably has an SPF value less than 15. If light gets through, but you can't really see through it, it probably has a SPF value somewhere between 15 and 50. If it completely blocks all light, it probably has an SPF value greater than 50 (*e.g.* heavy cotton denim). Cotton garments can be washed with a new product called *Sun Guard* from the makers of *Rit Dyes*. This treatment is purported to give garments an SPF rating of 30. (*Sun Guard* will not add sun protection to 100% polyester and acryllic fabrics.)

For excursions into the mountains beyond the dunes, no matter how warm it may seem, you'll need to pack warm clothes and rain gear for that fast moving afternoon storm or cold front. Protecting your body from sunburn is even more important at the higher altitudes of the Preserve, where the UVRs are even more intense.

FOOTWEAR

Yes, you do need footwear out on the dunes. The afternoon surface temperature of the sand on the dunes can reach 140° F (60° C). It might seem like a good idea, and fun, to hike without shoes, but you are advised to keep shoes handy when things start to heat up.

And, don't forget that your pet's paws can also burn on the hot sand.

PETS

Park regulations dictate that pets must be on a leash, not to exceed six feet (1.8m) in length, whenever they are outside of the visitor's vehicle. The foregoing applies to dogs, cats, other domestics and, yes, probably even your pet gerbil. Don't leave pets (or children) in a closed-up vehicle in the sun while you are out hiking on the dunes *for a few minutes*. In a very short time, a closed vehicle can easily reach temperatures of 120° to 140°F (48° to 60°C).

Backpackers with dogs along Medano Creek

Another *no-no* is to leave your pet tied up to a tree or fence post, where shade or water may not be readily available. Be considerate, be pet-wise. Always clean up after your pet.

WILDLIFE ENCOUNTERS

While most Park and Preserve visitors don't perceive wildlife as a threat to them, bad encounters are on the rise in Colorado. If you happen to unexpectedly encounter a bear or mountain lion while in the Park or Preserve, it is important that you keep in mind some common sense guidelines. You don't want to agitate anything that weighs between 200-450 pounds and can run up to 35 mph!

Most problems center around food. Don't feed wildlife, and hang your food out of reach when in the backcountry. Hiking at dawn or dusk may increase your chances of meeting a bear or mountain lion. Use extra caution in places where hearing or visibility is limited: in brushy areas, near streams, where trails round a bend or on windy days. Avoid hiking alone and keep small children close and in sight.

Do not run from a bear or mountain lion. Running triggers a predatory response and they are more likely to attack. Back away slowly while facing a bear. Avoid direct eye contact and give the bear plenty of room to escape. If on a trail, step off the trail on the downhill side and slowly leave the area. Use extra caution if you encounter a female bear with cubs. Avoid getting between cubs and their mother.

In the case of a threat from a mountain lion, stay calm and hold your ground or back away slowly. Stand upright facing the lion. Maintain direct eye contact and try to appear larger than you are. Don't crouch down. Mountain lions still have a healthy fear of humans in unpopulated areas, so aggressive behavior will often scare off the lion.

Backcountry Ethics

It should go without saying that in the Park and Preserve, natural features and man-made artifacts should be left in place for future generations to enjoy. There is one important — *and fun* — exception to this rule. You may go out and run on, jump on, slide on, dig in and generally disturb the sand on the dunes as much as you want, but keep in mind that a variety of critters, *including me*, call this place our home.

Your visit to the **Great Sand Dunes National Park and Preserve**, and the adjacent **Sangre de Cristo Wilderness Area**, should continue to protect and preserve these areas by following the rules and regulations that land management agencies have set up. Each of us needs to do our part, and together we can preserve these natural treasures for everyone. Whenever applicable, we have noted current rules and regulations in this book. But things change over time. Before you engage in activities at the Park and Preserve, be sure to check in at the Visitor Center for the latest rules meant to ensure that your activity is compatible with protecting the environment.

As a general guideline for activities in the backcountry, you should follow the principles of **Leave No Trace** (LNT). The LNT principles described below will help protect and preserve your Park resources for those visitors who will follow in your footsteps in the years to come.

1. PLAN AHEAD AND PREPARE

It is important to know information about the Park, so that you will know what to expect. Find out about its ecology, climate, topography and rules and regulations. Be ready to modify your behavior and expectations accordingly.

2. TRAVEL AND CAMP ON DURABLE SURFACES

Stay on the established trails. Don't take shortcuts that become unsightly and encourage erosion. Camp only in established or sanctioned campsites. Check in with the Park personnel at the Visitor Center for information about designated backcountry campsites with the National Park.

3. DISPOSE OF WASTE PROPERLY

Be prepared to pack out what you pack in. It doesn't take much effort to carry along a litterbag for those disposable items you are finished with. Pick up trash that you find along the trails. Pack out toilet paper and personal hygiene products. Please remove dog feces.

4. LEAVE WHAT YOU FIND

It is not permitted within the Park and Preserve to remove or deface plants, animals, rocks or archaeological artifacts. Look, but don't touch.

5. MINIMIZE CAMPFIRE IMPACTS

Where fires are permitted, use established fire rings, fire pans or mound fires. Avoid the typical *white man's fire*. It's not necessary to have the flames jumping 20 feet into the sky to enjoy a campfire.

Don't destroy the environment by creating fire rings, sawing down trees or otherwise altering the natural setting. Never abandon a campfire that is still burning or contains hot coals. Winds can arise which carry sparks into flammable materials or the coals can burn down into the ground and start an unwanted fire. Keep your human impact to a minimum.

6. RESPECT WILDLIFE

Do not attempt to follow or approach wildlife. Be especially careful not to come between mothers and their young, such as a sow and cubs or a cow elk and fawn. Don't bury or throw unwanted food on the ground as it tempts wildlife and creates abnormal feeding habits. Store food legally and responsibly.

7. BE CONSIDERATE OF OTHER VISITORS

Be courteous when on trails. Remember the rules of the road — everyone yields to horses; bicycles yield to pedestrians; pedestrians yield to each other where required. Consider the quality of your visit to the Park. Control the enthusiasm of the younger members of your group. Respect the privacy of other visitors. Crowding causes conflict. Camp a reasonable distance from other groups.

Everyone, including the vehicle owner, is distressed when a car alarm goes off in the middle of the night. Consider turning yours off temporarily. With the exception of emergency personnel, cell phones do not have a place at ranger campfire programs. Leave them in your car or at camp. We all survived being out of touch before cell phones existed, and there's hope that we can make it a couple of hours without them.

Late afternoon party

FRIENDS OF THE DUNES

Summer concert series presented by Friends of the Dunes

Their Mission Statement: "The **Friends of the Dunes**, Inc. is a non-profit citizen's support group for Great Sand Dunes National Monument (now Park and Preserve). In cooperation with the National Park Service, the Friends provide a forum for citizen involvement in planning decisions, focus public interest on issues and need, and provide volunteer and financial aid for projects beyond the scope of the monument's (now Park and Preserve) budget. The Friends assist in the educational facilities and programs for its visitors and promote recreational opportunities at the Dunes. Through cooperative agreement, the Friends conduct fund raising campaigns on behalf of the National Park Service and direct charitable donations toward improving facilities and services at the monument (now Park and Preserve)."

The Friends of the Dunes, Inc. (The Friends) was founded in 1989. The Friends have participated heavily over the past several years in the expansion and renovation of the Visitor Center. This project cost approximately $2 million to complete. The Friends provided a significant amount of funding toward reaching this worthwhile goal.

The Friends are also strongly involved in providing additional Park visitor activities in the form of artist workshops, science seminars, summer concerts, a 5K/10K run, photo workshops and of course, the all-important **sand sculpture contest**, to name a few. One event of special note is the **Castles, Kites & Concert**, a full day of fun in the sun. You don't want to miss this one! Contact The Friends or the Park Visitor Center for additional information regarding these exciting events.

Since its inception in 1989, the Friends of the Dunes has assisted the Park in numerous ways, including the facilitation of thousands of hours of volunteer work and the brokering of more than $1 million towards research, facilities improvement, and educational and interpretive projects that were beyond the ability of the NPS to finance. The Friends received the eight-state Rocky Mountain Region, *2002 Working Together Shoulder to Shoulder Award* from the National Park Service in recognition of their contribution.

Membership information for Friends of the Dunes can be found on their website: *www.greatsanddunes.org* Applications should be sent to: *Friends of the Dunes, Inc.* *11500 Highway 150* *Mosca, CO 81146* *(719) 378-2312   Ext. 227*

As you experience the Park, you will notice that litter is kept under control. The Friends sponsors an **Adopt-a-Highway** program, as well as an ongoing effort to keep the Park grounds free of litter. With over 300,000 visitors a year, it doesn't take long for litter to become a major problem. If during your visit to the Park, you see litter along the paths or other areas, take a few extra moments to pick up this unsightly mess and deposit it in trash receptacles that are provided for this purpose.

If you are in need of a **wheelchair** during your visit to the Park, you will be happy to know that The Friends have donated a chair that is capable of traversing the sand. This chair was funded by visitor donations and member contributions. This is just another example of how The Friends activities are helping enhance your visit to the Park. Why not drop a few *pesos* into the contribution container the next time you are in the Visitor Center. Everyone will thank you for your generosity.

The Friends currently has over 200 members. One of the benefits of being a member of The Friends is *The Hourglass*, a newsletter filled with informative articles, as well as a calendar of events. Archaeological opportunities exist for members of The Friends to participate as volunteers in ongoing archaeological activities as part of the National Park Service's **Volunteer-in-Park** (VIP) Program. Add your name to The Friends membership today!

Contributions may be made for specific projects such as the **Visitor Center Facility Fund**, the **General Research Fund** or the **Water Research Fund**. Contact The Friends for additional information. Donations made to The Friends are tax deductible to the extent permitted by current IRS tax regulations.

A portion of the revenue from the sale of this book will be donated to The Friends.

The National Park Service has a volunteer program called **Volunteer in Park**, or VIP for short. This program applies universally to National Parks throughout the country, as well as at the Great Sand Dunes National Park & Preserve. Interested applicants need only obtain and complete a form, aptly named the *Volunteer Application for Natural Resources Agencies*, available at the Park visitor center. This form provides space for indicating your areas of interest, as well as your availability and lodging requirements. Return the completed form directly to the Park.

As you might imagine, volunteers are needed in a wide variety of areas. Everything from desktop publishing, geology, multi-media and trail construction and repair, to "Other." Volunteer; it's good for you and it's good for everyone!

THE PLACE

Location
    How to Get There 35
    Climate and 36
        Weather
Natural History
    Eolian Geology 39
    Minerals 44
    Water 46
    Plants 48
    Animals 52
Cultural History
    First People 57
    Native Americans . . .58
    Spanish 60
        Conquistadores
    Zebulon Pike's 60
        Explorations
    Permanent 62
        Settlers
    Preserving a 66
        Natural Wonder
    Origin of Place 68
        Names

Wagon at Fort Garland museum

Rabbitbrush blooming near Visitor Center

Mule deer forage after a snow fall on the dunes

LOCATION

Great Sand Dunes National Park & Preserve
11500 Highway 150
Mosca, CO 81146-9798
(719) 378-6300
www.nps.gov/grsa/home.htm

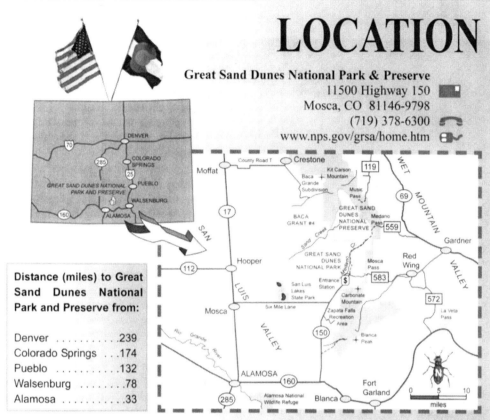

Distance (miles) to Great Sand Dunes National Park and Preserve from:

Denver 239
Colorado Springs . . .174
Pueblo 132
Walsenburg 78
Alamosa 33

The **Great Sand Dunes National Park and Preserve** is located between the San Juan and the Sangre de Cristo Mountains in southwestern Colorado's San Luis Valley. These two mountain ranges are the catalyst which provides material for building and maintaining the dunes. The Park is located northeast of Alamosa, Colorado, in the south-central portion of the state.

How to Get There

From the south, the entrance to the Park is located 19 miles (31 km) northeast from the junction of US 160 and CO 150. To reach this junction from Alamosa, travel 14 miles (23 km) east of town on US 160.

The Park may also be accessed **from the west** by traveling 14 miles (23 km) north from Alamosa, to just past Mosca, Colorado, on CO 17, turning east (right) on Six Mile Lane (County Road Ln 6N) for 16 miles (26 km) and then turning northeast (left) on CO 150 to the Park entrance. All access roads are two-lane blacktop suitable for passenger cars.

Access to the Park **from the east** is via US 160. From the stoplight at the intersection of Main and 7th Street in the town of Walsenburg, Colorado, proceed west for 59 miles (95 km) to the junction with CO 150. Turn right (north) on CO 150 and proceed 19.0 miles (30.6 km) to the Park entrance station.

Climate and Weather

The Great Sand Dunes National Park and Preserve is located in the **high desert** at an elevation of 8,175 feet (2,499m). The climate in regions of this type tends to run on the mild to cooler side of the temperature scale.

Late spring, summer and early fall months can present visitors with ideal daytime temperatures ranging from highs of 50° to 85° F (10° to 29° C) and nighttime lows of 30° to 50° F (1° to 10° C). When visiting the Park during October through April, visitors can expect daytime high temperatures to range from a pleasant 30° F to 60° F (1° to 16° C), to bone chilling nighttime lows of 0° to 30° F (-18° to 1° C). The highest temperature recorded at the Park was 96° F (36° C) in 1982, while the lowest temperature was -25° F (-32° C) in 1963, both extremes set in relatively recent times. Temperature differences of this magnitude are not that unusual for this part of Colorado.

The San Luis Valley is one of the sunniest locations in the country, with an average of nearly 300 days per year of sunshine. But visitors to the Park can expect occasional snow during the colder months and brief thundershowers during the warmer months. The average annual precipitation for the Park is 11 inches (28 cm), which can fall as either rain or snow. In 1997 the Park received a near record 20 inches (51 cm) of precipitation.

Southwestern Colorado experiences, what is commonly referred to as, the **monsoon season** during the months of July and August. Short but drenching

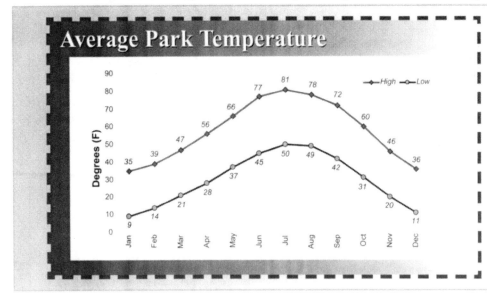

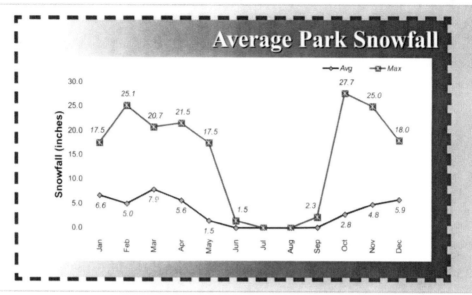

Average Park Snowfall

thunderstorms, accompanied by severe lightning and hail, can occur at any time of the day or night during these months. Always be alert for sudden weather changes.

The average annual snowfall for the Park is 38 inches (96.5 cm). The winter of 1991-1992 holds the record for having the greatest snowfall with 86 inches (218 cm) being recorded. Most snow normally falls during the month of March as a direct result of the mixing of warm, southwestern moisture with colder blasts of Canadian air. The adjacent Sangre de Cristo Mountains play a major role in the Park's weather patterns.

The sun in the summer can heat surface sand temperature to as much as 140° F (60° C). This temperature is as hot as the highest recorded air temperature in Death Valley. Protective clothing and adequate water intake are extremely critical in these conditions.

If the rain, snow or lightning don't get you, those spring winds might! The spring months of April, May and early June are known for occasional high-velocity wind storms. Combine the wind with sometimes cooler temperature readings and you have the makings of a downright cold day or night. Make sure you fasten your tent down extra well or it may end up in the drink at nearby San Luis Lakes State Park!

Ambient air temperature will decrease as you gain altitude. If you start at the Park visitor center, elevation 8,200' (2,499m) and decide to climb to the top of nearby Kit Carson Peak at 14,165' (4,317m) you will gain nearly 6,000' (1,829m) of altitude, and lose somewhere in the range of 20° to 33° F (-6° to 0°C) in temperature. This effect is referred to as the **Environmental** or **Adiabatic Lapse Rate.** Each 1,000' (305m) of altitude gained will result in an average ambient air temperature loss of 5.5° F (-14.7° C) when the air is dry or 2.2° F (-16.5° C) when the air is moist. Since the humidity is variable the actual temperature loss will range somewhere between the dry and moist adiabatic rates or about 3.3° F (-16° C).

NATURAL HISTORY

Sunset on the dunes

A bleak ghost forest stands where healthy ponderosa pines once thrived, smothered by escape dunes. A small river flows in surges, as miniature sand dunes below the water surface — antidunes — form and shift, producing waves up to a foot-high in the river. Unique insects, that can withstand surface sand temperatures of over 140° F, enjoy a barbecue dinner of the remains of less fortunate bugs. A small rodent survives in this desert environment without ever drinking water. Welcome to the surprising and dramatic world of the Great Sand Dunes.

Eolian Geology - It's all about the Wind

The Great Sand Dunes rise more than 700 feet above the surrounding valley, and cover approximately 39 square miles. Where did all that sand come from? Shouldn't there be an ocean nearby — or, how about a huge surrounding sandy desert? What are sand dunes doing in the Rocky Mountains of Colorado?

The Great Sand Dunes are a product of winds and "walls" formed by surrounding mountain ranges. What better place to learn about **Eolian Geology** — geology related to the wind?

The prevailing southwesterly winds blow sand across the San Luis Valley. When the sand reaches the high Sangre de Cristo mountains, they are deposited in the valley. If the southwesterly winds always had their way, the dunes would gradually shift toward the mountains.

However, powerful storm winds frequently blow from the northeast, shifting the sands back into the San Luis Valley. This is the primary factor which helps stabilize the size and location of the dunes. The barriers of Medano Creek and Sand Creek also help keep the margins of the dunefield relatively unchanged over time. The creeks cut into the edges of the dunefield, carrying sand downstream. Medano Creek disappears into the ground, leaving dry banks of sand to be blown back onto the dune field. Now that's recycling at its best! Mother Nature has built one of the greatest sand castles of all time. And she started only about 12,000 years ago — maybe longer, maybe shorter — this is another of Nature's mysteries that scientists are still trying to solve.

NPS interpreter shows how dunes are formed by a prevailing SW wind (left) and NE winds (right) pushing through high mountain passes

NE winds come down from passes in the Sangre de Cristo Range behind the dunes

UNIQUE DUNES

Ripples from wind action

Where did all that sand come from? Five billion cubic yards of sand seems like a lot to find in the middle of a high valley, 1,000 miles from the nearest ocean. Not only is there a lot of sand above ground, but there is another 350 feet of sand extending below the level of the valley floor.

The ash flows and lava of the San Juan Mountains to the west contributed much of the material, with the migrating rivers and streams that drained into seasonal ponds, or **playas**, playing a large role. Water helped erode the rocks of the San Juans, and carried the sediments down into the San Luis Valley where it was deposited along the shores of the playas. When the playas dried, the sandy beach deposits were exposed and blown into the dune system. During the ice age, alpine glaciers left debris in the valley as well.

Strong winds helped break down these particles further, as sand grains were bounced along the valley floor. There was a "sifting" effect over time. Larger, heavier grains of sand couldn't be lifted out of the valley as the winds reached the high mountains, but lighter dust particles were carried away.

Very small particles of dust and sand are moved by **suspension**; that is, they are suspended in the air by the winds. You may become especially aware of suspension if you wear contact lenses and the wind picks up just a bit. As the particles become a little larger, they bounce along the surface; a process called **saltation**. **Surface creep**, or rolling sands, accounts for movement of large grains of sand. And you thought surface creep referred to that nasty kid down the street!

The Great Sand Dunes are the tallest sand dunes in North America, rising approximately 750 feet from the base, to the top of the tallest dunes. That makes them slightly taller than the tallest office building in downtown Denver. But the **Alashan Plateau,** in China's Gobi Desert, lays claim to hosting the tallest dunes in the world, topping 1,200 vertical feet in height.

These dunes are different than many other dune fields in the world, according to geologist Andrew Valdez. They are very compact, covering about 30 square miles, and can be thought of as one giant dune, with smaller dune forms within it. Other large dune fields in the world often have flat areas within the boundaries of the field, but the Great Sand Dunes are continuous, and therefore make up one the largest dunes in the world.

Did you hear that? Sometimes you'll hear booming of the dunes — a very low — frequency sound that you'll also feel vibrating under your feet as dry, large slipfaces shift. Other times (especially as you run down a sand slope) you'll hear the sand squeaking, as tiny sand particles rub against each other.

One of the magical things about the Great Sand Dunes is the natural quiet. Other than noises from other people (music, conversation), sound monitors placed around the Park rarely exceed 40 decibels. For you musicians out there, that's equivalent to *ppp* — piano-pianissimo, or as soft as possible.

NOT ALL DUNES ARE ALIKE

Complex wind patterns vary in different parts of the dune fields, affected especially by three low passes in the Sangre de Cristo mountain range: Medano, Music, and Mosca Passes. The wide variety of dune shapes reflect the differing wind patterns that formed each dune.

You'll notice that many of the dunes along Medano Creek (a.k.a. the **Medano Creek Dune Range**) have a gradual slope on one side and a steep slope (the "slipface") on the other side. This shape is similar to what you see after a snowstorm with high winds. The snow (or in this case, sand) is blown from the windward slope and deposited on the leeward side. Like snow on a mountainside, the sand on the leeward face will avalanche when it reaches a critical angle, reshaping that side of the dune.

A few dunes have slipfaces which form an entire side of the dune. These are known as **transverse dunes**. However, if you look closely at the dunes in this area, you'll see where the slipfaces are confined to only the upper portion of the dune ridge. These are **reversing dunes**.

When the winds reverse their usual direction as storms pass through the area, the movement of the sand on the slopes of the dunes reverses as well. This can cause an unusual effect on the reversing dunes, that looks like the ridge tops have folded back on themselves. The whimsical name sometimes given to these ridge top formations is **Chinese Walls**. With just a little imagination, these formations resemble a model of the long, winding Great Wall of China.

Shadows highlight the Chinese Walls along ridge tops

As you hike on the Medano Creek Dune Range, note the closely-spaced ridges and the impressively steep, front face of this area of dunes, especially the **slip-face** in the vicinity of the Castle Creek picnic area.

Star Dune Complex from the Sand Ramp Trail, near the base of Mt. Herard

Sinuous curves of dunes present a new assortment of shadows as light changes during the day

Another interesting shape you may see as you explore the dunes is a **star dune**. These dunes have three or more slip-faces, and form a star pattern if viewed from above. Star dunes are formed when multiple wind directions shape the sand. **Reversing dunes** have a slip-face which can form on either side of the dune, depending on recent wind directions. They can have very sharp crests atop steep slopes which drop off in two directions. As you hike along the crests, you may find that you must straddle the top, keeping each foot on the opposite slope of the dune. Star dunes and reversing dunes tend to be the patterns found on the tallest dunes.

The **Sand Creek Star Dunes** at the base of Mt. Herard are the most complex dunes in the range of sand dunes. Winds can blow in almost any direction in this area, and the complex wind patterns result in numerous star dunes. This area of dunes consists of one central high point with a spider web of dunes radiating out from it.

Some of the dunes are crescent-shaped **barchan dunes**. The "wings" of the crescent point down-wind. **Parabolic dunes** have long arms — 2 or 3 miles in length — trailing behind their flanks as they migrate toward the main dune field from the valley floor south of the main dunes.

The sinuous curves of all these different dunes offer an infinite variety of photographic opportunities as the light changes throughout the day. And if the wind blows tonight, you'll be able to come out again in the morning to photograph a new assortment of shapes and shadows.

The Army Corps of Engineers has done research (perhaps "Desert Storm" was an incentive here) of *"Depositional Patterns and Transported Material Resulting from Wind"* — English translation: "Shapes of Sand Dunes." Did you know there are barchan dunes on Mars? No wonder the Great Sand Dunes have an other-worldly look to them.

MOVEMENT OF DUNES

Encroaching escape dune

There are some actively-advancing dunes that have "escaped" the main dune mass, and move up to 35 feet per year. The speediest **escape dune**, measured so far, managed to travel 20 feet in just 40 days. These dunes are mainly exposed to only one wind direction.

The escape dunes we see today may have first broken away from the main dune field during a drought period in the 1950s, when they managed their bold "dash" east across Medano Creek. As ranger and geologist Andrew Valdez puts it, *"Don't be a tree here."* The existing trees are smothered by the encroaching dunes, which eventually move on, leaving a **ghost forest** behind.

Cottonwoods tend to fare better than evergreens when attacked by the sand. Cottonwoods are capable of converting lower limbs to roots, which may help them continue to draw sufficient moisture from the surrounding sands to survive. However, the escape dunes often win the battle between tree and sand.

Ghost forest

Most of the dunes remain in place, despite the best efforts of the wind to move them. A huge **sand sheet** surrounding the dunes contains enough vegetation to stabilize the sand there and prevent it from being blown away. The **sabkha** is a salt-encrusted plain, mainly southwest of the dunes, where the sands have been cemented by the mineral deposits left by evaporation. The sands here are too hard for the wind to move. These two phenomena contribute to the stability of the sand dunes.

Photographs taken of the Great Sand Dunes over a century ago and compared to ones taken recently, show that while individual dunes change shape over the years, the dune field overall looks about the same. These dunes oscillate but don't migrate (for the most part).

The dune known as **High Dune** (the highest dune visible from the Visitor Center) has been surveyed regularly. It shifted 14 feet one year, and 30 feet in another year — but in different directions. Over time, however, the *elevation* of High Dune changed less than 3 feet.

Minerals

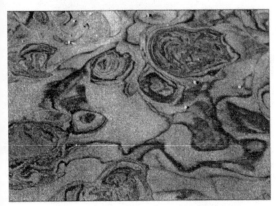

As you explore the dunes, note all the colors of sand. Black **magnetite** colors the surface in some areas, while pink feldspar, red and tan sandstone, green epidote, white quartz, and many other minerals provide a rainbow of color in the sand. If you happen to have a small magnet with you, run it through the sand to collect the appropriately-named magnetite.

Swirls of sand and magnetite

A walk along the Medano Creek streambed or other streams and springs can lead you to a rainbow of colorful rocks and interesting minerals. Look for strange, rusty-looking chips. Red-colored **bog iron** is created as iron bacteria oxidizes dissolved iron deposited along streambeds, and causes it to rust. Early settlers were able to build iron tools from bog iron.

Bog iron

The surrounding Sangre de Cristo Mountains also contain interesting rocks and minerals. While hiking to Willow Lakes, and other destinations in the Crestone region, you'll find the colorful mosaic patterns of **crestone conglomerate**. These distinctive rocks contain embedded cobblestones, or **clasts**, the size of *Rocky Ford cantaloupes* (a regional favorite in late summer) or larger. They were part of an ancestral Rocky Mountain range, worn down over millions of years, compressed under high pressure, then exposed again for our viewing pleasure. Unlike some conglomerate rock, these cobbles aren't just "cemented" to each other; they are completely fused with the surrounding rock — they don't separate out when the larger rock is broken.

Crestone conglomerate

LIGHTNING ON THE DUNES

As you walk among the dunes, watch for samples of **fulgurites**; strange-looking tubes of sand formed when lightning strikes the dunes. At first glance, you may think these dark-colored, tubular formations are the droppings of a strange, small animal. When you examine them more closely, however, you'll discover that they are hollow tubes of sand, with the insides of the tubes melted to a glassy finish. Many of the pieces found at the Great Sand Dunes range from about one to three inches in length, and are about the thickness of a soda straw. Occasionally, fulgurites measuring up to three feet have been found here, but they break apart when anyone tries to carry them. The world's largest fulgurite has three huge branches measuring 38 feet in total length — it was NOT found here at the Great Sand Dunes.

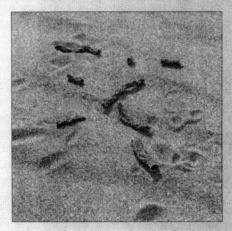

Fulgurites tend to be fragile, and can easily be broken into smaller pieces by the time you spot them on the surface of the dunes. These pieces of "petrified lightning" are said to aid in communication with extra-terrestrials, to act as an aphrodisiac, and to enhance healing. They have another, much less appealing, attribute if you attempt to stay out on the dunes to watch them being created, up close and personal, during a lightning storm. If you miss out on finding your own fulgurites, don't despair. The Visitor Center has an excellent collection for your viewing pleasure.

Speaking of **lightning**: it is quite common in this region. If you see a lot of clouds forming, or hear distant thunder, that is NOT a good time to be out climbing on the dunes!

Water

The San Luis Valley averages less than 10 inches of precipitation a year, making it a true desert, albeit a very high, cool desert. Yet, with the nearby mountains and springtime snow melt, small rivers and streams play an important role in bringing moisture to the area. Dramatic thunderstorms, very prevalent during July and August afternoons, can sometimes drop over an inch of rain in less than an hour. The dry, rocky slopes of the foothills absorb very little of the rain, and flash floods dig gullies in the ground that disappear almost as quickly as they appear.

In the springtime, you might enjoy wading in Medano Creek on your way to or from a hike on the dunes. *Médano* means "sand dune" in Spanish. The creek generally dries up during other times of the year, and may not flow at all in a dry year. Medano Creek flows in waves with an unusual **surge flow**. Water accumulates, especially when sand ridges called **antidunes** form below the surface. When they break, the increased water volume surges and creates waves. Stop and listen to the creek flowing. You'll hear the changes in water flow as the antidunes begin to form and then break. The creek disappears into the ground along the eastern side of the dunes, and reappears miles away.

Medano Creek's unusual surge flow makes an excellent "conveyer belt" for sand. The creek drives fresh sand into its channels in the spring and early summer. When the creek dries up later in the year, the winds blow the sand back onto the dune field.

People familiar with hiking around streams in the Colorado mountains may notice something odd about Medano Creek and the other creeks near the Sand Dunes. Generally, a mountain stream runs higher during the warmer part of the day and into the evening, as the sun melts snow in the mountains that feeds the stream. The creeks around here seem to behave just the opposite. They run higher during the cool of the night, then the flow drops during the heat of the day. What's going on? Researchers offer this explanation: cottonwoods and aspen trees growing along the sandy waterways rapidly draw

Antidunes forming
below the surface

Surge flow

water through the porous sand during the sunny part of the day, but slow down as they cool at night. Those are some really thirsty trees!

Water is becoming even more precious in this region. In aerial photographs taken in 1936, 88 wetland areas and 69 ponds could be seen. Today, there are only five ponds. Sand Creek's channel has lowered by about 10 feet, and a drought in the 1950s contributed to a redistribution of the water table.

The existence of the dunes depends largely on water. Geologists say that one reason that the dunes do not move much is due to their moisture content. While drier, surface sand moves freely, the wetter core of the dunes remains remarkably stable. Water flowing from higher elevations erodes the dunes and deposits sand downstream. Winds then carry sand back up onto the dunes. In places, the groundwater aquifers lie just below ground level, which allows Sand Creek and Medano Creek to flow and move sand downstream. If the natural water table were altered due to diversion by developers, these creeks might disappear into the ground far upstream from their usual flow. The sand wouldn't be deposited where it would be blown back onto the dunes, and the entire system would be dramatically altered.

Moisture in the core helps stabilize the dunes.

Fortunately, the people of the San Luis Valley, local and national politicians, the National Parks Service and many others have worked together to create the Great Sand Dunes National Park and Preserve. The major expansion of lands beyond the original boundaries of the Great Sand Dunes National Monument have made it possible for a single agency to manage an entire interrelated ecosystem, protecting the water and other natural resources of the area.

During a wet year, the surge flow can produce foot-high waves. Families bring along their favorite beach gear, and enjoy a day splashing in the water and savoring the views of the nearby snow-crested peaks.

Plants

*From the fall tundra of Mt. Herard to the
dunes, a drop in elevation of over 5,000 feet*

If you were a bit surprised by the appearance and the setting of the Great Sand Dunes, you have good reason to be. The variety of natural environments within a very small distance is quite amazing. Dunes education ranger Patrick Myers loves the diversity of the area. He explains, *"As the crow flies, it's three miles from the alpine tundra to the desert grasslands."* How many places in the world can you go from grassland, to dunes, to riparian, to Piñon/Juniper, to sub-alpine, and finally, to alpine tundra environments in such a short distance?

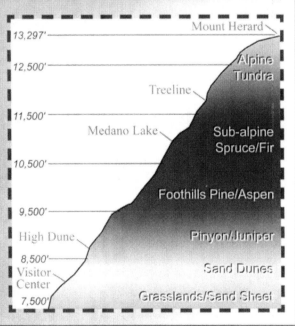

Mount Herard

13,297'

12,500'   Alpine
            Tundra

            Treeline

11,500'   Medano Lake   Sub-alpine
                           Spruce/Fir

10,500'

            Foothills Pine/Aspen

9,500'

            High Dune   Pinyon/Juniper

8,500'   Sand Dunes
Visitor
Center
7,500'   Grasslands/Sand Sheet

Blowout grass

B ecause of the incredible range in elevation from dunes to peaks, there are hundreds of species of plants found in the region. Pick up a *Plant Checklist* booklet at the Visitor Center for a list.

Temperatures are cool and water is scarce in this high desert region. Several species of plants have adapted to enable them to grow directly from the sand dunes, while other plants generally grow just outside of the sand, venturing onto the dunes only during moist years.

Blowout grass, **indian rice grass**, and **scurf pea** all grow directly on the dunes. Blowout grass grows tall, with long, thin blades which bend back to the sand, drawing delicate patterns as they are blown by the wind. Indian rice grass almost seems to glow with its own light, as its seed heads catch the sunlight in the early morning or late afternoon. The scurf pea, with its long horizontal stems (*rhizomes*), is well-designed to hold on tight when the winds blow and to spread out to find whatever moisture it can. When a plant in one part of the network of stems succumbs to the sand and heat, a new plant may sprout up from the same network, but in a more advantageous location. Look for its tiny sweetpea-like blossoms low to the ground.

Scurf pea

A slim, grass-like plant with a delicate flower was thought to be near extinction until the **slender spider flower** was found in the sabkha and other areas by the Great Sand Dunes. The Nature Conservancy has counted over 70 rare and imperiled species of plants and animals on the lands of the Medano-Zapata Ranch, which lies mostly south and west of the National Park and Preserve.

Prairie sunflower

Prairie sunflowers create a spectacular sight in late summer, especially in moist years, when they are able to flourish directly on the sand. During dry years, they still put on a beautiful show in the areas surrounding the dunes.

Not surprisingly, you'll discover a number of species of cactus and other desert-loving plants in the lower elevations near the dunes. **Prickly pear cactus** (*opuntia*) is common (along with the colorful **opuntia bug**, also called a cactus bug).

Be careful not to be stabbed by the long spike-like "leaves" of the numerous **yucca** in the area. Not surprisingly, Native Americans found these plants useful to create needles and thread, and mixed roots of this common plant with water to make a sudsy soap for washing.

Sage, **rabbitbrush**, **yarrow**, **mullein**, and **winter-fat** are

Prickly pear cactus

Fringed sage

Cottonwoods

Fairyslipper orchid

Aspen

Bristlecone pine

Phlox

also plentiful. Did you remember to bring along your allergy medicine? Sage we know as a tasty herb. Native Americans enjoyed it to add flavor to sweet corn. During World War II, a man in Alamosa tried to extract the small rubber content from the abundant rabbitbrush in the San Luis Valley to make tires. He soon discovered it wasn't worth the effort. Yarrow, another herb, is easily identified by its white cluster of flowers. It makes a good analgesic tea. Mullein, with its velvety leaves, has been nicknamed "Indian toilet paper" and "backpacker's delight." It can grow a flower stalk up to six feet tall, with clusters of yellow flowers. Winter-fat? Often mistaken for sage, this pale green, almost silvery-colored plant seen growing in the flat lands near the base of the dunes provides great browsing for deer and antelope, especially in winter (helping to keep some fat on the animals in winter — thus the name!)

Cottonwoods are common along the streamcourses, such as Medano Creek, that lead into the foothills. As you explore farther from the dunes and venture into the foothills, you'll find vegetation more typical of the mountains of Colorado. In the cooler, more moist areas among the trees, watch for **fairyslipper orchids**, **wild roses**, and **kinnikinnick** (which we love saying three times fast). **Wild strawberries** are abundant along many trails, especially at elevations above 9,000 feet.

Junipers and **piñon pines** are common at lower elevations, while **ponderosa pines**, **douglas fir**, and **aspen** dominate as you climb higher into the mountains. **Blue spruce** (the Colorado State Tree), **lodgepole pine**, **engleman spruce**, **douglas fir**, **white fir**, and **bristlecone pines** are some of the other trees you'll find in the area. **Mountain mahogany** is a common shrub that grows to be about 6 feet tall, and has feather-like seed heads in the fall.

At higher elevations you can enjoy many lovely and delicate tundra flowers. In essence the tundra is a cold desert, receiving less than 20 inches of moisture per year, mostly as snow. It's interesting that tundra plants share many of the same adaptations as the desert plants on the dunes, some 5,000 feet below — long tap roots to reach precious water and strategies to prevent desiccation. Among the most common that you'll find on the tops of the high peaks are **phlox**, **alpine forget-me-nots**, and **alpine sunflower**.

Enjoy the fragrances you'll discover as you get up close and personal with some of the trees, shrubs, bushes, herbs, and flowers. Break open a juniper berry with your fingernail and you'll recognize the distinctive smell these berries give to gin. The bark of the ponderosa pine is said to smell like vanilla or butterscotch. You won't soon forget the deliciously sweet scent of forget-me-nots. And pinch a few sage leaves to release their distinctive smell.

FIRE!

In April of 2000, a wildfire raged over 3,129 acres at the Great Sand Dunes and the surrounding areas. High winds helped the fire spread rapidly, destroying two buildings along with shrubs, grasslands and areas containing piñon pines, aspens, cottonwoods, and junipers. The piñon pines generally fared well; many were scorched, but they slowed the winds which caused the fire to burn out. Other stands of trees were more seriously damaged or destroyed. Some of the burned areas are clearly visible near the Visitor Center, which was not damaged.

Aspen regenerating at the Park after the fire

The burned areas are recovering quickly. Many new shoots of cottonwoods and aspens have appeared; and pines have hidden their scars with new needles.

The 2000 fire was probably caused by a spark from a fire set by humans near a development south of the dunes. However, fire has always been a tool of nature to destroy first, but then to provide an environment for new growth and new life.

Fire raging at the Great Sand Dunes in April of 2000

Animals

Animal tracks lead down toward Medano Creek

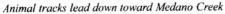

You'll find tips for viewing wildlife within the Park and Preserve, and the surrounding areas, on page 118 in the *Activities* section of this guide.

The Great Sand Dunes and their surrounding lands are home to a wide variety of animals. The sandy soils on and around the dunes make it easy to spot tracks of numerous animals, as well as the tiny tracks of insects.

Perhaps the most interesting creature is the nocturnal **kangaroo rat**. These small rodents are highly specialized to live in desert regions, especially in the sand dunes of the world. They don't sweat, and they don't drink. They are able to obtain all their water from the seeds they eat. Kangaroo rats have developed specialized organs in their nasal cavity to recapture moisture when they breathe, and their kidneys operate so efficiently that they return nearly all the water back into the bloodstream.

Coyotes "sing" in the distance, and **bobcats** leave their tracks in the sand, as they stalk the numerous **rabbits** in the area. If you are observant, you may notice "pounce" marks of these two predators. Kangaroo rats and rabbits also attract other efficient predators like **bull snakes** and **rattlesnakes**, who leave their own tell-tale pattern on the sand.

You're very likely to encounter **mule deer** as you travel through Great Sand Dunes National Park and Preserve. Note their long, mule-like ears; all the better to hear you with, my dear!

Bones among the blowout grass and sand

Pronghorn were reintroduced in the area in the early 1960s, so keep an eye out for these graceful antelope, especially in the flat, open prairie as you drive into the Park. These beauties are the fastest land animals in North America, so you won't have much luck trying to chase after them for a photo. From the road, you may also spot **elk**, especially in the winter when they move down from their summer range high in the surrounding mountains, or look for the huge herd of **bison** on the nearby Medano-Zapata Ranch.

Black bears, mountain lions, porcupines, and **bighorn sheep** can be spotted at higher elevations in the surrounding San Juan and Sangre de Cristo Mountains. Some of these animals may descend to the floor of the valley, and even wander along the dunes on occasion.

You may also know mountain lions by the names puma or cougar. They tend to be secretive, and will try to avoid people. Black bears (you won't find grizzly bears in Colorado) also prefer to be left alone. Human encounters with either of these creatures are very rare, especially if you make a little noise when hiking so you don't surprise them. We've included information elsewhere in this guide (see page 29) on what to do if you have a close encounter of the scary kind!

We've heard some people refer to the **marmots,** often found in high-elevation rock fields, as "rock-chucks." This seems to be a *flat-lander's* variation on the name of an animal with a similar appearance: the woodchuck. Don't let local hikers hear you call them rock-chucks; you may get laughed off the mountain. Cute little creatures called **pikas** *(PY - kuhs)* may chirp at you and scramble into small holes between rocks in the high country.

BIRDS

Can anyone resist shouting, *"Beep-beep!"* as a **roadrunner** dashes across the road in front of your car? Tiny **hummingbirds** whir past you, or hover to check out bright-colored clothing. Many other birds can be seen in the park: the noisy **magpie**, the beautiful blue trio of **Stellers jay, piñon jay** and **mountain bluebird,** and **Clarks nutcracker** to name a few.

For a guide to birdwatching in the Park and Preserve, and the surrounding areas, see page 100 in the *Activities* section of this guide.

Look up into the branches of the tall ponderosa pines, or high above you in the sky to see if you can spot a majestic **golden eagle** or a **bald eagle.** **Falcons** may swoop down from the trees to catch a mouse or

Kangaroo rat

Coyote

Bull snake

Pronghorn antelope

Bison

Marmot

Pika

Magpie

Mountain bluebird (female)

Ptarmigan

other small prey.   As you climb into the surrounding mountains, you may see a **ptarmigan** waddling across a trail or among the rocks. Numerous birds can be seen as you make your way along the Montville Nature Trail or further up the trail toward Mosca Pass. Find a pretty spot to sit quietly among the trees or along the stream, and your patience may be rewarded with melodic songs, the haunting *coo* of the **mourning dove** or the *rat-a-tat-tat* of **woodpeckers** searching for insects.

In the spring and fall, water fowl such as greater (and lesser) **sandhill cranes** often migrate through the area, as do **canada geese** and until recently, even the endangered **whooping crane**. Nearby Monte Vista, CO holds an annual Crane Fest in early March each year, when visitors to **Monte Vista National Wildlife Refuge** may see on the order of 20,000 to 25,000 sandhill cranes. Their unforgettable call may cause you to think you are in the midst of the world's largest french horn concert. And until recently, you might have caught sight of the very rare, endangered whooping crane, joining the migration of its smaller cousins. Unfortunately, this single bird has now died, but as introduction efforts from other flocks continue, whoopers may yet return. The Great Sand Dunes and San Luis Valley are full of surprises!

Bald and golden eagles and **rough-legged hawks** often spend their winters in the San Luis Valley. **Herons, snowy egrets,** several types of **hawks, avocets,** and **common snipes** breed here. Some of the best areas near the Great Sand Dunes for birdwatching are at San Luis Lakes State Park, Alamosa National Wildlife Refuge, Russell Lakes State Wildlife Area, and Monte Vista National Wildlife Refuge.

FISH

The threatened and endangered **Rio Grande sucker** and **Rio Grande cutthroat trout** were being crowded out of streams and lakes by non-native fish in this region. Recently, both have been reintroduced into Medano Lake and Medano Creek after removing the non-native competitors.   This waterway is a "closed basin" — the water flows from Medano Lake high in the Sangre de Cristos down to the Great Sand Dunes, where the creek disappears into the sand. That means that fish in the creek can't swim to another stream, and undesirable fish can't make their way upstream into this creek. These natives shouldn't face future habitat competition, unless people intervene as they did in the past.

The severe drought of 2002 caused the waters to warm and unfortunately kill many of the reintroduced fish. Hopefully, enough will survive to build up a healthy population again in the future.

INSECTS

The Great Sand Dunes are the only home of the **Great Sand Dunes tiger beetle**, known in scientific circles as *cicindela theatina rotger.* You won't find these bugs anywhere else in the world! This special type of tiger beetle is described as a "voracious carnivore" who likes fried food — unfortunate, small insects fried by the hot sand, which can reach 140° F at the surface. This colorful little beetle has green shoulders and head, with ivory and brown designs on its wing covers.

According to Phyllis M. Pineda, Resource Specialist, who studied the great sand dunes tiger beetle in depth for her master's thesis, *"Daily activity was classified into six categories: basking, searching, stilting, shade-seeking, burrowing at mid-day, and burrowing at evening."* Other than **stilting** (the beetle stands on "tip toe" to hold its body as far from the hot sand as possible), these behaviors sound a lot like those we observed of *homo sapiens* at Piñon Flats Campground.

Pineda continues, *"These behaviors appear to be influenced by surface temperatures of the sand . . . intended to maintain sublethal body temperatures."* In other words, the tiger beetles prefer not to be fried.

The dunes are also home to two species of **clown beetle** found nowhere else in the world. You'll have to be extremely observant to spot one of these critters; they are only about 1/4 inch long.

Almost as unique is the **giant sand treader camel cricket**, which also lives in a few other dune fields. This

Great Sand Dunes tiger beetle

insect's feet have been described as "snowshoes," which let it move across the sand with ease. Its hind legs and feet are adapted to dig sand efficiently, and it creates extensive burrow systems in the sand.

There are other unusual insects which can tolerate the extreme temperature changes, winds, and lack of water. The **circus beetle** is another insect endemic to the Sand Dunes; it entertains observers by standing on its head when threatened. The circus beetle was a semi-finalist for a trip to the Space Station, but lost out to a beetle from Alberta. The **flower beetle** is a tiny beetle with a drooping neck and a head that seems to dangle from its body. The **robber fly** is a fierce-looking, large fly, that snatches prey in midair above the dunes.

Many of the insects burrow into the sand during the day to avoid the hot sand. That sounds like a good plan for us large visitors too — did you bring along a pail and shovel?

CULTURAL HISTORY

Abandoned homestead in the San Luis Valley

As you visit the Great Sand Dunes, enjoy the pristine environment, nearly unchanged by human presence. Since this region was never permanently settled by significant numbers of people, you can play an imagination game to pretend that you are a visitor from hundreds, or even thousands, of years ago, and can see the land in much the same way people from your selected era saw it. This area has always been special — from the time of the early mammoth and bison hunters, to the time it was known as the "Land of the Blue Sky People," to the days of travelers and settlers arriving via the Mosca Pass toll road, to today's visitors from all over the world.

Ranger Fred Bunch describes the experience here beautifully as *"the opportunity to hear your own heartbeat,"* as you explore this quiet, high altitude desert and surrounding mountains, lakes, and valleys.

One sad note about modern visitors is that some people "collect" artifacts, such as arrowheads or bone fragments, or cause further damage to old structures already showing the effects of time. These acts may destroy valuable clues to the history of this magical place; clues that can never be recovered. We sincerely hope that those who visit this historic region will become as enchanted with it as we have, and will strive to see it preserved for future generations.

"Mountain man" reinactor at Sand Dunes event

First People

Two of the most significant archaeological sites for discovery of human history in North American lie near the Great Sand Dunes. Evidence of perhaps the earliest Americans was discovered near the towns of Folsom, Colorado (thus the name "Folsom people"), and Clovis, New Mexico (that's right, "Clovis people"). These ancestors of the Anasazi and Pueblo Indians are known to have hunted and camped near the Great Sand Dunes, possibly as early as 10,000-12,000 years ago.

Just west of the Park, archaeologists found a camp used for meat processing with artifacts that date back to this era. Archaeological sites within the park contain remnants of mammoth, camels, and an ancient bison that was about 1½ to 2 times the size of modern animals. Ask at the Visitor Center to see the huge mammoth tooth, similar to ones found in the Park. Its size and weight will astound you! It's easy to picture a camel walking along the sands today, but an immense, elephant-like creature is harder to imagine. It's possible that there were sand dunes in the area even back when the earliest people (and mammoths) passed through this area, 10,000-12,000 years ago.

Scientists have found tools, grindstones and burial sites, especially in areas featuring springs. An exciting discovery was made in 2000 by archaeologists Pegi Jodry and Becky DeAngelo. Subterranean dwellings formed by post-hole construction were found that date back 3,000 - 5,000 years, or possibly even a bit older. These **Basin Houses** were possibly dome-shaped, oblong to round, and covered with brush. The oldest known structures of this type have been found in California, and are about 10,000 years old. Pegi Jodry says they expect to find evidence of many more Basin Houses in the San Luis Valley.

These early people made use of a spear-throwing tool called an **atlatl** (pronounced: AHT-lat-el) to bring down large prey. The atlatl is a stick with a hook on the end of it. A spear fits in the end of it, and the atlatl is used to throw the spear. Hobey Dixon, a retired professor of biology and the president of Friends of the Dunes, made a "spear" out of two old ski poles, and tried a little target practice. He reports that it is difficult to learn to aim the atlatl accurately, but it is extremely powerful. Using an atlatl as a launching tool, he can drive his ski-pole spear through a 2 inch board!

Your Uncle Sam says, "Possessing, destroying, injuring, removing, digging or disturbing from its natural state any of the following is expressly prohibited:

1. Nonfossilized and fossilized paleontological specimens
2. Cultural or archaeological resources or the parts thereof
3. Mineral resources or cave formation or the parts thereof
4. Living or dead wildlife or the parts or products thereof
5. Plants or the parts or products thereof."

Let's leave the digging and collecting to the professionals. They know what to do and how to do it. If you are interested in archaeology, there are opportunities to join the professionals in this valuable work. Members of The Friends of The Dunes can participate as volunteers in ongoing archaeological activities as part of the National Park Service's **Volunteer-in-Park (VIP) Program**. Contact The Friends for further information (pg. 32).

Numerous rock chips found in and near the house-pits, such as pieces of obsidian, are not found naturally in the San Luis Valley area, and are thought to have been brought to the area from southern New Mexico and Arizona. Based on bones found at the site, at least one group of people dined regularly on small mammals, such as rabbits and perhaps — are you ready for this — mice and lizards.

Over the centuries, cycles of wet and dry periods in the San Luis Valley have strongly influenced human habitation. During wetter times, ponds and marshes were common, as were a wide range of vegetation and animal life. These conditions attracted people, who could find the food and water they needed to survive. During times when water became scarce, archaeologists find little evidence of prehistoric human habitation.

Native Americans

The Ancestral Puebloans likely spent time in and around the Great Sand Dunes starting about 3,000 years ago. Descendents of these cliff-dwelling people, the Tewa and the Tiwa Indians of northern New Mexico, have a creation story of the first humans emerging from the underworld through a hole in a lake near the Great Sand Dunes, possibly San Luis Lake, and tell of their ancestors living in the San Luis Valley.

The Navajo believe they were put upon the Earth by the Creator within the boundaries of four sacred mountains. The Sacred Mountain of the East is Blanca Peak. The impressive Blanca massif, with its four 14,000-foot peaks radiating outward like spokes on a wheel, can be seen as you look south from the dunes. In the center, **Blanca Peak** (14,345') is the 4th tallest mountain in Colorado.

On the slopes of Blanca Peak, archaeologists have excavated a hearth and earth oven, used around 2,000 years ago to slow-bake plant materials. The people using these oven-heated rocks, wrapped the food in various materials, and then buried it to slow-cook — kind of a predecessor to today's crock-pot recipes.

In more modern times, probably beginning around 1400 A.D., Apache, Arapahoe, Cheyenne, Comanche, Kiowa, Navajo, and Ute Indians migrated to the San Luis Valley and other parts of the Southwest. The Ute people, in particular, left numerous signs of their lives in the valley over a period of centuries. They likely spent summers here, hunting and making excellent use of native plants. Jicarilla Apache people have a traditional name for the Dunes — *Sei-nanyldi* — translated as, *"It goes up and down."*

The San Luis Valley was referred to as the "Bloodless Valley" by the Utes and Navajos. They considered the area sacred, and would not shed blood in battle here.

The Blanca massif

CULTURALLY PEELED TREES

The Ute people surely could have given us a lesson on the expression, *"Waste not, want not."* Some of the most fascinating signs that remain of their lives and culture, from the late 1700s through the early 1900s, are the partially peeled **ponderosa pines** in the Park. About 100 or so old pines along Medano Creek, at the east edge of the dunes near Indian Grove, have been "culturally peeled" by Native American peoples. As you walk among the **peeled trees**, in a lovely meadow under the majestic beauty of Mt. Herard, you can almost sense the presence of the people who were here hundreds of years ago.

Native Americans were careful not to kill the trees when they used a sharp piece of wood to peel chunks of bark from the ponderosas. The bark was used to make trays, baskets and cradleboards, and was also useful as a building material. Resin and pitch were used for adhesives and waterproofing. Inner bark and sap had medicinal properties, and provided a source of food, which according to Ute elders who visited the area recently, was probably considered to be a delicacy. After pounding the inner bark, it was boiled, baked, or smoked to prepare it for consumption. The inner bark could also be used to thicken soup or stew, or to make tea.

nner bark is quite nutritious and high in fiber and vitamin C. One pound of inner bark contains as much calcium as 9 glasses of milk!

Zuni Indians were known to grind up the material to use as "flour" in making something like a tortilla. The Kutenai Indians tell stories of giving the sweet inner bark to kids as a candy-like treat in the springtime. As archaeologist Marilyn Martorano puts it, the trees were a sort of *"mini 7-11 store."* As people journeyed through an area like this one, they might peel a tree, have a snack, pick up some supplies, and continue on their way.

Although the trees have survived for centuries after being peeled, the passage of time will eventually kill these historic sentinels. The lifespan of a Ponderosa is 300-600 years. Because of their cultural significance, the trees at Indian Grove were added to the National Register of Historic Places in 2000.

WICKIUPS

Nearly every child knows about teepees, but **wickiups** are another type of shelter used by Native Americans. Wickiups are temporary shelters shaped like teepees, and erected by wedging trees together.

Very few wickiups remain standing in Colorado, yet 5 have been found in the Sand Dunes area. The dry conditions in the San Luis Valley have helped preserve the wickiups, which are roughly 200 years old. The Park Service doesn't disclose the location of these structures in order to protect them.

Spanish Conquistadors

The Spanish arrived in the San Luis Valley in 1599, bringing dramatic changes to the region. They utilized the well-established trails of the Utes, Apache, and Navajo to move people, wagons, and livestock into the region. Portions of **Los Caminos Antiguos**, The Ancient Roads, can still be followed as they pass close by the Great Sand Dunes and surrounding areas.

Just one year before the Spanish arrived, New Mexico was "claimed" by Spanish conquistador Don Juan de Oñate for the Spanish crown. Although the supposed goals of the Spaniards were "pacification" and "Christianization" of the Indians, for some a higher priority was to find rumored silver mines and other riches. The same year the conquistadors arrived in the San Luis Valley, Oñate ordered an attack on the Indians at Acoma Pueblo in New Mexico in retaliation for an attack on a small group of soldiers en route to join Oñate's men. The Spaniards killed 800 men, women, and children, and took 500 more captive. Oñate ordered his men to cut off the right foot of every captive male over the age of 25, as a message to other native people in the region. Oñate established the first permanent Spanish settlement in New Mexico in 1598, but the Spaniards found the San Luis Valley too inhospitable to settle for some time. It wasn't until 1708 that the San Luis Valley was "claimed" for the Spanish crown.

By the mid 1600s, native people benefited from the introduction of horses to the region, and the Utes in particular became proficient riders. But, of course, in the long run, the clash of cultures proved to be to the advantage of the Europeans and to the detriment of the lives and cultures of the Native Americans living here. For those who survived the likes of conquistadors like Oñate, there was the huge devastation wrought from European diseases previously unknown to the Native American people.

Zebulon Pike's Explorations

On Thanksgiving Day in 1806, explorer **Zebulon Montgomery Pike** failed in an attempt to climb the peak later named for him — Pikes Peak. Pike declared that no one would ever reach its summit. Contemplate that while you eat a fresh doughnut in the coffee shop at the top of the peak. Of course, Pike's group was half-starved, inadequately dressed, and were climbing through deep snows in -4°F temperatures. Pike and his men then traveled south and west, continuing their exploration of the southern portion of the newly-purchased Louisiana Territory.

On January 28, 1807, the group climbed over either Medano Pass or Mosca Pass (depending on which historian you listen to), heading west over the Sangre de Cristo Mountains. We can imagine their astonishment as they made their way down into the San Luis Valley, and began to view glimpses of the dunes in the valley below, peering through the trees surrounding them. You might say this was the first of Pike's "Peek" of the sand dunes. But we don't have to simply imagine what they thought, because Pike wrote in his journal:

> *"The sand hills extended up and down at the foot of the White mountains, about fifteen miles and appeared to be about five miles in width. Their appearance was exactly that of a sea in a storm (except for color) not the least sign of vegetation thereon."*

After establishing the night's camp near Medano Creek, Pike climbed "one of the largest hills of sand" and was able to see a large river in the distance. Pike (the same guy who didn't think anyone could ever reach the top of Pikes Peak) thought he had found the Red River within the Louisiana Purchase, when in fact he was encroaching on Spanish territory on the Rio Grande River. He may have "discovered" the Great Sand Dunes on behalf of its new United States owners, but he didn't really know where he was.

Spanish soldiers "greeted" Pike later in 1807, about a month after he built a stockade near present-day Alamosa. They let him know that he and his men were trespassing on Spanish lands, and escorted them first into Mexico, and eventually back to United States territory.

SANGRE de CRISTO MOUNTAINS

When Pike came across the Great Sand Dunes, he wrote that they were at the foot of the "White" Mountains. We know this range today as the **Sangre de Cristo** or *Blood of Christ* mountains.

This name may have simply originated from the beautiful red glow of the snowy peaks in the sunset. Or, as legend has it, *"¡Sangre de Cristo!"* were the dying words of a Spanish priest as he gazed one last time upon these dramatic peaks.

Sunset on one of the Sangre de Cristo peaks, east of the Park entrance road.

Permanent Settlers

First Spain, and later Mexico, found that issuing land grants in the San Luis Valley was an efficient method for attracting settlers, and in turn, establishing their "ownership" of the area. One of the largest in the valley, the **Luis Maria Baca Grant**, was ceded in the 1800s. Over the years, the grant passed through several hands, largely intact, before eventually becoming important to the establishment of the new National Park and Preserve.

Rugged individuals and families moved into the harsh region, built communities, and began farming here. The region remains rich in Spanish place names, and in Hispanic culture. Over 40% of the residents of Alamosa County, and nearly 70% of the residents of both Costilla and Saguache Counties consider themselves to be of Hispanic/Latino origin, according to the 2000 U.S. Census. About 2.3% of the residents of the three local counties listed themselves as American Indian or Alaskan Native, compared to about 0.9% for the nation as a whole.

The Mexican-American War resulted in the San Luis Valley becoming part of the Territory of Colorado in 1852. Fort Massachusetts was established at a spectacular setting at the foot of Blanca Peak as an outpost to protect American settlers and travelers. It was moved to its Fort Garland site several years later, in 1858. Kit Carson served as its commander in 1867 and 1868. In 1883, after the Utes were confined to reservations, the post was abandoned, but the town has survived. Some of the original fort buildings now house the **Fort Garland Museum and Visitor Center**.

The legendary Buffalo Soldiers (left) served at Fort Garland (below)

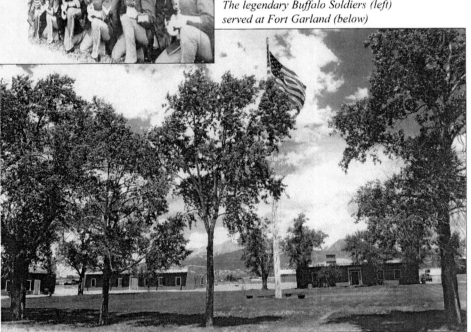

THE RAILROADS

In 1848-1849, **John C. Fremont** led a group of men attempting to find a railroad route through the central Rocky Mountains. Although Fremont was warned that traveling through the San Luis Valley and into the San Juan Mountains in winter was not wise, Fremont insisted on continuing to search for a route that would be passable, even during the winter months. The explorers dropped into the San Luis Valley from Mosca Pass. They continued west into the San Juan Mountains, where they were caught by a January blizzard. The men survived by eating their mules (and, it was later rumored, by resorting to cannibalism). Ten members of the exploratory group died before the rest of the party was led through the San Luis Valley, to safety in Taos, by a rescue party organized by Kit Carson.

A few years later, Fremont passed this way again, this time arriving at the Great Sand Dunes via Medano Pass. Although this was another winter journey, the weather was far milder than on his previous trip, and he charted what he believed would be a feasible railroad route.

Lieutenant **John W. Gunnison** soon followed Fremont in 1853, dispatched by the War Department with orders to also search for a feasible rail route. Gunnison's party had a somewhat easier time of it, successfully getting their wagons over the Sangre de Cristos and the San Juan Mountains, and on to Utah. In their passage through the valley, they noted the dunes and also made the first written record of what we now call the **Crestone Peaks**, those magnificent summits that today lie just beyond the northern boundary of the Park and Preserve.

By 1878, a narrow gauge railroad brought settlers to what is now the town of Alamosa, but the route was not the one suggested by Fremont. Alamosa became a hub for train travel in the region within the next ten years, thus establishing itself as the most important town in the valley.

For a taste of what rail travel was like in this region, book a trip on the **Cumbres & Toltec Railroad**, which once ran from Alamosa through Antonita, CO and Chama, NM, and on to Durango and Silverton, CO. The Alamosa portion of the trip isn't available nowadays, but you can still experience a ride on a genuine steam train running on narrow-gauge tracks, and pulled by locomotives dating to 1925. The train now originates at Antonito, 28 miles south of Alamosa on US 285. Call 888-286-2737 for information.

Steam engine on display in Alamosa

THE TOLL ROAD TO MONTVILLE

The Wellington cabin

Meanwhile, prospectors, traders, and other travelers had become interested in this region. In 1871, the railroad wasn't yet available for travel to the San Luis Valley. So, a fellow by the name of **Frank Hastings** obtained a charter from the Territory of Colorado, and improved an existing trail over Mosca Pass, turning it into a toll road. The tiny town of Montville (also known as Orean) formed near an old trading post at the mouth of Mosca Creek.

Montville included about 20 houses and a general store/post office which was run by Hastings. A short Nature Trail now marks the site of the town of Montville, destroyed by a flash flood around 1911. Don't worry; your admission fee to Great Sand Dunes National Park covers the old, $2 toll charged for a team and wagon back in the 1890s.

Life wasn't easy for homesteaders in the dry San Luis Valley. In 1927, the Wellington family hand-dug a ditch for irrigation from Mosca Creek to Buck Creek. The **Wellington Ditch** can still be seen as you hike along the appropriately-named Wellington Ditch Trail within the park. This one-mile trail runs from the campground to join the Montville loop trail. Between this trail and the paved road heading to the Piñon Flats Campground, you can spot the remains of the cabin built by the homesteading family. The cabin is most easily reached by walking from the paved road just north of the intersection with the road to the dunes and picnic area. You can peek in through the windows, but don't go inside or you may end up with an old ceiling plank falling on your head!

Kids collect magnetite using magnets

There's gold in them thar dunes!
At least, that's what brought some prospectors to the dunes in the 1920s. The black streaks you see in the sand are **magnetite**, a volcanic mineral believed to indicate the presence of gold. While prospectors did find a fine "flour gold" within the sand, very few made any money for their efforts. However, it was reported that in 1938 George Opincar of Blanca, CO developed a process that enabled him to recover 21¢ worth of gold from 2½ tons of sand.

THE FRENCHMAN, ULYSSES HERARD

Another local figure and early settler was **Ulysses (Ulus) Herard**, whose family homesteaded along Medano Creek, and what is now the Medano Pass Primitive Road, starting in 1876. Ulus suffered an unfortunate accident as a young man, when he was kicked in the jaw by a horse, rendering him nearly deaf. He managed to communicate by having people shout into the end of a hollowed-out cow horn which he held to his ear.

Bighorn sheep investigate the site of the Herard homestead

The Herards established a fish hatchery, raised thoroughbred horses, and also managed a herd of cattle. Ulysses' wife was postmistress of the Herard Post Office, an extension of their family home. If you drive or hike along the upper portions of Medano Pass Primitive Road, you'll be able to visit the site of their home and post office, although very little remains of the buildings.

Ulus Herard was known as a very hospitable man who always left his cabin door unlocked so travelers could have a place to stay. They were expected to clean up after themselves, however, and refill the wood box.

Remember the story about culturally peeled trees? In 1935, Herard told his grandson, Jack Williams, his recollections of the Ute Indians peeling and using the inner bark of the Ponderosa Pines on his homestead for food, and of their annual fall harvesting of chokecherries.

In 1984 the Board of Geographic Names approved the renaming of Mount Seven to be Mount Herard. **Mount Herard** is the most visually prominent peak towering over the Great Sand Dunes, and reaches a lofty elevation of 13,297 feet.

Locals say that in 1895, three miners were prospecting in North Arrastre Canyon, above what is now Oasis Campground. They struck gold and wanted to celebrate their good fortune, so they sent one fellow into town to buy them "some good alcohol." Somehow the salesclerk in Mosca thought that they wanted to buy "some wood alcohol." Sadly, the three miners drank the deadly substance in what was their final toast in life.

Miners buried within the Oasis Campground, near the old train car where new grave markers were recently placed above each grave

Preserving A Natural Wonder

GREAT SAND DUNES NATIONAL MONUMENT

Fortunately for the preservation of this unique natural wonder, residents of the San Luis Valley worked hard to have the dunes designated a National Monument. The Monte Vista (Colorado) Chapter of the P. E. O. Sisterhood (The *Philanthropic Educational Organization* is a national social service organization for women founded in 1869) launched an intense campaign in 1930 to gain support for National Monument status from numerous organizations, newspapers and political figures. In just 2 years, President Hoover signed a proclamation on March 17, 1932, stating, *"Whereas it appears that the public interest would be promoted by including the lands hereinafter described within a national monument for the preservation of the Great Sand Dunes and additional features of scenic, scientific, and educational interest . . . now therefore I, Herbert Hoover . . . do proclaim and establish the Great Sand Dunes National Monument . . ."*

A new road was opened to the Dunes in that first National Monument year, but the drive was over a dusty, unpaved road. Effects of the Great Depression made other improvements to the new Monument a low priority. Eventually, in 1938, road improvements were made, and construction began on a park headquarters building and superintendent's residence. World War II soon put construction on hold again.

The 1960s saw more development within the **Great Sand Dunes National Monument** as a new Visitor's Center, a campground, and an amphitheater were built. A non-profit organization called **Friends of the Dunes** (see page 32) was formed in 1989, as a public support group for the Dunes. This volunteer organization has raised funds and obtained grants to help remodel facilities, helped bring a specially-designed wheelchair to the Visitor Center that can be used on the Dunes, and has supported studies of the natural history of the area, including publishing books on the subject.

Wheelchair, specially designed to travel on the dunes

Ranger on patrol within the dunes

Superintendent Steve Chaney speaks at the dedication ceremony for the newly expanded area in September of 2001

CREATING A NATIONAL PARK AND PRESERVE

On November 22, 2000, President Clinton signed the **Great Sand Dunes National Park and Preserve Act** of 2000, which authorized the expansion of the National Monument into a National Park almost four times its original size. Roughly 42,000 acres of National Forest Wilderness Area were immediately transferred to NPS management, and renamed the Great Sand Dunes National Preserve.

One major hurdle before the "Monument" becomes a "Park" is the purchase of the Baca Ranch — nearly 100,000 acres of land lying west and northwest of the Dunes. The inclusion of this land, along with the addition of the Preserve lands, makes it possible for a single entity to manage and protect an entire natural system. A broad coalition of local groups, conservation groups, and the National Park Service worked to stop the sale of water from this region to the Front Range cities of Colorado. Their extensive studies revealed that a lowering of the water table would impact dune movement, vegetation, and many species of animals and insects. The strong relationship between the surface and ground water, and the importance of the entire physical, biological, and cultural system of this area of the San Luis Valley were found to be crucial to the protection of this unique and complex place.

In early 2002, The Nature Conservancy announced that they would purchase the Baca Ranch as part of a plan for the federal government to eventually own the land and make it part of the National Park and Preserve. Funds donated by Yale University (which owned shares in a partnership involved with the Baca Ranch), appropriations from the U.S. Land and Water Conservation Fund, and loans from other foundations and trusts helped supplement the private fundraising by The Nature Conservancy to make the transaction possible.

Steve Chaney, Superintendent of the Great Sand Dunes, emphasizes the significance of basing the boundaries of the Park and Preserve on natural systems rather than political boundaries, *"If we could create a National Park from scratch, this is what it would look like."*

Origin of Place Names

A number of people who passed through the San Luis Valley and the Great Sand Dunes have been recognized by having mountains, rivers, towns and counties named after them. Many of the streams, passes and peaks in and around the Great Sand Dunes have Spanish or Native American names.

Alamosa County, Alamosa (town) — Spanish for "cottonwood grove."

Baca Ranch - Back when they "ruled" the region, the government of Spain granted to Luis Maria Baca a huge parcel of land covering portions of what is now New Mexico and Colorado. After the Mexican War of 1848, the U.S. government promised to uphold the land grant, but homesteaders and squatters had settled portions of the original grant. Baca's heirs received other lands to replace the original parcel. One of those areas became known as the Baca Ranch (Luis Maria Baca Grant No. 4, to be precise), some of which is now a part of the National Park and Preserve.

Blanca Peak (14,345') Sierra Blanca Range, Blanca (town) — Most likely the "white" of the snows atop Blanca Peak and the Blanca massif was the inspiration for the name.

Cochetopa Pass, Cochetopa Creek, Cochetopa Canyon — This melodious name comes from the Ute word meaning "Pass of the Buffalo."

Conejos County, Conejos River — *Conejo* is Spanish for "rabbit," a common creature found in the San Luis Valley and surrounding areas.

Culebra Peak (14,047'), Culebra Pass, Culebra Creek — *Culebra* is Spanish for snake.

Del Norte (town), Del Norte Peak — Means "of the North" in Spanish.

Fremont County, Fremont Pass — The County is located northeast of the Great Sand Dunes, while the Pass lies between Copper Mountain ski area and Leadville, Colorado. John C. Fremont led numerous exploratory parties to survey parts of the West and later ran for President. The written accounts of his western travels proved to be quite popular, and likely influenced numerous people to travel west to fulfill the Manifest Destiny. Do you think they still would have gone west if they also knew of the extreme winter conditions Fremont and his men endured on their trip through the San Luis Valley into the San Juan Mountains?

Gunnison (town), Gunnison River, Mt. Gunnison (12,719') — John W. Gunnison was another explorer who passed through the San Luis Valley in 1853, staying at Fort Massachusetts for a time. The Gunnison party continued out to Utah where their leader was killed by Indians.

Hayden Peak (13,561'), Hayden Pass, Hayden Creek — Ferdinand V. Hayden passed this way in the 1870s. Not just another explorer and surveyor, Hayden was the first director of what became the U.S. Geological Survey. He was also a key player in establishing our first National Park, Yellowstone.

Huerfano County — *Huerfano* is Spanish for "orphan."

Kit Carson Mountain (14,165') — This peak is named after Christopher "Kit" Carson. Carson was a trapper, military scout, Indian agent, rancher and soldier. He spent several years working as a guide for John C. Fremont.

Herard, Mount — This prominent peak to the north of the dunes (and often used as a backdrop in photos) was named after Ulysses Herard. Herard homesteaded in this area in the 1870s.

Mt. Herard in winter

La Veta (town), La Veta Pass — *Veta* means vein; not as in "blood," but as in "ore."

Medano Pass, Medano Creek — *Médano* is Spanish for — *surprise!* — sand dune.

Mosca Pass, Mosca Creek — *Mosca* means "little fly" or "mosquito" in Spanish. This name is best understood at dusk on a summer evening.

Palmer Divide, Palmer Lake (town) — William Jackson Palmer finally succeeded where others had failed. In the 1870s Palmer's Denver & Rio Grande Railway laid tracks from Denver to Pueblo, over La Veta Pass, and on to Garland City, 6 miles northeast of Fort Garland, then to Alamosa, and beyond.

Pikes Peak (14,110') — When you travel by land from the east across Colorado, Pikes Peak is the first sign you see of the Rocky Mountains. This famous peak is named after Zebulon Pike. Pike was the first U.S. citizen to report on the wonders of the Great Sand Dunes.

Poncha (town), Poncha Pass — Some people have tried to find a Spanish origin for *poncha,* and have come up with anything from "gentle" and "mild," to some plant that was smoked like tobacco, to a misspelling of the word for "belly." A more plausible origin is the Ute term for "footpath."

Saguache County or Sawatch — (alternate spellings of the same name) — The Ute people used a single term for a blue-green color, *saguache* is generally translated as "blue-green earth."

Zapata Falls, Zapata River, Zapata Ranch — Although *Zapata* is a famous name usually associated with the Mexican Revolution, here the place names may simply be derived from the Spanish word for "shoe." The name *zapato* (masculine) may have been used originally, but we're told that when the Linger family bought the Medano and Zapato Ranches in the 1920s and ordered stationery for their operation, the printer in Alamosa accidentally changed the spelling to Zapata. So, why are these places named after a "shoe?" There are so many stories, we don't know what to do.

Zwischen, Mount — In German, *zwischen* means "between." Mount Zwischen is a visually-prominent peak located about midway between Mosca Pass and Medano Pass.

FACILITIES

Park Facilities
  Visitor Center 72
  Services Within 74
    the Park
Emergencies

Local Facilities
  Services Outside 79
    the Park
  Campgrounds 80
  Lodging 82
  Restaurants 85
    and Groceries

Teepee, GSD Oasis

Ranger-led program

*Rainbow arches over
Piñon Flats Campground*

PARK FACILITIES

Entrance to Visitor Center at the Great Sand Dunes

Welcome to the Great Sand Dunes! As you drive into the Park and Preserve, you'll come to a familiar sight — an entrance station. As of 2002, the **entrance fee** per adult is $3. Children 16 and under may enter for free. If you have a Golden Age, Golden Access, National Park Pass, or Annual Permit, you and your car passengers may also enter for free. Entrance fees are good for seven days.

OPTIONAL PASSES

One of these *optional* passes may be a good choice for you if you plan on returning to the Park within the year or if you plan on visiting other parks in the National Park Service system. The ranger at the entrance station can accommodate you. Your options include:

Great Sand Dunes Annual Permit (good for entrance fees to Great Sand Dunes for one year from month of purchase): *$15*

National Parks Annual Pass (good for entrance fees to NPS areas for one year from month of purchase): *$50*

Golden Age Permit (lifetime pass good for entrance fees to NPS areas if you are a US Citizen 62 or older): *$10*

Golden Access Permit (lifetime pass to NPS areas if you are a US Citizen with a permanent disability): *Free*

Visitor Center

The Visitor Center should be your first stop in the Park. There you'll find Park staff and volunteers on duty to answer your questions, you'll find information about **daily programs**, **nature walks** and other events, you can obtain necessary **backcountry permits**, **books** or **maps**, and you'll enjoy the **interactive displays**.

Interactive displays

Ranger-led "porch" talk

Bookstore at the Visitor Center

If you're like most folks, your first stop after you enter the Park will be — the restrooms. OK, so maybe your second stop will be at the **Visitor Center**. Happily, both restrooms and the Visitor Center are located a short drive from the entrance station, and share a common parking area. Watch for the first left turn after entering the park.

The Visitor Center is open from 9:00 AM to 6:00 PM during the peak "tourist season" from Memorial Day to Labor Day. During other times of the year the Visitor Center closes earlier. The building is closed for Thanksgiving, Christmas, and New Year's Day. Even if you've been to the Park before, it's well worth stopping for another look, especially since additional displays and improvements are being made on an ongoing basis.

With the expansion of the Park and Preserve, even more improvements are on the way. Starting in the fall of 2002, the Visitor Center building will be closed for expansion and redesign, with additional displays, a new audio/visual room, and a larger assortment of books and other materials. Administrative offices will also be added to this building. But don't despair if the Visitor Center is under construction when you visit. Just go a short distance further along the paved road to the next left turn, head to the **Dunes Parking Lot**, and there you'll find a temporary Visitor Center building with all the expected services. The Visitor Center remodeling project is expected to take two years.

Even if you arrive after Visitor Center hours, the Park and Preserve are never closed! However, if you plan to spend the night within the Park boundaries, you must either camp in Piñon Flats Campground (pay the fee at the Fee Station at the entrance to the campground), or obtain a free backcountry camping permit at the Visitor Center (only an option if you stop by while it is open).

Map of Park Facilities

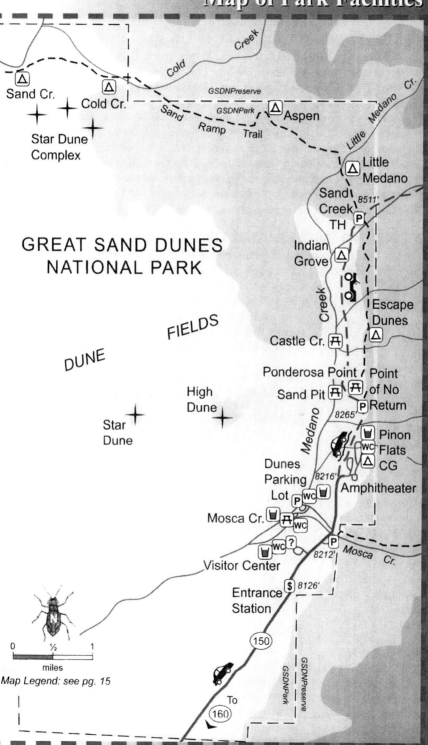

GREAT SAND DUNES
NATIONAL PARK

Sand Cr.

Cold Cr.

Star Dune
Complex

Cold Creek

Sand Ramp Trail

GSDNPreserve

GSDNPark

Aspen

Little Medano Cr.

Little
Medano

Sand
Creek
TH

8511'

Indian
Grove

Escape
Dunes

DUNE FIELDS

Creek

Castle Cr.

Ponderosa Point

Sand Pit

Point
of No
Return

High
Dune

8265'

Medano

Star
Dune

Pinon
Flats
CG

Dunes
Parking
Lot

WC

8216'

Amphitheater

Mosca Cr.

WC

WC   ?

8212'

Mosca Cr.

Visitor Center

Entrance
Station

$ 8126'

150

N

0   ½   1
miles

Map Legend: see pg. 15

To
160

Services Within the Park

RESTROOMS

Once you've entered the Park and Preserve, you'll find restrooms in four areas: the Visitor Center, the Dunes Parking Lot, the Mosca Creek Picnic Area and the Piñon Flats Campground. So, if you find yourself hiking up on the dunes and hear the call of Mother Nature, don't look around for an outhouse up there. If hiking back to the parking lot is not an option, you may be able to find a strategic spot among the hills and valleys of sand to take care of business. Imitate a pet kitty in a sand box: dig a cat hole 1" deep, and thoroughly cover it up when you are done. (Note that *Dunes toiletry etiquette* is slightly different than when you are in normal backcountry conditions. Generally, when hiking where there is soil, you dig a 6" hole for your "deposits.") Remember the principles of **Leave No Trace** (see page 30) and pack out your toilet paper, rather than leaving it to blow in the wind.

DRINKING WATER AND BEVERAGES

Don't venture out onto the dunes or on any other hike without carrying plenty of drinking water with you. You can fill your water bottles at the Visitor Center, or at any of the other restrooms listed above. The Piñon Flats Campground has water hydrants located near each restroom. These provide a much higher water flow than regular drinking fountains, and will expedite the filling of multiple bottles (or larger water containers).

A soda pop machine is located outside the Visitor Center, and at a small kiosk at the entrance to *Loop #2* of Piñon Flats Campground during warmer months.

SHOWERS

Cats like to roll in the sand and dirt as a prelude to a really thorough bath. Since you'll probably feel like you've been rolled in the sand and dirt after a few days of camping and playing on the dunes, you may want to seek out a way to bathe, other than licking the dirt off your legs.

On a hot day, you may enjoy rinsing off using the outdoor **cold showers** and **foot washes** located beside the Dunes Parking Lot. Understand that these are not private showers — you will be in full view of the parking area and the front range of the sand dunes. And remember that this is a family area — no nudity allowed, except for toddlers, two or younger (that's not an official NPS rule).

TELEPHONES

Within the Park and Preserve, phones are located beside the Visitor Center and at the entrance to Piñon Flats Campground. You can make **free local calls** from these phones. For long distance, you must use a phone card or place a credit card or collect call through the Operator — these are NOT pay phones, and there is no way to put money into them.

You'll find many additional services close-at-hand at the **Great Sand Dunes Oasis Store**, just outside the Park entrance station; including hot showers, groceries, meals, laundry and lodging. The Oasis has limited hours and services during the winter months. For even more choices, your best bet is to drive to **Alamosa**, 33 miles away (see page 87.) See the section on *Local Facilities* for full information.

IMPORTANT! If you leave the Park, remember to retain your **entrance fee stub** to show at the entrance station upon Park re-entry.

PICNIC AREAS

For easy access — *and location, location, location* — the **Mosca Creek Picnic Area** is an excellent choice for a picnic. Conveniently located by the Dunes Parking Lot, it offers two large picnic areas (one at the entrance and one at the far end of the loop), and numerous smaller picnic spots within a grove of cottonwoods. There are tables, grills (charcoal fires only), water and restrooms. Mosca Creek flows through the area, offering the kids a chance to splash around a bit while you're getting the food unpacked.

To reach Mosca Creek Picnic Area, drive north past the Visitor Center, and turn left at the first intersection. Follow the road toward the dunes, and turn left just before reaching the Dunes Parking Lot.

There are also several primitive (no water or restrooms) picnic spots along the **Medano Pass Primitive Road** (see page 103,) but you'll need a robust, four-wheel drive vehicle to make it through the deep, soft sand, or a willingness to do a bit of walking. To reach the road, continue on the Park access road, north past both the Visitors Center and the turnoff for the Dunes Parking Lot. When you reach the Amphitheater Parking Lot, turn left.

Passenger cars can drive to **Point of No Return** — a small parking area about 1 mile from the start of the sandy road. From there, walk (or drive, if you dare) to **Ponderosa Point** (0.3 mi / 0.5 km), **Sand Pit** (0.7 mi / 1.1 km), or **Castle Creek** (1.0 mi / 1.6 km) picnic areas. Each of these spots is equipped with one or two picnic tables in the shade of ponderosa pines (guess which picnic area that is!) or cottonwood trees. All offer great views of the sand dunes.

Mosca Creek Picnic Area

Ponderosa Point

Sand Pit

Castle Creek

CAMPGROUND

Piñon Flats Campground offers a beautiful setting amidst a large grove of — you guessed it — **piñon pines**. By the way, you'll also see this tree name spelled as "Pinion" or "Pinyon" or even "Pinon" when someone couldn't figure out how to draw the Spanish *tilde* (that's the squiggly line over the "n"). This is the only developed campground within the Park, with **88 campsites** available

FEES (as of 2003)
$12 per campsite per night / **$6** with Golden Age or Golden Access pass (maximum of 6 people per site.)

on a first-come, first-served basis (no reservations). Come early, and choose a site with great views of the dunes, or one nestled in the trees, or a site beside a small stream. You can even choose a site next to the bathrooms. Speaking of which — the campground has several bathrooms with cold running water, flush toilets, and electricity. Several sites are set up for handicap access.

You'll find a picnic table, fire pit, and space for your tent in each site. Be sure to pitch your tent within the area marked by stonework for your site. In past years, people had been pitching tents on nearly every open spot of land within the entire campground, destroying much of the ground vegetation between sites. Help the area continue to recover by using the flat areas in your site for your tent.

Many sites have enough parking space to accommodate a **recreational vehicle** up to 35 feet long. There are no hookups. Generator operation is limited to the hours of 7 - 9 AM, Noon - 2 PM, and 5 - 7 PM. Quiet hours are from 10 PM to 6 AM.

Just before entering the campground, recreational vehicle owners can use the dump station and refill their water at the service area located in the Amphitheater Parking Lot. At this location you can also get free air for your tires (read more about tire pressure in the section on driving on the Medano Pass Primitive Road on page 103). A large trash dumpster is also at

Late afternoon at Piñon Flats Campground

this site, as well as receptacles for recycling aluminum cans. The dump station and water hose are NOT available during winter months.

Are you looking for a campsite for a large group? There are three **group campsites** at Piñon Flats Campground. These sites may be reserved in advance (and reservations are highly recommended), and cost $3 per person per night. Your group can consist of anywhere from 12 to 50 people. For group reservations or more information, ☎ (719) 378-2312 x220.

Please don't feed or tempt local wildlife to steal your food. Your food isn't healthy for the local critters, and having a bear go after your cooler is definitely not a good thing. The mule deer who hang around the campground will sometimes walk right up to you, looking for a handout. Chipmunks will scurry across your picnic table, attempting to take a nose-dive into your dinner. One managed to dig its way into a zipped pouch attached to one of our backpacks, pulled out a plastic baggie, chewed it open and ate all the *Tums* inside. We figure it must have eaten too much people food, and needed to settle its stomach. Our packs go inside the car from now on.

BACKCOUNTRY CAMPING

For those looking for more of a **wilderness experience**, see the section on *Backcountry and Wilderness Camping* on page 92. The Park has several designated campsites; some as close as a few hundred yards to parking and wheelchair accessible, and others in remote wilderness.

EMERGENCIES

(Unless otherwise noted, all phone numbers are within the 719 Area Code.)

For **medical, fire,** or **law enforcement emergencies,** ☎ 911. Telephones are at the entrance to Piñon Flats Campground and at the Visitor Center.

For **Poison Control,** ☎ *(800) 332-3073.*

For less dire emergencies, stop at the **Visitor Center,** or ☎ *378-6300* during regular business hours, or after hours ☎ *589-5807.*

If you feel the need to visit a hospital, you'll find one in Alamosa:
SLV Regional Medical Center
🏢 *106 Blanca Avenue*
Alamosa, CO 81101
☎ *589-2511*
🖳 *web site: www.slvrmc.org*

For a dental emergencies:
Alamosa Dental Clinic
🏢 *201 Carson Avenue*
Alamosa, CO
☎ *589-9691*

For **towing,** see the *Driving 4WD Roads* section, page 105.

LOCAL FACILITIES

The Cottonwood Inn Bed & Breakfast, Alamosa

Mural on the Crestone Store

The Great Sand Dunes National Park and Preserve is located in a sparsely-populated area of Colorado, nearly 250 miles from Denver by car. Because of its remote location, you won't find a *huge* selection of motels or campgrounds in the immediate vicinity. But that doesn't mean you don't have a number of great options for comfortable lodging or fine dining.

The nearest town large enough to have a variety of motels and restaurants is historic **Alamosa**, about a 40-minute drive southwest of the Park. This old railroad town, and now commercial center for the San Luis Valley, has a population of about 8,800. Other small towns close to the Dunes — such as **Mosca, Hooper, Blanca** and **Fort Garland** — have limited services. But in all you'll find the friendliness of small-town America, a slower-paced way of life and pride in the residents' Anglo/Hispanic heritage. Whether you explore the early-settler style of the **Great Sand Dunes Oasis** "village" or partake of *huevos rancheros* at **Lu's Mainstreet Cafe** in Blanca, relax and enjoy this friendly region.

Sharing ice cream at GSDO Campground

Services Outside the Park

SHOWERS

The **Great Sand Dunes Oasis** complex at the entrance to the Park offers private, hot showers as part of their camping fees. If you are staying elsewhere, you may use a shower at the Oasis for $4 (2002 rates). The Oasis complex is only fully-open from approximately April 1 to November 1 of each year. Hours and services are limited during the winter months.

LAUNDRY

Now that you've had a nice hot shower, you'll want to put on some clean clothes. The Oasis complex has coin-operated washers and dryers available. Alamosa is home to at least two laundromats as well, if you happen to be driving that way: **B&Ds Laundromat**, *510 La Veta Avenue*, *(719) 589-6441* and **Sunshine Laundry**, *217 Market Street*, *(719) 589-5254*.

INTERNET

If you've just gotta get online, stop by the **Public Library** in Alamosa to use one of their internet-connected computers. There is no charge, but you are limited to 30 minutes if anyone else is waiting to get on.

The Library is located directly next door to the **Alamosa Visitor Information Center**. If you are driving into Alamosa from the Great Sand Dunes, take the first right turn after crossing the bridge over the Rio Grande. Library hours are 10:00 AM to 8:00 PM Monday through Thursday; 10:00 AM to 5:00 PM Friday and Saturday; 1:00 PM to 4:00 PM Sunday.

PUBLIC TRANSPORTATION

United Express, *(800) 241-6522*, offers several flights daily between Denver and Alamosa. **Greyhound Bus Lines**, *(719) 589-4948*, has daily bus service linking Alamosa to Denver (to the north) and Albuquerque (to the south).

RENTAL VEHICLES

If you are flying into Colorado and arriving at the major gateways of Denver, Colorado Springs or Pueblo, you'll find numerous automobile rental agencies at the airport or around town. However, when you get away from these larger cities, things can become a bit more limited.

If you are renting a vehicle, and are contemplating driving along the Medano Primitive Road or one of the other rugged four-wheel drive roads (such as the roads to Music Pass or Medano Pass,) DON'T attempt these roads in a mini-SUV, such as a *Subaru Forester* or *Toyota RAV4*. Think "big" and "robust" and "tough" when selecting a vehicle for these challenging roads — think *Blazer* or *4Runner* or *Explorer.*

In Alamosa, **L&M Automobile Rental**, *(719) 589-4651*, *email: autos@amigo.net*, has locations at the Alamosa Airport, as well as a main office on West Avenue. They are open for limited hours Monday through Friday, weekends by reservation only. **Budget Car Rental**, *(800) 527-0700 or (719) 589-0103*, has economy cars starting at about $55 per day, and SUVs start at around $145 per day. This national chain is located at the Alamosa Airport.

Campgrounds

CAMPGROUNDS OUTSIDE THE PARK

Just outside of the Park's entrance on CO 150 is a privately-owned "village," the **Great Sand Dunes Oasis Campground & RV Park**, consisting of a combination gift store/convenience store, a full-service restaurant, a gas station, an RV Park, and a campground (all part of the Great Sand Dunes Oasis). A small motel is also located in this area (Great Sand Dunes Lodge), but it is a separate entity from the "Oasis" facility.

> **FEES** (as of 2002)
> ▌ 70 tent sites, **$12** per night for 2 people.
> ▌ 20 RV sites with full hookups, **$18.50** per night for 2 people.
> ▌ **$2.50** per night for each additional person age five or older.

Campers enjoy the ice cream

Visitors may stay at one of the tent sites located along dirt roads that take you back among the trees. Group campsites are also available. For an extra fee, you can set yourself up in one of the four small cabins. The cabins are very basic, including bunk beds and a double or single bed with cushions, a small table and chairs, and cooking grills and picnic tables located outside each cabin. There are no private bathrooms, no running water, and no other cooking facilities for these cabins.

Another option (for an extra fee) is to spread out your sleeping pads and bags on a wooden platform under a large teepee. Again, you'll find a cooking grill and picnic table outside the entrance to each teepee.

All campers (whether sleeping at a tent site, cabin or teepee, or within your own RV) may use the restrooms with running water, hot showers, laundry, game room, horseshoe pit, and basketball court. On Saturday night, don't miss the **Ice Cream Social** — only $1 (2002). Bring your own bowl and spoon, and be ready for dessert!

The **San Luis Lakes State Park/Mosca Campground** (closed during winter), ☎ *(719) 378-2020*, is on Country Road 6, 13 miles from the Great Sand Dunes entrance, east of CO 17 and west of CO 150.

This state park has 51 sites with fine views of the surrounding mountains, the Great Sand Dunes and San Luis Lake. These are suitable for either RV or tent camping. RVers will find electrical hook-ups and a dump station, but no sewer hook-ups. All campers can enjoy sheltered tables, fire grates, drinking water, hot showers, flush toilets and laundry facilities.

> **FEES** (as of 2002)
> ▌ **$3** day-pass (good from the day purchased until noon the next day.)
> ▌ *Annual State Pass* is $50. Colorado residents 62 years or older qualify for $10 *Aspen Leaf Annual Pass*. Aspen Leaf holders can camp free Sunday through Thursday nights ($3 electrical fee charged.)
> ▌ Camping fee, **$14** per night.

CAMPGROUNDS NEAR ALAMOSA

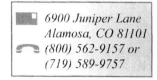

*6900 Juniper Lane
Alamosa, CO 81101
(800) 562-9157 or
(719) 589-9757*

The well-kept **Alamosa KOA**, 3.5 miles east of town on US 160, has grassy sites within a grove of mature cottonwood trees and great views of the Sangre de Cristo Mountains. It has laundry facilities, hot showers, a convenience store, a playground, "Kamping Kabins" and even dataports — all the comforts of home! 38 RV sites and 12 tent sites are available. This campground is open May through October.

Alamosa Economy Campground, Mini-Golf & Go Karts has 12 RV pull-through sites 45 feet or longer with room for slideouts, and 20 tent sites in a separate area. Hot showers are available — useful after paint-ball target practice, driving go-karts, or playing volleyball, horseshoes, mini-golf, or other entertaining activities. Located on US 160, 2.5 miles east of Alamosa, it's open all year.

*12532 Hwy 160 E
Alamosa, CO 81101
(719) 589-5574*

CAMPGROUNDS NEAR BLANCA/FORT GARLAND

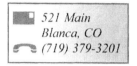

*521 Main
Blanca, CO
(719) 379-3201*

The **Blanca RV Park & Store** has shaded, grassy tent sites (but only 5 of them!) and 26 RV sites with full hookups and pull-thrus. Firewood, laundry facilities, and showers are available. The on-site store has groceries, souvenirs, gasoline, LP gas and fishing supplies. There's even a modem connection available for you technophiles out there. On US 160 in Blanca, it's open all year.

Also open year-round is the **Ute Creek RV Park**,  *Box 188, Fort Garland, CO 81133*, (719) 379-3238.

CAMPGROUNDS NEAR HOOPER/CRESTONE

Nanu, nanu! The aliens have landed, and you can camp among them, watch for them from an elevated platform or buy alien souvenirs at the gift shop.

At the **UFO Watchtower & Campground**, 2.5 miles north of Hooper on CO 17, you'll find 24, long RV sites with room for slideouts on two sides, plus 24 tent sites. If you like trees and grasses when you camp, this is not the place for you. However, this campground offers excellent unobstructed views of the Sangre de Cristo Mountains and the San Juan Mountains, and

*2502 CR 61
Hooper, CO 81136
(719) 378-2271*

of course the Sand Dunes are featured in the vista as well. A central modem connection is available for emailing aliens or friends. No showers, restroom facilities or hookups are available. It's open all year.

The US Forest Service's **North Crestone Campground** has 13 sites in a beautiful mountain environment at 8,300' elevation, each with a picnic table and fire ring, nestled in a pine forest. Drinking water and vault toilets are available. The campground can accommodate vehicles up to 25 feet in length, *barely.* It's open June through October.

To get to the campground, drive into the town of Crestone. Follow the main road as it zigzags through this tiny town. Continue north out of

*46525 State Highway 114
Saguache, CO 81149
(719) 655-2553*

town, following the signs on Forest Road 950. Although a sign says that the campground is 1.0 mile out of town, we measured closer to 1.3 miles.

Lodging

LODGING OUTSIDE THE PARK

Great Sand Dunes Lodge

Immediately outside the entrance to the Park, tucked within the Oasis Village, you'll find the motel located closest to the Dunes. For those who prefer sleeping in queen-sized beds, using their own private bathroom, and the convenience of a telephone and color TV, the **Great Sand Dunes Lodge** offers all this, plus a convenient location And a swimming pool! And in-room coffee *(hurray!)*

This facility has only a small number of rooms, so make your reservations early. The owners are warm and friendly, the rooms are clean and modern and from your private patio, each room has a great view of the Dunes and the backdrop of high peaks. Rates start around $85 per night and the lodge is open from April to October.

7900 Highway 150 N
Mosca, CO 81146
(719) 378-2900
web site: www.gsdlodge.com
email: information@gsdlodge.com

The **Great Sand Dunes Oasis** is located immediately outside the Park entrance. This "village" offers a campground (see the section on *Campgrounds*, page 80) cabins, teepees and two, *count 'em*, two motel rooms. Rates start around $70 per night and lodging is available seasonally (closed in the winter.)

5400 Highway 150 N
Mosca, CO 81146
(719) 378-2222

The two rooms are actually located in a small, rectangular modular building that sits on a lonely stretch of CO 150 about a mile south of the Oasis Village and Park entrance — sort of a *Little House on the Prairie* setting. The building may lack the visual charm of the Ingalls' log cabin, but the views are outstanding. If you're looking for a place that is far from the madding crowd, this is for you.

LODGING IN ALAMOSA

If you really want to treat yourself, consider staying at the **Cottonwood Inn Bed & Breakfast and Gallery**, one of the loveliest places you'll find in this region. Located in a Craftsman-style house built in 1912, this *B&B* is beautifully restored with antiques, reproductions, and local fine artwork. The bedrooms are warm and inviting, and each has its own bathroom. The delicious breakfasts will get you ready for a day at the Dunes.

The Cottonwood Inn also offers an option to stay in one of the apartments next door. Each apartment includes a living room, one bedroom, a private bathroom, and a kitchen with a small eating area. The decor is very 1930s, with the original linoleum in the kitchen, claw-footed bathtub, and the original kitchen sink. It may remind you of a place you lived in as a kid. Yet furnishings are modern and comfortable.

123 San Juan Ave.
Alamosa CO 81101
(800) 955-2623, (719) 589-3882
web site: www.cottonwoodinn.com
email: relax@cottonwoodinn.com

The Cottonwood Inn has a number of packages available combining a stay at the Inn with other activities, such as golf, horseback riding, a visit to local hot springs or a train ride on the Cumbres-Toltec line. Rates start around $70 per night during high season (March to October.)

The following motels are located on US 160. *Days Inn* and *Holiday Inn* are on the east end of town, while the rest are on the west end. The west end of Alamosa is also home to such familiar sights as *K-Mart*, *McDonalds*, and most other national chains.

Best Western Alamosa Inn
1919 Main Street
Alamosa, CO 81101
(719) 589-2567

Comfort Inn of Alamosa
6301 County Road 107 S
Alamosa, CO 81101
(800) 228-5150
(719) 587-9000

Days Inn
224 O'Keefe Parkway
Alamosa, CO 81101
(800) 325-2525 or (719) 589-9037

Grizzly Inn
1919 Main Street
Alamosa, CO 81101
(719) 587-2722

Holiday Inn of Alamosa
333 Santa Fe
Alamosa, CO 81101
(719) 589-5833 or
(800) HOLIDAY

Super 8
2505 W Main
Alamosa , CO 81101
(719) 589-6447
(800) 800-8000

(The *Grizzly Inn* recently split off some rooms from the *Best Western* in an adjoining building. The quality of the rooms is similar in both motels, and both have been recently remodeled. Summer rates start around $90/night; winter rates start around $70/night)

LODGING IN BLANCA/FORT GARLAND

The **Fort Garland Motor Inn** in town along US 160 is immaculately clean and modern. A coin-operated laundry is conveniently located across the street, and an ATM is within a stone's throw of the front entrance, for those cash emergencies that seem to come up when we're on a

Chris and Anna Rajkiewicz
PO Box 96
Fort Garland, CO 81133
719-379-2993
email: frontdesk@fone.net

trip. Rates start around $55 per night. Handicapped-accessible rooms, as well as rooms including kitchens with full-sized appliances, are available for a higher rate.

LODGING IN MOFFAT/CRESTONE AREA

The **White Eagle Village** hotel and conference center offers an attractive setting and pleasant, comfortable rooms, along with an on-site restaurant, massage therapy, and fitness center. There is no smoking inside the buildings.

67485 County Road "T"
Moffat, CO 81143
(719) 256-5865 or 1-800-613-2270
web site: www.whiteeaglevillage.com/
email: info@whiteeaglehotel.com

This is a "get-away-from-it-all" sort of place, with no TV or phones in the rooms. Instead, entertain yourself at the golf course next door *(Challenger Golf Club),* or enjoy fantastic hiking and fishing opportunities just minutes away in the Sangre de Cristo Mountains.

Hotel rooms start at $45 per night. Shared "hostel" rooms are also available for $15 per night. Special "Stay and Play" packages for lodging, plus golf, are available.

Other fun places to stay in the Moffat/Crestone area are:

Willow Spring B&B
Formerly the historic *Forbes Hotel* built in 1910 as part of the railroad land boom. Rates start at $45 per night, single occupancy
P.O. Box 500, Moffat, Colorado 81143
719-256-4116
web site: www.willow-spring.com

Silver Star Bed & Breakfast
Rates start at $40 per night, single
557 Panorama Way, PO Box 476, Crestone CO 81131
719-256-4686
web site: www.angelfire.com/co2/SilverStar

Rainbow Bed & Breakfast
Rates start at $40 per night, single
223 Rainbow Overlook, Box 293, Crestone, CO 81131
719-256-4110, (800) 530-1992
web site: www.angelfire.com/co/rainbowbb

Restaurants and Groceries

I thought YOU brought the cooler! If you're running low on food supplies, don't despair. There are several places (at least during "tourist season") very close to the Park entrance, and plenty of places in nearby towns where you can buy groceries or get someone else to do the cooking.

As we traveled through this portion of the San Luis Valley, we found numerous little cafes and diners with menus featuring, what we began to refer to as, *standard southwest diner* fare. Burgers, BLTs, turkey or ham sandwiches, soups, salads, and chicken-fried steak are readily available at many of these spots. The **southwest influence** also adds burritos, tostadas, tacos, and chile rellenos to many of these menus. Many of the diners are open for breakfast, where you can find inexpensive, hearty portions of eggs, pancakes, French toast, and *(this is the southwest, folks)* breakfast burritos and huevos rancheros.

For those seeking a change of cuisine, head for the towns of Crestone and Alamosa. Note that all restaurants in Alamosa are smoke-free.

RESTAURANTS OUTSIDE THE PARK

The **Great Sand Dunes Oasis Restaurant** is located in Oasis "village," just outside the Park entrance. It's open seven days a week, 8:00 AM to 7:00 PM (8:00 PM Memorial Day through Labor Day), closed from November through March.

Without a doubt, the highlight of the food here is the fresh **home-made pie.** If you're lucky enough to stop in for a treat on one of the days that the baker ("Grandma") has been hard at work, you may find yourself with such a huge choice of flavors that you'll have trouble making up your mind. By the second day, the selection may be more limited, since others before you have been involved in pie-eating frenzies. That's OK; even the leftover pies are probably the best you've ever tasted. We're lobbying Grandma to adopt us.

Grandma's pie

Breakfast is inexpensive and features the usual egg dishes, pancakes, french toast, and an excellent (and huge) breakfast burrito. Lunch and dinner items include many typical All-American items, such as sandwiches, hamburgers and fish & chips, plus some southwestern items like burritos, chili, and *Navajo Tacos.* At dinner,

*5400 Highway 150 North
Mosca, CO 81146
(719) 378-2222*

steak, chicken, chicken-fried steak, and liver & onions are added to the fare. Yes, this is the *standard southwest diner,* with some extras.

GROCERIES OUTSIDE THE PARK

The nearest place to purchase groceries, as well as **gasoline** and sundry items, is at the **Great Sand Dunes Oasis Store** at the Park entrance. The general store is only open occasionally during the winter months of November through March. The store stocks a limited supply of groceries. As you might imagine, due to their location, they seldom have fresh fruit or vegetables. However they do carry canned goods, pancake mix, dry pasta, as well as milk and eggs. And let's not forget the beer and *Haagen-Dazs* ice cream bars!

RESTAURANTS IN ALAMOSA

PRICES (as of 2002)
$ under $10
$$ from $10 to $20
$$$ from $20 to $30

Alamosa has a number of restaurants, ranging from the typical national, fast-food chains, to steakhouses, to Chinese and to Mexican cuisine — *lots of Mexican cuisine!* Most of the action is concentrated on the main drag in town (US 160), appropriately named Main Street. Here are a few of the choices available.

You'll find a wide range of dishes available at the **Grizzly Inn Restaurant & Pub** *($$-$$$)*, including Caesar salad, steaks, chicken dishes, seafood and pasta. The salad bar is cleverly presented in an old covered wagon. Ask for the wine list, and check out the dessert specials. There is a very reasonably-priced daily breakfast special, Sunday brunch buffet and a taco bar on Friday nights. They're open seven

1919 Main Street
Alamosa, CO 81101
(719) 587-2722

days a week, 6:00 AM to 10:00 PM. The restaurant is next door to the *Grizzly Inn,* an attractive alternative to the name-brand motels in the area.

Oscar's Restaurant *($-$$)* is one of our favorite Mexican restaurants anywhere. Try the fajitas or whatever is on special. Actually, try anything on the menu — we've never been disappointed.

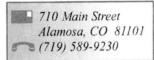
710 Main Street
Alamosa, CO 81101
(719) 589-9230

For those among you who don't think you like Mexican food, you can always order a steak, a burger or a sandwich. They're probably quite good too, but we're telling you that you're missing out on some great Mexican food. Oscar's is open Sunday through Thursday, 11:00 AM to 8:00 PM; Friday and Saturday, 11:00 AM to 9:00 PM.

Another excellent choice for lunch or dinner is the **Hunan Chinese Restaurant** *($-$$)*. We were pleased with the very fresh taste of the food (not like some restaurants that seem to keep dishes on a steam table for days on end), and the extensive selection of dishes available. We counted 39 different entrees for lunch, but lost count of the options available for dinner. A *Thai-style* dish that was the special one night was particularly

419 Main Street
Alamosa, CO 81101
(719) 589-9002

delicious, with just the right degree of spiciness for an American palette to handle. Check them out Monday through Saturday, 11:00 AM to 9:00 PM; closed Sunday.

In addition to a variety of espresso drinks, lattes, mochas, and teas at the **Milagros Coffeehouse** *($$)*, you can also enjoy sandwiches, quiche, salads, soups, bagels and ice cream at this comfortable coffeehouse, located in downtown Alamosa. Local musicians entertain with live music about twice a month, with styles ranging from jazz, to folk, to light rock. Milagros is a non-profit establishment which raises funds for *La Puente,* a homeless shelter that also provides job readiness training to help people return to the

529 Main
Alamosa, CO 81101
(719) 589-9299

workforce. Their hours are Monday through Saturday, 7:00 AM to 6:00 PM; open Sundays for special events only.

GROCERIES IN ALAMOSA

You can't go wrong with either of these huge, new supermarkets, both located along US 160. There's **Safeway**, ▮ *1301 Main Street, Alamosa, CO 81101,* ⌒*(719) 587-3075,* and **City Market,** ▮ *131 Market Street, Alamosa, CO 81101,* ⌒ *(719) 589-2492,* with a salad bar that is truly impressive.

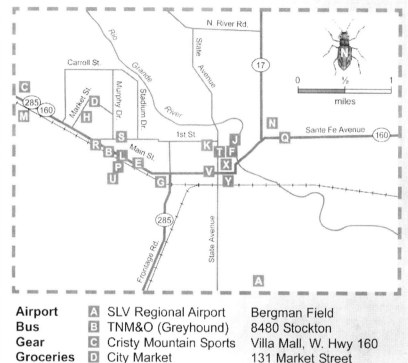

Airport	A	SLV Regional Airport	Bergman Field
Bus	B	TNM&O (Greyhound)	8480 Stockton
Gear	C	Cristy Mountain Sports	Villa Mall, W. Hwy 160
Groceries	D	City Market	131 Market Street
	E	Safeway	1301 Main Street
Info.	F	Chamber of Commerce	Cole Park
Laundry	G	B & D Laundromat	501 La Veta Avenue
	H	Sunshine Laundry	217 Market Street
Library	J	Alamosa Public Library	423 4th Street
Lodging	K	Cottonwood Inn B & B	123 San Juan Avenue
	L	Best Western Inn	1919 Main Street
	M	Comfort Inn	6301 County Road 107 S
	N	Days Inn	224 O'Keefe Parkway
	P	Grizzly Inn	1919 Main Street
	Q	Holiday Inn	333 Sante Fe
	R	Super 8	2505 W. Main Street
Medical	S	SLV Medical Center	106 Blanca Avenue
Post Office	T	Alamosa Post Office	505 3rd Street
Restaurant	U	Grizzly Inn Restaurant	1919 Main Street
	V	Oscar's Restaurant	710 Main Street
	X	Hunan Chinese Rest.	419 Main Street
	Y	Milagros Coffeehouse	529 Main Street
Showers		Alamosa Rec. Center	(719) 589-2105

RESTAURANTS IN BLANCA/FORT GARLAND

As you drive through the town of Blanca along U.S. Highway 160, you can't miss seeing **Lu's Mainstreet Cafe** *($$-$$$)* on the south side of the road. This place has a 70s look to it, with wood

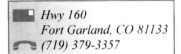
609 Main Street (Hwy 160)
Blanca, CO 81123
(719) 379-8646

paneling on the walls. Walk on in, seat yourself (smoking and non-smoking areas are provided), and dig in to some typical American fare or try out the Mexican food.

Breakfast options include giant hot cakes, malted Belgium waffles, fresh cinnamon rolls, breakfast burritos, omelets, biscuits & gravy or even steak & eggs. Lunch and dinner selections include hot and cold sandwiches, hamburgers, steak, pork chops, chicken fried steak, fish & chips, salads and Mexican items such as enchiladas, burritos, tacos, tostadas, and rellenos. Pie and cake can top off your meal. Lou's is open seven days a week, 6:30 AM to 8:00 PM (or later if they're busy)

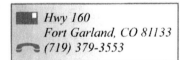
Hwy 160
Fort Garland, CO 81133
(719) 379-3357

Elvis posters (and clocks) are complimented by a few Marilyn Monroe posters at **Del's Diner** in Fort Garland *($$-$$$.)* Yes, you can enjoy a burger, a BLT, chicken, ham, or fish, chicken fried steak and chili while you enjoy the 50s theme. You'll even find meals for the kids ranging from about $1.25 to $3.50. Decent food at reasonable prices. It's open daily, 6:30 AM to 8:00 PM (no credit cards accepted.)

The small **Ute Café** *($$-$$$)* is located on the north side of US 160 in the town of Fort Garland. The menu includes the expected *standard southwest diner* items, but focuses on Mexican dishes. There are also some unusual items, such as the "Half Breed" (we wouldn't make up a name like that) which consists of Italian sausage on a flour tortilla, served with a side of spaghetti smothered in green chile. You

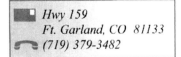
Hwy 160
Fort Garland, CO 81133
(719) 379-3553

won't find that on every menu! Another adventurous dish is the Chicharrone burrito. That's fried pork skin and refried beans wrapped in a tortilla and smothered in green chile. It's an acquired taste.

For dessert-lovers, try the apple pie with cinnamon ice cream, a specialty here. The Ute is open Sunday through Friday, 8:00 AM to "dinnertime" depending on how busy they are (non-smoking only.)

GROCERIES IN BLANCA/FORT GARLAND

Hwy 159
Ft. Garland, CO 81133
(719) 379-3482

The **Old Fort Market**, one block south of US 160 on CO 159 and next to the Fort Garland Museum, is larger than your typical "general store," but is much smaller than a "supermarket." However, they do stock fresh meat, vegetables and fruit, along with a wide assortment of packaged foods. They even have one of those chicken roasters where you can buy a whole roaster right off the spit (smells great!). A nice bonus is the hot coffee bar where you can grab a cup of coffee, tea or hot chocolate. The market is open 7:00 AM to 7:00 PM Monday through Saturday; 8:00 AM to 4:00 PM Sunday.

RESTAURANTS IN CRESTONE

Baca Townhouse Complex
Crestone, CO 81131
(719) 256-4402

Time for a delicious and healthy meal at **The Desert Sage Restaurant** *($$-$$$)!* It's open daily 7:00 AM to 1:30 PM and 5:30 PM to 8:30 PM. The dinner menu changes nightly, depending on the chef, but a recent sample included: cornmeal-crusted, ruby-red trout filet with onion and bacon compote, herb-marinated chicken breast on mashers with vegetables, beef tenderloin, salmon, ahi steak and fried rice with vegetables and tofu.

The salad bar here is as wonderful as the entrees. Consider picking up a freshly-baked loaf of bread while you're here. Yum!

Iktomi's Kitchen *($$),* *(719) 256-5157,* is located in the miniature "shopping center" just east of the Crestone Store. Try a breakfast burrito, huevos rancheros, buffalo burger, veggie burger or the specialty of the house, a *Potato Skillet.* Smoothies are another specialty, and the chef selects nightly specials for your dinner dining pleasure. You can even sample a dish made with local goat cheese. Rumor has it that the *organic, free-trade* coffee here is the best around.

Iktomi's is open daily for breakfast and lunch, and open Friday, Saturday, and Sunday for dinner. The exact schedule seems to change frequently.

GROCERIES IN CRESTONE

Just when you think this is a typical little general store, look more closely at the items on the shelves of the **Crestone Store.** You may spot sauces and ingredients for Thai, Indian, Japanese, and Polynesian dishes. "Natural" and "organic" labels are everywhere. For the kids' breakfast, you can choose anything from *Mother's Peanut Butter Bumpers Cereal* to *Enviro Kidz Organic Orangutan-O's Cereal.* Just remember that Crestone is a very "spiritual" community, and is home to a Zen center, Baptist church, Ashram, Episcopal church, Tibetan stupa and other religious and spiritual organizations. Then again, that doesn't mean the people here can't enjoy drinking a *Bud* and cheering on participants in a pie-eating contest.

Gas is also available from pumps just outside the store.

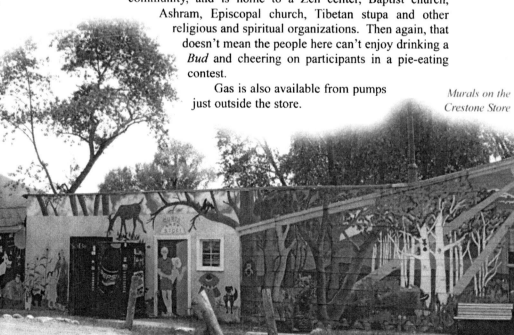

Murals on the Crestone Store

ACTIVITIES

Backpacking up Willow Lakes Trail

Hiker on Revelation Point

Things To Do

Backcountry and 92
 Wilderness Camping
Birdwatching 100
Driving 4WD 103
 Roads
Dune Skiing, ...107
 Boarding, Sledding,
 & Rolling
Horseback Riding . .108
Hunting & Fishing . .111
Mountain Biking 112
Park Organized 115
 Activities
Photography 116
Watching Wildlife . . .118

Hiking

Hikes In the Park . .122
Eastern Access 154
 Hikes
Western Access . . . 172
 Hikes
Hikes in Zapata . . . 176
 Falls Recreation Area

Climbing

Climbs in 184
 the Preserve
Climbs South of . . .188
 the Park & Preserve
Climbs North of 190
 the Park & Preserve

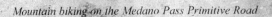

Mountain biking on the Medano Pass Primitive Road

THINGS TO DO

Enjoying the view on top of High Dune (highest point on the dune fields)

Snowboarding on the dunes

The Great Sand Dunes National Park and Preserve is a great place to camp in the wilderness, to discover the lives of critters through birding or watching for other wildlife, to bike or drive a remote mountain track, or take photos, ride a horse, and, if you like — take an exciting run, jump, roll or slide down a shifting slope of sand!

You'll undoubtedly be drawn out on to the dunes to explore. You can climb as high as you like on these mountains of sand. Your reward will be seeing exciting views of the San Luis Valley and the surrounding mountain ranges, capped by 14,000-foot peaks. Perhaps this will inspire you to extend your adventures into the vast backcountry beyond the dunes. You can use this chapter to help plan most of your activities (hiking and climbing are covered in the next two chapters.)

While most activities can be self-planned, the Park Service also schedules lot of fun and interesting activities for visitors. You'll want to stop at the Visitor Center and check out ranger-led **nature walks** and **campfire programs** during the summer months. Concessioners also operate in the Park and Preserve, offering horseback riding and 4WD touring. And the **Friends of the Dunes** (see page 32) offer special activities, such as their annual Christmas bird count, that you might want to join in on.

Backcountry and Wilderness Camping

Backcountry camping

Are the official campgrounds starting to remind you a little too much of home? Want to get away from neighbors, TVs, generators, and Frisbee games? For those looking for more of a *wilderness experience* within the Park, consider obtaining a free **backcountry camping permit** at the Visitor Center. No permits are needed to camp in the Preserve.

Within the Park, there are several **designated primitive backcountry sites** available, or consider a unique adventure of camping somewhere on the dunes for the night! There is even a wheelchair-accessible site along the Medano Pass Primitive Road, with a fire grate and outdoor privy.

When you get your free backcountry camping permit, the staff at the Visitor Center will let you know where you may leave your vehicle overnight. You must display your **overnight parking permit** on your car and park in the area assigned to you.

If you plan to cook anything while camping in the backcountry, take along a gas stove. No wood or charcoal fires are allowed. Pitch your tent within 50 feet of the "arrowhead" sign that marks each designated backcountry campsite. Inquire at the Visitor Center before you leave about the availability of water near your site. Some sites may be near water during the spring months, but the streams may dry up at other times of the year, so plan ahead. Don't drink untreated water — **giardia** may be present in any stream or pond. The water may look clear and taste great, and you won't experience the nasty symptoms due to giardia right away. However, once it "hits" in one to three weeks, your world will center around being very, very close to a bathroom. Boil, filter or chemically treat all drinking water obtained from streams, and life will be good.

Some of the backcountry sites have a designated privy. For those that do not, take a little walk away from your campsite, and at least 200 feet away from any water sources, and dig a little "cat hole" six inches deep (one inch deep on the dunes) and bury your "droppings."

Pack out all trash — no one will be coming by to pick it up for you! Keep your food stored so you don't attract wildlife to sample your energy bars and *Twinkies*. Never feed any wildlife; many human foods are harmful to birds and animals. If we feed them, they lose their natural behavior around people and can become a nuisance, or even a danger to campers.

CAMPING ON THE DUNES

With a backcountry permit in hand, take a hike of a mile or more out onto the dunes from the designated overnight parking to a spot of your liking (as long as it isn't a *day-use only* area), and set up your camp.

Consider starting your hike just after dinner, to reduce your load and to avoid extremely hot sand on a sunny day. Brief afternoon and early evening thunderstorms are quite common during the summer, so plan accordingly. Remember, there is no water up here on the dunes. You'll need to carry all your water, and remember to bring a backcountry stove and fuel, if you plan to cook.

Watch the shadows shift and lengthen as the sun sets, and enjoy the beautiful display of stars above you. This region is blessed with clear skies on most nights, almost no light pollution from nearby towns, and is very, very quiet. Camping on the sand dunes will take your mind and spirit far away from the world of rush hours, cell phones, meetings and deadlines. Lie back on the sand and sense the slow rotation of the earth, as the stars shift above you. Listen for the haunting voices of coyotes or the scuffling of small animals emerging from their shelters beneath the surface of the dunes.

You'll miss a lot of the magic of this special destination if you choose to sleep in a tent. However, the dunes exist because of wind. Light winds can coat you, and your gear, with a layer of fine sand and dust; stronger winds can give you a sand-blasting demonstration, with you as the target. If strong winds are forecast, consider rescheduling your overnight experience on the dunes for another night. If the winds do pick up, you can always bury your head inside your bag. For those warmer summer nights, though, covering your face with a breathable, lightweight shirt or scarf may be more comfortable. Finally, consider bringing along ski goggles to protect your eyes in case of bothersome winds, especially if you wear contact lenses.

Oh, and one other thing — you've probably realized there aren't any privies out on the dunes. If the need arises, dig a hole in the sand one inch deep (not the usual six inches, recommended for normal soil) and cover it up, cat-box style, when you are finished. Pack out all paper — *including you-know-what kind* — and other trash. Plastic bags are very helpful for this matter.

"Lie back on the sand and sense the slow rotation of the earth, as the stars shift above you."

Camping out on the dunes without a tent

DESIGNATED BACKCOUNTRY SITES

The Park Service maintains several **designated backcountry sites** within the Park. To reach the following campsites, drive up the **Medano Pass Primitive Road** which is suitable for passenger cars for one mile (1.6 km) to Point of No Return. If you have a high-clearance, four-wheel drive vehicle with a low gear, you may be able to drive further along the road to an overnight parking area closer to your selected campsite. Discuss this option with the Park staff when you obtain your overnight parking permit at the Visitor Center. The minimum towing fee here is $100, so review the cautions in the *Driving 4WD Roads* section, page 103.

> **IMPORTANT!** Water is a major issue when camping in the backcountry. If you are backpacking into these sites, you'll need a minimum of a gallon of water, per person, per day. (Let's see: water weighs a pound per pint, so two gallons for two days weighs 16 pounds. *Ouch!*)

While most of the backcountry campsites aren't far from streams, many of these streams dry up and disappear over the course of the summer. Be sure to ask a ranger for an update on the flow of streams near your selected campsite before you set out!

For **Sawmill Canyon Campsite** (8,400'), drive up the Medano Pass Primitive Road, approximately 0.8 miles (1.3 km) from its start near the amphitheater, to the gated parking area on your right. Follow the gentle path as it works its way gradually uphill to the campsite, about 175 yards from where you parked. The trail is only slightly sandy, and is very well maintained, allowing **wheelchair access** to the site.

This campsite is outfitted with a picnic table, fire pit, bear boxes for storing food and a composting toilet, which is handicapped-accessible. Nestled among tall trees, with an intermittent stream (Sawmill Creek) close by and glimpses of surrounding peaks above the trees, it offers a true backcountry experience, while still being easy to get to.

Sawmill Canyon Campsite can be reserved in advance. Note that there is a locked gate at the entrance to the campsite, so don't forget to check in at the Visitor Center for a permit before heading out!

To reach **Escape Dunes Campsite** (8,500'), drive up the Medano Pass Primitive Road one mile (1.6 km) to the Point of No Return parking area. Look for the large trailhead sign

To find your way around, see the *Park Facilities Map* on page 73!

Encroaching escape dune near Escape Dunes Campsite

Mule deer near Escape Dunes Campsite

by the parking area, describing the **Little Medano Trail** (renamed in 2002 as the **Sand Ramp Trail**.) Hike 1.4 miles (2.3 km) north along the Sand Ramp Trail, past Castle Creek. A sign along the trail will direct you to turn right and walk a short distance to the campsite. This campsite is shaded by tall ponderosa pines, and lies close to several **escape dunes**, and the remains of trees smothered by the sands. We encountered a small herd of mule deer grazing beside this camp.

In a wet spring, you may be able to obtain water from Castle Creek, which you'll cross shortly before arriving at the camp. However, often you'll need to carry all your water to this camp.

For **Indian Grove Campsite** (8,500'), either hike the Sand Ramp Trail, starting at Point of No Return, or hike/drive north from Point of No Return along the Medano Pass Primitive Road.

The site is 2.9 miles (4.8 km) beyond the Point of No Return parking area. If you hike along the Sand Ramp Trail, you'll cross Castle Creek and hike past the turn for the Escape Dunes Campsite. Continuing along, a sign by the trail will direct you to turn left to reach Indian Grove. Take a break here to explore the beautiful grove of ponderosa pines and to examine the **peeled trees** in this area. These trees had sections of

Examining peeled trees

bark peeled by the Ute Indians, who passed through this area from the late-1700s through the early-1900s.

If you are traveling to the Indian Grove Campsite along the Medano Pass Primitive Road, look for the sign directing you to the campsite. From the road, the campsite is to your left (west). Groves of peeled trees can be found on both sides of the road.

Now you're ready to go set up camp. Follow the trail west, cross the Medano Pass Primitive Road and continue on the trail as it drops into a low, flat area within another grove of ponderosa pines, near the foot of the dunes. This campsite has a self-composting toilet, surrounded by a privacy fence, so you won't need to do your cat-sandbox thing when you stay at this site. Water may be available from Medano Creek near this campsite.

The **Little Medano Campsite** (8,800') is the next one you will reach as you continue hiking north along the Sand Ramp Trail. It offers great views of the dunes, as well as **Mt. Herard** to the north and the **Blanca Peak** massif to the south. Since it lies between Medano Creek and Little Medano Creek, there is often a reliable water supply within a reasonable distance of this site. The Little Medano Campsite lies only about 0.5 mile (0.8 km) from the Sand Creek parking area on Medano Pass Primitive Road, so it can be a short hike for those driving a robust, four-wheel drive vehicle, capable of navigating the dreaded *Sand Pit* section of the road. This can be a good "beginner" backpack destination (if you can drive to Sand Creek Trailhead) due to the short hiking distance from that point. Those walking from Point of No Return face a 3.9 mile (6.5 km) walk along the trail.

Aspen Campsite (9,200') is our favorite backcountry campsite. It is along the Sand Ramp Trail, 5.7 miles (9.5 km) from the Point of No Return parking area and 2.3 miles (3.8 km) from the Sand Creek Trailhead. It's also the highest of the designated sites, provides good views of the dunes from an angle most visitors never see, is nested in a grove of aspen trees and lies beneath the picturesque **Heavenly Valley** (a local name for a lovely area.) But remember — since it is at a higher elevation, that means you'll be hiking up several long, sandy hills to get here. We recommend pumping water from Little Medano Creek (if it is still flowing) when you cross it on the way to this camp. Be sure to ask about where you can obtain water before you set out; you may have to pick

Sunrise on the dunes from Aspen Campsite

up water from Medano Creek (which means hiking south on the Sand Ramp Trail from the Sand Creek Trailhead parking), or it is possible that you will need to carry all your water with you.

If you camp here, you may want to set aside most of a day to hike and explore Heavenly Valley, a beautiful backdrop to this fine campsite.

From the Aspen Campsite, continue climbing uphill along the Sand Ramp Trail to a point above the tallest dunes, with a great view of the dune field, then drop *down, down, down* into a valley, with Cold Creek flowing near the **Cold Creek Campsite** (8,400'). Or, perhaps you'll encounter a dry streambed instead (ask the rangers before you go.) This camp lies within a stand of ponderosa pines, with a steep, vegetated dune between it and the main dune field, 8.9 miles (14.8 km) from Point of No Return and 4.8 miles (8 km) from the Sand Creek Trailhead. This valley is popular with wildlife, including mountain lions, bear, elk and deer.

An ominous sign that this really is the end of the trail at Sand Creek Campsite

Hike a short distance further along the Sand Ramp Trail for a view of the **Star Dune Complex** section of the Park. This region features numerous **star dunes** with three or more slip-faces.

A long hike (or ride on horseback) brings you to the end of the Sand Ramp Trail and the **Sand Creek Campsite** (8,800'), 10.5 miles (17.5 km) from the Point of No Return parking area and 7.1 miles (11.8 km) from the Sand Creek Trailhead. In the future, there are plans to extend this trail to the north, to hook up with the trail up Sand Creek, near the ghost town of Liberty.

When Sand Creek is flowing, you can enjoy fishing in the shade of a large grove of cottonwoods. (Don't forget to obtain a Colorado fishing license before you set out.) Elk and riparian birdlife may be seen in this area, which features a much different natural environment than the rest of the designated backcountry camps.

Sunset on the dunes

WILDERNESS CAMPING AND BACKPACKING

Packing up the Medano Pass Primitive Road

If you set out to explore some of the wonderful hiking trails that lead you into the National Preserve, you may want to turn your adventure into a multi-day **backpacking trip**. Once outside the boundaries of the National Park, you may camp virtually anywhere without a permit.

You'll find detailed descriptions and maps for all the trails in the Park and Preserve in the section on *Hiking*, page 120. Many of these can be joined up for an extended backpacking trip of almost any length. **Medano Lake** is a popular destination, by packing up the Medano Pass Primitive Road, starting at either end. Also very popular is the beautiful pack over **Music Pass**, from the east side of the Sangre de Cristo Range, providing access to the spectacular alpine lakes of upper Sand Creek. Those who have established a car shuttle may continue west over so-called **Cottonwood Pass**, exiting into the San Luis Valley at the Baca Grande subdivision. In the future, the Park plans on developing accesses on the west side of the range, within the newly acquired portions of the old Baca land grant, for possible wilderness pack trips into the alpine headwaters of Sand Creek, Pole Creek and Deadman Creek.

Be aware of **hunting season** when you are in the Preserve, and wear festive colors (blaze orange is best) during these times. You don't want someone to mistake you for an elk, do you? Hang your food in a tree, or close it up within your vehicle whenever you aren't in the process of cooking your meal or eating. Don't invite the bears to your picnic!

Most important of all — enjoy the quiet wonders of the spectacular Sangre de Cristo Mountains. You'll take home some incredible memories from a backpacking trip into the alpine wilderness.

When in the National Preserve, always keep the guidelines of *Leave No Trace* in mind (see page 30), and focus on these rules in particular:

▌ Pick a campsite where others have already camped. Place your tent within the marked boundaries, where you won't be damaging additional vegetation.

▌ If you must have a fire, use only existing fire rings. Do not cut down any trees or branches — use dead wood already provided by *Mother Nature*. It's preferable to use a backpacking stove for cooking.

▌ Park your vehicle no further than 100 feet from the road, and only drive on established roads and access "driveways."

▌ Follow the same rules already described for camping within the Park, regarding carrying out your trash and dealing with *calls of nature*.

Wilderness camping in the Preserve after a fall snow storm

MEDANO PASS ROAD CORRIDOR CAMPING

The upper, six-mile portion of the **Medano Pass Primitive Road** (within the National Preserve) is lined with 25, marked and numbered, **roadside campsites**. Many of these sites are nestled in the trees. Some offer views of rock outcroppings along Medano Pass, and all are within a short distance of Medano Creek, which zigzags back and forth along the road.

Wildlife is abundant in this area. During one particularly interesting summer day, we spotted a herd of bighorn sheep, a buck with a good-sized rack and a big, healthy-looking bear searching for food. We made sure our food was closed up inside our car (which is also where we were, at the time.)

Be sure to set up your tent within the marked boundaries of the site you've chosen, and use the existing **fire rings** rather than building your own.

No permits are needed to camp in the established sites, or any other sites within the National Preserve.

The Medano Primitive Road can be accessed from within the National Park (where deep, soft sand often stops even four-wheel drive vehicles in

You may also camp in other, unmarked spots along the road, as long as you follow these guidelines:

▮ Don't camp where signs indicate the spot is closed to camping.

▮ Don't build new fire rings, and don't build a wood fire.

▮ Drive and park on the roadway or within an existing parking area only.

their tracks.) Before you try this access, read our cautions in the *Driving 4WD Roads* section, page 103. An alternative is to reach the road from the Wet Mountain Valley to the east, and up over Medano Pass. We call the access roads to the key passes from the Wet Mountain Valley *the Good, the Bad and the Ugly.* The road to Medano Pass from the east is merely *bad.* We wouldn't try it in most passenger cars, but if you have a four-wheel drive vehicle — even a mini-SUV — you can probably manage the drive. Follow the driving instructions on page 156 to reach Medano Pass from CO 69. From the pass, drive down the steep dirt road to a "T" intersection, where you'll turn left to continue down the Medano Primitive Road toward the Great Sand Dunes.

The Medano Pass Primitive Road is closed during the winter.

Camping at a marked site along the Medano Pass Primitive Road

Birdwatching

Birding in the Park

The Park and Preserve, and surrounding portions of the San Luis Valley, offer wonderful bird watching opportunities for the experienced birder, or for anyone who just likes looking at these feathered creatures. Situated on a **major flyway**, the valley sees a large number of species, as great waves pass through on annual migration.

Also contributing to the variety of bird species is the rich diversity of habitats in a small area. The wetlands and marshes of the valley floor attract huge numbers of waterfowl and shore birds. The cottonwoods and willows along the Rio Grande River are the best songbird habitat in the valley. And the elevation gradient in the Park and Preserve — from desert grasslands to alpine tundra — creates ecological niches that elsewhere might be hundreds of miles apart. Compressed in a small distance is a very diverse band of bird species.

Common birds within the Park and Preserve itself include: **red-tailed hawk**, **American kestrel** (a falcon), **mourning dove**, **common nighthawk**, **white-throated swift**, **broad-tailed hummingbird**, Lewis' and **downy woodpeckers**, **Say's phoebe**, **horned lark**, **violet-green swallow**, **Steller's jay**, **piñon jay**, **magpie**, **common raven**, **mountain chickadee**, **bushtit**, **mountain bluebird**, **Townsend's solitaire**, **yellow-rumped warbler**, **western tanager**, **pine siskin**, **black-headed grosbeak**, **green-tailed towhee**, **chipping sparrow**, **gray-headed junco** and **blue grouse**. Perhaps you'll even spot an *American ball-capped camera-toter* in or near the Visitor Center.

Speaking of the Visitor Center, you can pick up *A Checklist of the Birds of Great Sand Dunes National Monument* for just 50 cents in the bookstore. You may also want to bring along a field guide, complete with photos and detailed descriptions of birds. The **Montville Trail**, and the connecting **Mosca Pass**

Blue grouse

Trail, are excellent areas for spotting birds. Find a comfortable spot among the trees or at the edge of a meadow, and keep your eyes and ears open. Mountain bluebirds are often seen in open areas, and along the roads.

Nearby **Zapata Falls Recreation Area** also attracts birds. The falls area is one of a few known Colorado breeding sites for the uncommon **black swift**, which nests in the dark recesses and spray of large waterfalls.

Greater sandhill cranes

WILDLIFE REFUGES

Also nearby are the **Alamosa** and **Monte Vista National Wildlife Refuges**, located southeast and west of the town of Alamosa respectively. See the *Attractions* section, page 204 for driving directions.

In the spring, the San Luis Valley is noted for the arrival of tens of thousands of **greater sandhill cranes** (and a few thousand **lesser sandhill cranes**, as well). Celebrate the migration of these wonderful birds with over 7,000 other bird *aficionados* at the annual **Crane Festival** weekend, held in early to mid March, centered at the Monte Vista Refuge. These amazing birds may fly at elevations as high as 30,000 feet (along with commercial jets), and average 45 miles per hour. When thousands take off from the wetlands in the early morning, the sight and sound is unlike anything you've ever experienced. As writer Aldo Leopold so eloquently described in *A Sand County Almanac*, "When we hear his call we hear no mere bird. We hear the trumpet in the orchestra of evolution. He is the symbol of our untamable past . . . Their annual return is the ticking of the geologic clock. Upon the place of their return they confer a peculiar distinction."

At one time, in the midst of thousands of sandhill cranes, you might have spotted, with luck, a larger crane, standing nearly five-feet tall, with snow-white feathers, black wing tips, and red and black head. This was the rare and endangered **whooping crane**, brought back from the edge of extinction. Efforts to increase the wild populations of this majestic bird, with a wingspan of 7½ feet, have been very creative. Whooping crane eggs were transferred to sandhill crane nests, so that the adoptive birds would learn to migrate with the large sandhill flocks. The *whoopers* adjusted to their new families a bit too well. Instead of wanting to mate with other whooping cranes, they were attracted to sandhills instead. *Oops.*

The next effort was to teach whooping crane chicks to follow an ultra-light aircraft and learn their migration pattern from the little plane. This method is still being evaluated. The good news is that the cranes don't try to mate with ultra-light planes or hang-gliders.

Unfortunately for now, the last of the whooping cranes known to migrate through the San Luis Valley, a 19-year old female, died recently in an apparent collision with a power line. Maybe we can borrow an ultra-light and a few whooping cranes from another part of the country?

Although the best viewing location for all these cranes is at the Monte Vista Refuge, cranes can also be seen along 6 Mile Lane, especially near San Luis Lakes, and near other wet areas in the valley, such as the Alamosa National Wildlife Refuge.

Canada goose

Turkey vultures

Western meadowlark

It's possible that we're beginning to see an effect of the recent drought in Colorado on the wild bird populations in the San Luis Valley. According to two separate counts conducted in December of 2002, as part of the National Audubon Society's 103rd annual **Christmas bird count**, results in the Monte Vista Wildlife Refuge and in the Great Sand Dunes Park and Preserve were unusually low, both in species and numbers of individuals. At Monte Vista alone, the count was 50% below that of 2001.

The Dunes count is organized annually by **Friends of the Dunes**. Contact them for details about participation in future counts (see page 32.)

Consider a drive to nearby **San Luis Lakes State Park**. As you might imagine, this lake environment attracts many additional birds that don't often venture closer to the Dunes. Species observed at San Luis Lakes include **bald** and **golden eagle**, various **hawks**, **American kestrel**, **peregrine** and **prairie falcons**, **common loon**, various **grebes**, **american white pelican**, several **bitterns**, **heron**, **egret**, **tundra swan**, **canada** and **snow goose**, numerous species of **ducks**, **turkey vulture**, **plover**, **sandpiper**, various **gulls**, **tern**, **rock dove**, **great horned owl**, **snowy owl**, **belted kingfisher**, **mountain bluebird**, **mockingbird**, **shrike**, various **swallows**, **wrens**, **warblers** and **towhees**, **red-winged blackbird**, and **western meadowlark**. *Whew!* And that's just the short list.

A long-time Alamosa resident passed along an interesting tip for spotting golden and bald eagles in the San Luis Valley. As you drive through the flat valley (especially in the springtime), watch the fields for cows with very young calves. Eagles find the **afterbirth** of cows to be quite a treat, and will hang around (usually watching from treetops) waiting for a new arrival, so they can clean up after the birth. If you see young calves, and a tree anywhere in view (remember that eagles have extremely good vision), get out the binoculars and look closely for an eagle waiting for dessert.

Driving through the Wet Mountain Valley, the eastern approach to the Park and Preserve, we've often spotted red-winged blackbirds, sitting on the barbed wire fences along the roads leading to Music, Medano, and Mosca Passes.

We've come to think of FSR 119, leading toward Music Pass, as *red-winged blackbird lane,* since we've seen at least a dozen of these birds, with their distinctive red markings, every time we've passed by. Perhaps we've also discovered the origin of the name of the town of **Red Wing** near Mosca Pass!

Red-wing blackbird

Driving 4WD Roads

Sign warns of extremely soft sand

The only 4WD road which exists within the Park is the **Medano Pass Primitive Road**. The road starts directly across from the amphitheater and recycling center, and proceeds for 11 miles (17.6 km) up to Medano Pass. After reaching the pass, it is possible to continue down to CO 69. This extension to the drive adds another 10 miles (16 km) to the trip.

The Park Service suggests that you reduce your tire pressure to 10-15 psi when traveling on the road due to deep sand that could trap your vehicle. Free air is available at an **air station** in the amphitheater/recycling parking lot. You'll be able to return your tires to their proper inflated pressure on your return. But be aware that there is no air station after you go over Medano Pass and drop down to CO 69! If that is your plan, you may want to carry along your own portable air compressor.

The road contains numerous sections of deep sand which have been known to trap less-than-robust 4WD vehicles. During wet spring and early summer months, you may run into problems with swollen streams that cross the road. On the other hand, when conditions have been quite dry, the sand can become "bottomless", and vehicles can sink in to their axles. Drive with your lights on to warn oncoming vehicles of your approach, and watch for hikers and

Driving near the Sand Pit area

Drivers confer at a spot with deep, soft sand

equestrians on the road.

About 1.0 mile (1.6 km) after leaving the paved road you will come to **Point of No Return**, where 2WD vehicles are encouraged to park. Notice the sign that indicates that the towing fee beyond this point is a minimum charge of $100. (This is an old sign. Expect the cost today to be at least $300.)

If you are driving a 4WD, mini-SUV, with only moderate clearance and/or no extra-low gear, park here. While your vehicle may be fine on the upper portions of this road (where you'll be navigating through steep, rocky sections at times), don't underestimate the difficulty of driving up a slight hill in extremely deep, soft sand. Experience driving in deep, heavy snow may be helpful, although sand can be even trickier than snow.

Continue on the road as it winds past the **Ponderosa Point Picnic Area**, around the curve to the dreaded **Sand Pit** (which loves to eat four-wheel drive vehicles) and on up to the **Castle Creek Picnic Area**. Keep your vehicle moving steadily through this section of road. The dunes in this area have especially tall and steep slip-faces, terminating suddenly at Medano Creek. This can be a fun (and tiring!) place to play on the dunes.

Once past Castle Creek, continue on for about 1.5 miles (2.4 km) to a point where **Medano Creek** crosses the road. At times, the water in the creek can be quite deep, so exercise extra caution as you attempt this crossing. This spot is known as **Shockey's Crossing**. Look for the old cabins on the left side of the road, just after crossing the creek. Please do not disturb anything in the vicinity of these historic structures.

In another 0.5 miles (0.8 km) you will come to a fenced parking area, off to your left. This is the beginning of the Sand Creek portion of the **Sand Ramp Trail**. The **Sand Creek Trailhead** is also the terminus of the Little Medano Trail (also part of the Sand Ramp Trail), which joins the road from your right.

Congratulations! The worst of the soft sand is behind you. Depart the Sand Creek Trailhead, and follow the road as it begins climbing toward Medano Pass. You'll pass out of the National Park and into the Preserve in less than ½ mile.

Medano Creek crosses the road at several spots

The Preserve has a number of backcountry campsites along the Medano Pass Primitive Road. As you'll soon discover, these sites are conveniently located close to Medano Creek, which winds its way back and forth across the road eight times (including Shockey's Crossing, which you've already navigated). Each crossing is marked with a numbered sign so you can keep track of your progress. Many bears live in this area. Store your food legally and responsibly.

Map of Medano Pass Primitive Road

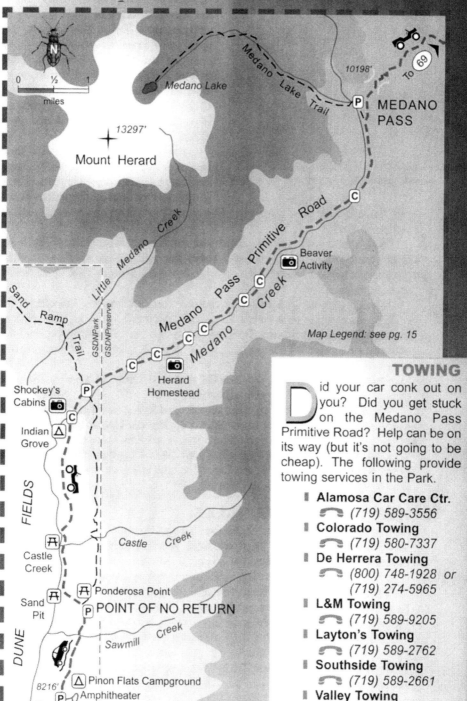

N

0   ½   1
miles

Medano Lake

Medano Lake Trail

10198'

MEDANO PASS

P

13297'

Mount Herard

Little Medano Creek

Medano Pass Primitive Road

C

Beaver Activity

C

C

C

Sand Ramp Trail

GSDNPark
GSDNPreserve

Medano Creek

C
C
C
C
C

Herard Homestead

Shockey's Cabins

P

C

Indian Grove

FIELDS

Castle Creek

Castle Creek

Ponderosa Point

Sand Pit

POINT OF NO RETURN

DUNE

Sawmill Creek

8216'

Pinon Flats Campground

Amphitheater

To 150

Map Legend: see pg. 15

TOWING

Did your car conk out on you? Did you get stuck on the Medano Pass Primitive Road? Help can be on its way (but it's not going to be cheap). The following provide towing services in the Park.

- **Alamosa Car Care Ctr.**
  (719) 589-3556
- **Colorado Towing**
  (719) 580-7337
- **De Herrera Towing**
  (800) 748-1928 or (719) 274-5965
- **L&M Towing**
  (719) 589-9205
- **Layton's Towing**
  (719) 589-2762
- **Southside Towing**
  (719) 589-2661
- **Valley Towing**
  (719) 580-0311

Smooth portion in the upper part of the road

After **Crossing # 3**, look for a herd of **bighorn sheep**, who often hang out in the meadows on your right, or on the cliffs to your left. This is also the location of **Frenchman's Cabin** — the ruins of the Herard homestead, built around 1875. See *The Frenchman — Ulysses Herard* in the chapter on *Cultural History* for more information about the Herard homestead and post office.

Just before **Crossing #6**, the road becomes quite narrow, with large boulders on each side of the road. Then, in case you've been getting a little bored with the *relatively* good road, after **Crossing #7** you'll enjoy a steeper, rockier section of road.

Watch for a long meadow, filled with marshes and beaver dams, just a bit higher up the road. You'll probably notice that you're close to this spot when you see that beavers have chopped down aspen trees to obtain building materials for their projects.

About 6.0 miles (8.8 km) after crossing the Park/Preserve boundary, you will encounter a spur road taking off to your left (west), with a sign pointing to the **Medano Lake Trailhead**, 0.5 miles (0.8 km) away. This is the trailhead for **Medano Lake** and **Mt. Herard** (a.k.a. Mt. Seven). Parking and camping are available in this area.

Back on the main road, continue for another 0.5 miles (0.8 km) as the road climbs steeply up to the top of Medano Pass.

Once at the pass, you will need to make a decision whether to turn around and head back to the Park, or to continue down the east side to CO 69. The first 2.5 miles (4.2 km) down the east side are steep and rocky, suitable for most 4WD vehicles. The remaining 7.0 miles (11.7 km) out to CO 69 are along a pleasant, gravel road. See the chapter on *Eastern Access Hikes* on page 156 for more details regarding this section of the road.

OTHER TYPES OF VEHICLES

Motorcycles, permitted within the Park and Preserve on the same roads as other motor vehicles, must be **street legal**, meaning they must have a license plate and be operated by a licensed driver. Off-road travel is not allowed.

There are an abundance of possibilities for motorcycle adventures outside of the Park & Preserve. The forest service roads and trails on the east side of the Sangre de Cristo Range are a good example. Try rides from CO 69, up any of the passes described in the *Eastern Access Hikes* section of this guide.

For a backcountry motorcycle experience, we especially recommend a loop ride up the **Colony Lakes Road** (FSR 120) and over to the **Music Pass Road** (FSR 119), via the **Rainbow Trail**. There are side excursions to be had by actually going up to the Music Pass and South Colony Lake parking areas.

Off-road vehicles (including ORVs, OHVs and ATVs) currently are NOT allowed in the Park or Preserve.

Dune Skiing, Boarding, Sledding, Rolling

Heading out to play

Yee-haw!!

Saucer-boy

Perfect tele-turn

Emptying out shoes afterwards

Shredding

All you really need to play on the dunes is a playful spirit. Most visitors simply walk up a dune of their choice, and walk, run, roll or somersault back down. However, some of us look for creative ways to ride down, on some sort of contraption.

For those visitors physically unable to walk out on the dunes, ask at the Visitor Center about borrowing a **specially-designed wheelchair** that can open up access to the sandy terrain for you and an assistant. The wheelchair is not designed to handle steep ascents or descents, however.

What can you use to slide down a dune or two? Cardboard covered with duct tape seems to be a popular choice. However, it doesn't seem to hold up too well. Saucer-style, **plastic sleds** are also popular, and work well for little, light-weight people. Most adults seem to bog down in the sand after sliding a short distance.

And then there are **downhill skis**, **cross-country skis** and **snowboards**. We discovered that it is very important to thoroughly remove all wax from the bottom of our skis before trying to slide on the sand. Silicon spray or *WD-40*, liberally applied, made the run down the sand slope feel a lot more like a run down a groomed snow slope. The good news — *no lift lines!* The bad news — *no lifts!*

So get on up there and enjoy the trip back down!

Horseback Riding and Pack Animals

Capture the spirit of early visitors to the Great Sand Dunes and surrounding areas by enjoying a ride atop a horse — you can bring your own, or hire horses through an outfitter and enjoy a guided outing.

If you're bringing your own horses or other pack animals into the Park and Preserve, be sure to pick up the latest copy of the *Horse Use Guidelines* at the Visitor Center. **Horses, mules, burros, donkeys, asses** and **llamas** may be used as pack animals.

PLACES TO RIDE

Most of the Park, and all of the Preserve, is open to horse use. Review the map available at the Visitor Center showing areas that are closed to horse and pack animal use. Basically, the rules aim at keeping horses out of the highest-use pedestrian and traffic areas. Here are the general guidelines for the Park:

No horses are allowed in the **Piñon Flats Campground**, or immediately around the Visitor Center Parking Lot or on the Nature Trail. Stay away from the **Dunes Parking Lot** and the **Mosca Creek Picnic Area**.

Only pedestrians are allowed on the dunes and in Medano Creek directly west of the Dunes Parking Lot. This area extends as far as the **High Dune**.

No horses may be ridden on the **Montville Nature Trail**. However, you may lead your horse on this trail, in order to access the **Mosca Pass Trail**, where you can mount up again. No horses are allowed on the **Wellington Ditch Trail**, **Dunes Overlook Trail**, or the **Sand Ramp Trail**, south of Point of No Return.

Keep horses off all paved roads, except to cross the road.

Backpackers with llamas on the Music Pass Trail

Turning from *no* to *yes* — yes, you can ride along the **Medano Pass Primitive Road**. As you start up that road, you'll see a **signed horse trail** on your right (just a short distance beyond a sign for the pedestrians' *Dunes Trail*) that leads from the Piñon Flats Campground area out toward the dunes. This is an excellent spot to leave the road and head toward the dunes. Once near the dunes, a ride north along **Medano Creek** is a particularly enjoyable option. Or, stay on the Medano Pass Primitive Road for a longer distance, and go exploring the vast areas around you.

PARKING TRAILERS

Trailers can be parked at the amphitheater parking lot (please don't block access to the RV dump station), the **Montville Trail Parking Lot** and at **Point of No Return** (day-use only). This is a small parking area, so consider how much space is available before parking here.

If you are coming into the National Preserve from the eastern access (Wet Mountain Valley), you may leave your trailer at parking areas next to trailheads in the Rio Grande National Forest. This includes **Mosca Pass**, the **Rainbow Trail** parking area and **Music Pass**.

CAMPING WITH HORSES

Obtain a free permit at the Visitor Center, then enjoy camping with your horses at the following designated backcountry sites within the Park: **Little Medano, Aspen, Cold Creek** and **Sand Creek**. See the *Backcountry and Wilderness Camping* section (page 92) for directions and other info on using these sites.

You can also get a permit to camp in most of the wilderness portions of the National Park. Your group size can be no larger than six people and up to six horses.

You can camp anywhere in the **National Preserve**, as long as your camp is at least 300 feet from any lake and 200 feet from any stream. In the Preserve, you may have a group of up to ten people. The total number of people plus horses cannot be more than 25. Follow guidelines provided by the Visitor Center for minimizing the impact of your camp.

ENCOUNTERING HORSES ON THE TRAIL

Remember that horses have **right-of-way** over hikers, bicyclists and ATV vehicles. They are big, heavy, strong and don't always understand that a bike or off-road vehicle isn't a danger to them.

If you are on a bike, make verbal contact and stop. Wait for the horse to pass or for the rider to tell you it is OK to continue. If you are on a motorized vehicle, it is advisable to shut off the engine, especially if the horses seem to be spooked by the noise. Horses may also calm down once they understand you are human — try taking off your helmet and speaking calmly to the horse and rider.

Even hikers can sometimes frighten a horse because it doesn't recognize you as human with that enormous backpack. Try removing it slowly, speaking calmly as you do. If you do encounter horses on the trail while hiking, use these safety guidelines to avoid startling the horses:

∎ Step off the trail to let the horseback riders pass.

∎ Speak in a normal tone of voice, and avoid sudden movements.

∎ If possible, allow the horse to be on the uphill side of you and the trail.

∎ Follow suggestions from the equestrian, who may know their horse's "personality" and know what might startle it.

GENERAL GUIDELINES FOR PACK ANIMALS

To limit spreading non-native weeds in the National Park and Preserve, horses must be fed **weed-free hay** for 24 hours before entering the region, and all feed you take with you must be certified weed-free. Dogs must be leashed at all times. Shovel and remove manure from your parking area before your ride, and after putting your animals in their trailer. And be careful when riding on the dunes. Steep dune faces are loose and potentially dangerous.

Others should yield the trail to horseback riders and pack animals. If you are concerned that the hikers, bicyclists or ATV riders are not going to behave in a way that your animal will tolerate, be pro-active. The best action may be for you to get off the trail, letting your animal face the approaching people. Be sure to communicate (calmly!) with others you meet on the trail, to help them know how to avoid spooking your horse or pack animal.

Outfitter-led rides can be a wonderful way to see the Park and Preserve! **Red Mountain Outfitters** offers daily rides (summer only), with a minimum of two people per trip. A two-hour ride is **$55** per person. Contact the outfitter, or bookings are also available at the Oasis Store, just outside the Park entrance.

P.O. Box 893
Alamosa, CO 81101
(719) 589-4186, Jim Flynn
www.redmountainoutfitters.com

As we said, rules can change. We've tried to give you a general idea of what to expect when you bring your pack animals to the Great Sand Dunes, but your best bet is to pick up the latest information at the Visitor Center before you unload your animals.

Guided group passes through
Great Sand Dunes National Park

Hunting and Fishing

HUNTING IN THE PRESERVE

First, the *fine print* — hunting is ONLY allowed in the **Great Sand Dunes National Preserve** and the adjacent **Rio Grande National Forest**. Hunting is NOT allowed anywhere within the confines of the **Great Sand Dunes National Park**. Firearms which are within your vehicle must remain unloaded at all times. You must be in possession of a valid Colorado **hunting license** to carry a loaded firearm outside of your vehicle.

All hunting is to be done in accordance with existing rules set down by the **Colorado Division of Wildlife** (DOW). You can obtain licenses and hunting brochures from sporting goods stores and other licensing agents in the

6060 Broadway
Denver, Colorado, 80216
(303)297-1192
web site: wildlife.state.co.us/regulations

valley. Among game available in the surrounding San Isabel and Rio Grande National Forests, and other public lands, are big-game species such as mule deer, elk, pronghorn, big-horn sheep and bear, as well as small game, turkey and waterfowl. In particular, elk are especially abundant — Colorado has the largest elk herd in the world. Both the San Luis Valley and the Wet Mountain Valley possess large bison herds, but these are on private ranches and not available for public hunting. Length of seasons and regulations change each year, so be sure to check with DOW well ahead of time.

FISHING IN THE PARK AND PRESERVE

First, the *fine print* — all fishing is to be done in accordance with existing rules set down by the Colorado Division of Wildlife (DOW). Be sure to check with DOW for all of the latest fishing rules and regulations.

Now for the *fun stuff* — You can enjoy **Free Fishing Days** during the first full weekend of June, when you can fish in Colorado without a license. At all other times you'll need a license, available at area sporting goods stores, as well as the **Great Sand Dunes Oasis** complex at the entrance to the Park.

There are a wide variety of opportunities for fishing in streams and lakes, both within the Park and Preserve, as well as in the surrounding area.

WITHIN THE PARK AND PRESERVE
- **Medano Creek** — Rio Grande cutthroats *(artificial flies and lures ONLY, catch and release ONLY)*
- **Medano Lake** — Rio Grande cutthroats *(fly, bait and lure fishing)*
- **Sand Creek** — brooks & cutthroats
- **Little Sand Creek Lake** — brooks and cutthroats
- **Lower Sand Creek Lake** — brooks and cutthroats
- **Upper Sand Creek Lake** — brooks and cutthroats

OUTSIDE THE PARK AND PRESERVE
- **South Zapata Lake** — never been stocked
- **San Luis Lake** — rainbows
- **Lower Willow Creek** — cutthroats
- **Lower Willow Creek Lake** — cutthroats

Mountain Biking

Because bicycles are permitted only on established vehicle roads within the National Park, and not on trails, biking within the Park is effectively restricted to a few miles of paved roads and to the Medano Pass Primitive Road.

MEDANO PASS PRIMITIVE ROAD

The **Medano Pass Primitive Road** provides the only real mountain biking experience within the Park. The road is rated as 4WD for vehicles, and contains

10.5 miles (17.5 km)
1,800' (549m) gain

some nasty sand traps — nasty enough to defeat Tiger Woods!

Warning: Wear a bicycling helmet. Be alert for oncoming vehicles; they won't be making as much noise on the sand as you will when you become a hood ornament for someone's SUV! And don't overexert yourself. Remember you are biking at 8,000 feet (2,434m) elevation.

This is a grueling ride, with deep, soft sand in many places and steep hills. For some sections of the road, you may end up carrying your bike more than riding it. Putting it plainly, your experience riding the road may be akin to your dentist drilling deeply into one of your molars — without any pain killer! If you're still thinking about it, we suggest you find a large rock and strike yourself sharply in the forehead. When you regain consciousness, maybe you'll have a better outlook on the situation — or will have forgotten the whole crazy notion!

Biking along the road, with Mt. Herard in the background

The road begins just across from the amphitheater and recycling station. Leave the pavement and begin your journey toward Medano Pass. In about one mile (1.6 km) you will come to the spot called **Point of No Return**, where 2WD vehicles are encouraged to park. Notice the sign that indicates the towing fee beyond this point is a minimum charge of $100!

Continue up the road 0.3 mile (0.5 km) to **Ponderosa Point Picnic Area** and take a few minutes to enjoy the spectacular view. A short rest here is important, as you are only 0.4 mile (0.7 km) from the dreaded **Sand Pit** section of the road. Okay, it's back on the bike through the Sand Pit area and on up to **Castle Creek Picnic Area**, which is located about 2.0 miles (3.2 km) from the start of the road.

Depart Castle Creek and continue on for about 2.0 miles (3.2 km) to a junction with the Sand Ramp Trail at the **Sand Creek Trailhead**. There is a vehicle parking area located on your left at this point. Just prior to reaching the Sand Creek Trailhead you will cross Medano Creek. Depending upon the time of year, and amount of moisture this area has received, you may need to carry your bicycle across the creek; and a refreshing event it is sure to be!

Leave the Sand Creek Trailhead and follow the road as it begins climbing toward Medano Pass. In approximately 6.0 miles (9.6 km) you will encounter a road taking off to your left (west) with a sign pointing to the **Medano Lake Trailhead** 0.5 miles (0.8 km) away. This is the trailhead for both Medano Lake and Mt. Herard (also known as Mt. Seven).

Continue on (if you can) for another 0.5 miles (0.8 km), as the road climbs steeply up to **Medano Pass**. If you have a car shuttle in place, you may elect to bike down the other side of the pass to CO 69. The first 2.5 miles (4.2 km) are steep and rocky, a challenging downhill for all riders. The remaining 7.0 miles (11.7 km) out to the highway are along a pleasant, gravel road. See the chapter on *Eastern Access Hikes* on page 156 for more details regarding this section of the road.

The Alamosa Chamber of Commerce has a **mountain biking guide** available for areas in the **San Luis Valley**. Contact them at ☎(719) 589-4840 for more info.

Take along all of the water and food you think you will need to complete this journey, as there are no "convenience stores" along the way. Happy trails!

SAN LUIS LAKES STATE PARK

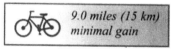

9.0 miles (15 km) minimal gain

There is an easy, 9-mile (14.4 km) riding-path located at **San Luis Lakes State Park**. The gravel path is level, as it winds around the lakes and marshes of this interesting area. Be advised that to enter this state park, you are required to pay an entry fee or have a *Colorado State Parks Pass*. Refer to the section on *San Luis Lakes State Park* on page 200 for a map and more details.

ZAPATA FALLS RECREATION AREA

Mountain biking enthusiasts will find a series of four enjoyable, moderate, *single track* riding trails located in the **Zapata Falls Recreation Area**. You can put together a full day's riding adventure by starting at the Piñon Flats Campground in the Park and riding to the Zapata Falls parking area, approximately 4.0 miles (6.7 km) south of the Park entrance on CO 150. After

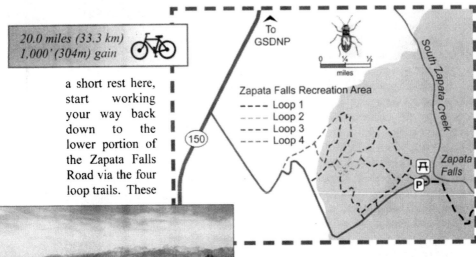

20.0 miles (33.3 km)
1,000' (304m) gain

a short rest here, start working your way back down to the lower portion of the Zapata Falls Road via the four loop trails. These

loops have signage at almost all trail junctions. The loops interconnect so that you can make your ride as long, or as short, as you like by putting together different combinations of loops.

This would be a good workout for most folks, as you may cover 20 miles (33.3 km) or more of riding on pavement, moderate-grade gravel roads and single track. Sound like fun?

Riding on the Zapata Falls trail system

THE RAINBOW TRAIL

An interesting loop trip on the eastern side of the Sangre de Cristo Range, starts at the 2WD parking area on the **South Colony Lake Road** (FSR 120) and connects up with the **Rainbow Trail**. The adventurous (and experienced) biker will ride to FSR 119, the **Music Pass Road**. It is then possible to bike back down to the junction with FSR 120 and return to the parking area. This loop covers 14.5 miles (23.2 km) and gains 2,250 feet (686m) for a fine day of riding.

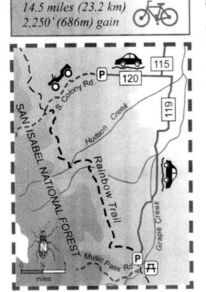

14.5 miles (23.2 km)
2,250' (686m) gain

To reach the start of this ride, from 4.4 miles (7.3 km) south of Westcliffe on CO 69, turn onto **Colfax Lane** (FSR 115). Where this ends, turn right on **S. Colony Road** (FSR 120), driving 6.5 miles (10.8 km) from the highway on an increasingly rocky road to the 2WD parking area. If you have 4WD, you may keep on; but otherwise bike up the road another 2.0 miles or so (3.3 km) to the intersection with the Rainbow Trail. Take a left and follow the single track about 5.0 miles (8.3 km) to the junction with FSR 119. This well-built trail has plenty of challenging ups and downs through pine and aspen. Finally turn left on FS 119 and ride back on this gravel road to complete the loop at FS 120.

Park Organized Activities

While visiting the Great Sand Dunes, you'll have many opportunities to learn more about history, botany, geology, climatology and biology of this area. You can participate in a fun interpretive program presented by Park rangers that leaves you saying, *"Wow! That's pretty cool."*

Ranger-led nature walk

During the summer, check at the Visitor Center for a schedule of daily, 10-minute **porch talks** (held on the porch at the back of the Visitor Center) and for **ranger-led walks**. In the evenings, take a stroll from your campsite at **Piñon Flats Campground** over to the **amphitheater** for a slide show or other presentation. Topics and times for these shows are posted at the Visitor Center and on bulletin boards in the Piñon Flats Campground. The presentations are given in a way that will fascinate and enlighten the adults in the audience, and also entertain the kids.

You'll come away from these programs with a better understanding of the natural world around you, and you'll be able to impress your friends with your knowledge!

FOR KIDS

Kids from 3 to 12 can begin the process of learning to care for and protect our natural environment while having a great time. How? By becoming a **Junior Park Ranger**, of course!

Start by picking up a Junior Ranger workbook for just 50¢ at the Visitor Center. Activities that lead toward the goal of *Junior Rangerhood* (we made that up) are divided into three age groups. The book is filled with puzzles and challenges, including our favorite — *Dunes Bingo*. Instead of listening to someone call out *"G-5,"* kids look for specific plants, animals, birds and natural features (has anyone seen a *sand dune* around here?) to mark their bingo card.

Once a child has completed the training activities in the book, they can have an adult ranger check their book and then take the **Junior Ranger Pledge**:

"As a Junior Park Ranger, I promise to help keep nature clean and beautiful; to protect plants, wildlife and their habitats; and to learn more about National Parks."

Now your Junior Ranger can proudly wear the official Great Sand Dunes Junior Park Ranger badge.

After reviewing the workbook, we think all the "big kids" from 13 to 102 would benefit from this training, too.

Photography

A tripod will help steady your shots

The stark beauty and haunting solitude of the Great Sand Dunes draws both amatuer and professional photographers, intent on capturing the essence and mood of this special place.

Great photo opportunities are always close at hand. Several spots along the entrance road (CO 150) to the National Park are popular for photographing the dunes complex against a backdrop of Mount Herard. Likewise, the patio behind the Visitor Center is convenient for taking in the immense panorama of dunes and peaks. But for those who are willing to go further out onto the dunes or into the surrounding backcountry, your efforts will be rewarded by experiencing the dunes first-hand and in discovering spectacular vistas, seldom photographed by most Park visitors.

Professional photographers know that early or late in the day are best for optimum color saturation in your photographs, avoiding intense mid-day light. If your interest is in photographing wildlife, you will find that animals are more likely to be seen at those times of the day. For best results, use a tripod to steady your shots. Sand can wreak havoc on delicate equipment. Protect it in plastic bags.

Early morning at the Great Sand Dunes

TIPS FOR PHOTOGRAPHING

▌ **Medano Creek** is only a short walk from the Dunes Parking Lot and is a favorite in late spring for photographing people splashing and frolicking in the surge flow of the creek. The three-day, Memorial Day Weekend is usually one of the best times for capturing people having wet fun.

▌ For those looking for more action shots, take a short 15 to 30 minute walk out on the dunes to discover people sliding, snowboarding and skiing down the steeper sand faces. These types of shots are always sure winners. Be sure to have a telephoto lens for close-ups and fast-speed film to cover the action.

▌ The views of the surrounding high mountain peaks from the top of **High Dune** (see Hike #5) are always spectacular, especially in the spring when the mountains are still snow covered. Plan on two to three hours of moderate hiking in sand to reach this vantage point. Late afternoon is good, when you will have the sun at your back. But early evening can be even better, as the Sangre de Cristo Mountains may glow crimson red before sundown.

▌ If you are not a serious sand hiker, and you have a couple of hours to invest, we suggest that you hike up to **Dunes Overlook** (see Hike #8), a 2.0 mile (3.2 km) easy, trail walk. From this point, you get a fantastic panoramic view of the dunes complex, including Medano Creek and Mount Herard. Take along a wide-angle lens to capture all of it. Morning is the best time.

▌ For the more adventurous photographer, the summit of **Mount Herard** offers a unique birds-eye view of the entire dunes complex from a vantage point 5,000 feet above the valley. This strenuous trip (see Hike #17) is best done in mid-September when aspen and tundra are both in their best fall colors.

▌ One of the finest views in the state is your reward for the short hike to **Music Pass** (see Hike #18) in the National Preserve. Early morning is the best

time for photographing alpen glow on the rugged high peaks that ring Sand Creek basin. Take a short walk down the west side of the pass for excellent opportunities to photograph wildflowers. You'll want a close-up lens and a small piece of cardboard for a windblock.

▌ Drive up photo opportunities are also available outside the Park. Try the view from the **Zapata Falls** parking area for a good scenery shot of the San Luis Valley and dunes complex. This is best done with a wide-angle lens and a polarizing filter to block haze.

▌ Another of our favorites is the view across **San Luis Lake** at San Luis Lakes State Park. When the water is calm, it is possible to capture beautiful reflections of the majestic Sangre de Cristo Mountains.

▌ For places to photograph wildlife, see some of the suggestions in the *Watching Wildlife* section, starting on the next page. You'll definitely want a telephoto lens for bison at the Medano-Zapata Ranch. But if your quarry is *Sandy,* bring a good close-up lens!

Watching Wildlife

Bison

Mule deer

Elk

The Great Sand Dunes National Park and Preserve, and the surrounding forests, mountains, lakes and streams, are wonderful places to spot a wide variety of fascinating animals. The flat grasslands along 6 Mile Lane and CO 150 are home to a large herd of **bison** on the Medano-Zapata Ranch, as well as **elk, pronghorn** and **mule deer**. **Bighorn sheep**, the males sporting their dramatic, curved horns, are often seen in high alpine meadows, but may also visit the dunes during the winter. A large herd of bighorn can often be seen in the valley below Music Pass, near the trailhead to Upper Sand Creek Lake.

Campgrounds are frequently visited by opportunistic **chipmunks, ground squirrels** and mule deer, looking for an easy snack of food, spilled by humans. **Crows** and **magpies** loudly announce their search for food as well. **Black bears** also visit the campgrounds when natural food grows scarce, with an eye out for coolers and other food containers carelessly left in reach. **Coyotes** are more often seen than heard, as they throw back their heads and howl loudly at the sky. **Bobcats** and **mountain lions** (cougars) are secretive and stealthy, and are rarely spotted.

If you hike to higher elevations in the surrounding Sangre de Cristo Mountains, you may spot a number of different animals and birds. When hiking near treeline, especially near Carbonate Mountain, we've often encountered **blue grouse**, large birds with coloring that blends well with tree trunks. Higher, often above treeline and in boulder-strewn areas, you may find little **pikas** darting around (and *eeeeking* at you) or encounter a **ptarmigan** waddling past. The ptarmigan's feathers turn white in winter, so they can blend in with the snow, then change to dappled browns in summer to blend in with the alpine tundra. Larger **marmots** also like to hang out in boulder fields, and will take any opportunity to get into your food or chew on your backpack straps when you aren't close by.

How can you improve your luck in seeing wildlife up close (but not too close)? Binoculars or a good telephoto lens on your camera will let you observe much more detail than you'll generally manage with the naked eye. For fun, consider carrying a field guide to the birds and animals likely to be found here in southern Colorado, and then check off a list of the critters you've spotted.

Animal pelts on display at the Visitor Center

Early mornings or evenings are generally good times to find animals out and about. When the sun is beating down on you at noon, and you are headed for the shade, many animals, birds and insects are probably doing the same thing.

If you've brought *Fido* with you (on a leash, of course!), you'll have much less luck spotting wildlife. Even if your dog doesn't bark at the other animals, they may smell him and regard him as a danger.

OK, so now you've spotted a pronghorn or mule deer, and want a little better look (or a little better photo). Move slowly and quietly toward the animal, but don't give it the impression that you are a predator. Not only is growling a bad idea, but so is staring at the animal or walking directly toward it. Pretend you're really more interested in searching for something on the ground in front of you. Glance up at the animal now and then, but act nonchalant about it. Wear sunglasses and drab-colored clothing.

If you are with other people, be sure you don't end up surrounding the animal (especially a larger animal) or someone may get hurt when that elk decides it is unhappy with the situation. If the animal is trying to move away from you, let it go. If it shows any signs of becoming aggressive, then it's definitely time for you to go. Be sure you know what to do if confronted by a dangerous animal such as a mountain lion or bear. Never offer food to wild animals. Our food isn't good for them, and teaching wild animals to get food from humans isn't good for anyone! (See page 29 for more safety information.)

Another fun activity in the sands of the dunes is to try to identify **tracks** and **scat** on the ground. From tiny *tire tracks* in the sand made by small insects such as the **circus beetle**, to the large, deep prints of big mammals such as mountain lions, the sand captures a whole world of movement by a variety of creatures. Look for the interpretive signs next to the Dunes

Casts of animal tracks at the Dunes Parking Lot

Parking Lot for identified samples of **animal tracks**.

Animal droppings are often rather distinctive in appearance, and you will probably "spot" numerous animals by what they've left behind. Not only can you find reference books on tracks and scat (check the bookstore at the Visitor Center), you can even find scat t-shirts and scat scarves to help you learn to identify animals by what they've left behind.

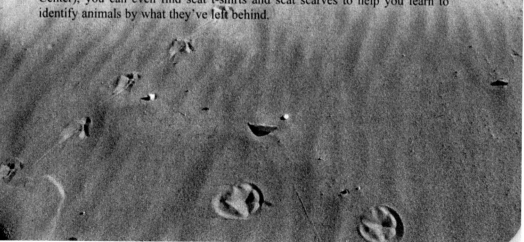

HIKING

Hiker on the Sand Ramp Trail

There's a lot more to your Park and Preserve than just the Visitor Center and the Dunes Parking Lot! Don't constrain yourself by coming to the Park and just spending 30 minutes, or even an hour. Come and spend the day or spend the night. Give yourself time to hike the trails in this unique place. Hiking options range from a stroll along the **Visitor Center Interpretative Trail** to challenging, high-altitude mountain adventures. Come explore with us some of the diverse treasures that await you.

The map on the facing page shows the location of the hikes described in this chapter, grouped into four areas: **hikes in the Park, western access hikes, eastern access hikes** and **Zapata Falls Recreation Area hikes**. The latter three are hikes originating outside the Park, either in the Preserve or in the surrounding National Forests. Due to numerous stops you will undoubtedly be making for photographic purposes, we have used approximate hiking times in our descriptions. Also, you'll find that hiking in the sand takes longer than on a normal trail. (After hiking for a few hours in the sand, your calves may be screaming for mercy!)

A box with each hike lists the one-way **hiking distance** and approximate **elevation gain** for that hike. While some hikes are described with optional destinations, the distance listed is to the farthest described destination. All right, grab your pack and water bottle, stick a feather in your cap for luck, *and let's go!*

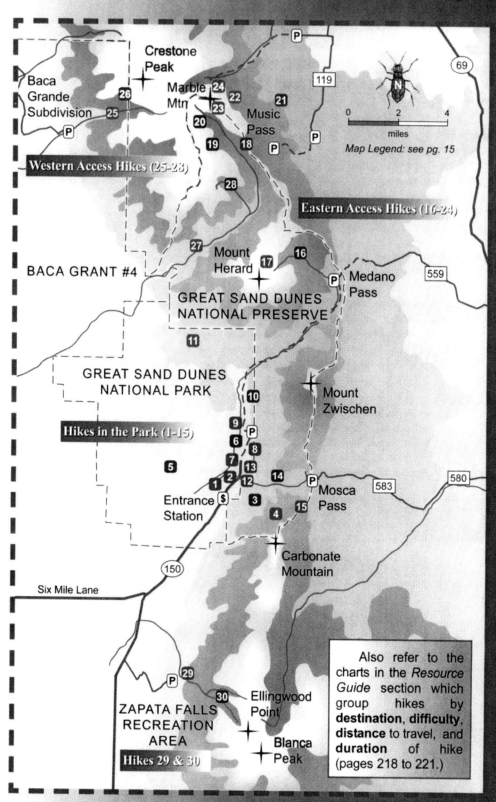

Crestone Peak

Baca Grande Subdivision

26

25

P

Marble Mtn

24

23

22

21

20

Music Pass

19

18

P

69

119

0   2   4
miles
Map Legend: see pg. 15

N

Western Access Hikes (25-28)

28

Eastern Access Hikes (16-24)

27

Mount Herard

17

16

P

Medano Pass

559

BACA GRANT #4

GREAT SAND DUNES NATIONAL PRESERVE

11

GREAT SAND DUNES NATIONAL PARK

10

Mount Zwischen

Hikes in the Park (1-15)

9

P

6

8

7

13

5

1   2   12

14

P

Mosca Pass

583

580

Entrance Station

$

3

15

4

150

Carbonate Mountain

Six Mile Lane

P

29

30

Ellingwood Point

ZAPATA FALLS RECREATION AREA

Hikes 29 & 30

Blanca Peak

Also refer to the charts in the *Resource Guide* section which group hikes by **destination**, **difficulty**, **distance** to travel, and **duration** of hike (pages 218 to 221.)

Hikes in the Park: From Visitor Center

Important! Starting in September of 2002, the **Visitor Center** will be closed for expansion and remodeling. A *temporary* Visitor Center will be set up at the Dunes Parking Lot for about two years while the improvements are being made. For hikes beginning at the main Visitor Center, you'll have to park elsewhere. Either park at the **Dunes Parking Lot** and follow the trail from the Mosca Creek Picnic Area to the Visitor Center, or park at the lot for the **Montville Nature Trail** and follow the trail toward the main Visitor Center.

VISITOR CENTER INTERPRETATIVE TRAIL

This very informative one-half mile (0.8 km) loop trail is referred to as *The Story of the Dunes Trail.* This gravel trail starts and ends at the Visitor Center. You will find numerous **interpretative signs** along the path that explain the wide variety of plant life that exists in this wonderful high-desert area. Experience first-hand the destruction and subsequent plant regeneration resulting from the fire of April 2000. You would not have wanted to be standing in this area when the fire swept through here!

This short, enjoyable walk provides you with panoramic vistas of the dunes and the adjacent San Luis Valley. Observe the **fire research areas** and ask yourself the question, "Is fire the end of something or the beginning of something else?" Actually it is both.

As we follow the pathway, notice how some species of plants are being replaced with others. Take a few moments and relax at one of the benches along the path. Reflect upon how many times fire, like the one in April of 2000, has reclaimed this land. Fire is important in the cycle of these early colonizers, which have adapted to move quickly into burnt-over areas, eventually to be replaced by the piñon/juniper and pine/fir climax forests of this area.

| 1 | 0.5 miles (0.8 km) minimal elev. gain | |

Start of the Interpretative Trail

Follow along this trail to see who the original inhabitants of this land were, where they came from, what they saw and who followed in their footsteps.

This is a good opportunity to examine the role the **sand sheet** plays in the propagation of the dunes. (Read the section in this guide on *Eolian Geology*, to better understand the complex roles that wind and water play in this ongoing drama, page 39.) Although the dunes are not appreciably growing, neither are they static.

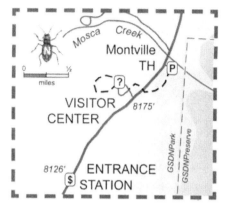

Read the information signs and understand their message. Finish your tour by visiting the patio at the back of the Visitor Center, which has more informational signs and displays. Try to time your walk to take advantage of one of the nature **patio talks** given by the rangers on the Visitor Center's patio. Schedules are posted at the Visitor Center.

MONTVILLE-VISITOR CENTER TRAIL

Starting from the lot for the Montville Nature Trail

Please note that while the Visitor Center is being expanded, and its

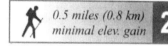

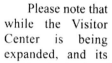

0.5 miles (0.8 km) minimal elev. gain **2**

parking lot is closed, (starting in September of 2002), this short round-trip walk should be started by parking at the Montville Nature Trail. Once construction is completed, you can choose to start at the Visitor Center instead.

Park in the lot for the **Montville Nature Trail**, and walk up a few steps to the start of the trail leading toward the Visitor Center. Note a trail sign pointing to your right. This short trail passes through the dramatic, stark beauty of the remains of trees burned in the fire of April 2000. Look closely for new growth made possible by the fire that barely missed the Visitor Center.

Soon, you'll cross the paved road, and continue walking among burned and new vegetation. This makes a great late afternoon or evening stroll. After a walk lasting only about 10 minutes, you'll arrive at the parking area for the Visitor Center. As you retrace your path back to the Montville Nature Trail, enjoy the dramatic late-day lighting of the dunes. We have some great sunset-watching opportunities here!

Visitor Center visible through the fire-ravaged forest

REVELATION POINT (LITTLE BALDY)

This moderate hike begins directly east across the road from the Visitor Center. It is another of those *must do* hikes. **Little Baldy** or **Revelation Point** (both are unofficial local names)

3	2.0 miles (3.3 km) 1,335' (407m) gain

is the high grassy knob you can see as you look east from the Visitor Center, with higher peaks behind it. The elevation gain, a modest 1,335 feet (407m), contains just one short, steep, uphill section toward the end of the hike. This hike requires a little more *back country* savvy than most of the hikes in the Park, as the last section includes some bushwhacking and route finding.

Cross the road from the entrance to the Visitor Center parking lot, taking care to watch for vehicle traffic, and walk slightly to your right to the trail sign. The trail is well defined at this point, and starts out by heading east, and then southeast, as it crosses several small drainages.

Trail begins across the road from the Visitor Center

As you start up the trail you will pass by the skeletons of **aspen** trees off to your left which were incinerated during the fire of April 2000. In a lush area near this sadly departed grove is another feature which was once more resplendent that it is currently. Look carefully and you can see the remains of what was once a thriving **beaver dam**. Imagine how active this area once appeared, with water cascading over the beaver dam, along with a thick growth of plant life lining its shores. Today it is still active, although quietly. The nutrients left behind over the years have spawned growth of another kind in the life cycle of this beautiful area. The pond that once housed a beaver dam now hosts a cornucopia of vegetation. Cattails and various other foliage abound.

Continue along the trail, walking through the new aspen grove which has sprung to life since the fire. In May of 2002, two years after the fire, these trees were a mere five feet tall (1.5 m). When you pass this way, you can use this height as a benchmark for determining how fast these trees grow.

Follow the somewhat sandy path as it gradually gains elevation. Those wooden poles which have been placed periodically across the trail are referred

Lush growth around former beaver dam

to as **water bars**. They are used to control erosion on the trail. The water will pool up behind the water bar and be diverted either left or right, instead of creating an unsightly, destructive gully if it were to rush down the trail.

Stop occasionally, as you gain elevation, to look back in the direction you have just traveled. Those views of the dunes complex and surrounding area will just keep getting better.

The abundant cactus you see along the trail are mostly of the **prickly pear** variety. You'll also see **yucca, sage** and **winterfat** (white sage). This area of the trail is also home to large colonies of ants, as is evidenced by the occasional, very large ant hills. Conventional wisdom suggests viewing these creatures from a safe distance!

Shortly you will encounter a **service road** intersecting the trail. Turn left and follow the road as it goes past a horse corral and barn, and on up toward the white water storage tank. As you approach the water storage tank, the road forms a "Y". Take the right fork, and in just a moment, you will arrive at a beige-colored, stucco/adobe building. This is **Well House 3**. The trail takes a right turn just past the Well House, as it crosses the **Morris Gulch** drainage and begins to head uphill.

In a few more minutes you may notice an excavation area on your left. During June/July of 2002, geologists examined the old **earthquake fault scarp** along this area of the trail. Do not enter this or any of the several other open pits you may encounter along the trail.

The trail is well-defined at this point as it follows the Morris Gulch drainage, gradually climbing up through stands of **ponderosa pine, piñon pine** and **juniper** trees. These trees provide adequate shelter from the wind, thus making this an ideal hike to do on those spring days when the wind is raging. Breathe deeply and enjoy the scent of all these wonderful trees and grasses. Now, let's just hope you don't have allergies!

Fault research trench

After passing the National Forest **wilderness boundary**, you may notice a small cross off to your left which likely marks the grave of someone's departed pet. Please do not disturb this site. Continue uphill into the ponderosa forest. The ponderosas are soon joined by stands of mature aspen. The contrast of the dark green of the pines and the light green, or brilliant gold in autumn, of the aspen is wonderful. Stop and listen for the sounds of water which may be running near the trail. Watch how the leaves of the aspen *quake* in the slightest breeze. The Native Americans called aspens *the trees with the eyes.* This name was probably the result of the distinctive eye-like markings on the bark of the tree. However, most folks simply refer to aspens as *quakies* because of the way the leaves quake in the breeze.

View of dunes area from the summit of Revelation Point

In 1.2 miles (1.9 km) the trail makes a turn to the left. You may notice that a faint trail seems to head straight ahead. This is merely a **game trail**, of which there are many in the area. Follow the left branch as it crosses Morris Gulch and walk up through an open area to a hillside of piñon pines. The drainage on your right is dominated by magnificent ponderosa pines. Soon you'll encounter **rocky formations** above the trail on either side — how quickly the views can change. As the trail begins to head uphill, it becomes somewhat faint, but not impossible to follow. Always be looking ahead to determine where the trail is heading. Generally stay in or slightly above, and to the left (north) of, the drainage while hiking up the drainage.

At the 1.6 mile (2.6 km) point you'll encounter an old **prospect mine** immediately to the left (north) of the trail. This particular dig is identified by light colored rock, fanning out and down the hillside. A few minutes of additional hiking will bring you to a point where the trail appears to merge back to the right into the drainage. Uphill to your left you should see a **cairn** (a neatly stacked pile of rocks). There will be a drainage coming in from your left. (If you have a GPS receiver, this point is located at *UTM 456420mE, 4174490mN*.)

Head left at this point and traverse steadily up the hillside toward a **saddle** that is just east of Revelation Point. This section of the hike is a bushwhack, so you won't see anything that resembles a trail. Trust your instincts and keep to the left the drainage, always heading uphill, and you will arrive alive at the saddle. Once at the saddle, turn left (west) and hike the remaining distance to the top of **Revelation Point**, elevation 9,510 feet (2,899 m).

The panoramic views from Revelation Point are impressive. Facing west you can see the Visitor Center, dunes complex, and in the distance, the **San Juan Mountains**. To the north is the **Sangre de Cristo Range**, with Mt. Herard dominating the view. To the south, scan the expanse of the **San Luis Valley**. To the east is the bald ridge leading to **Carbonate Mountain**. Look off slightly northwest and you may see Medano Creek snaking its way down along the edge of the dunes. Let's hope you brought your camera to capture this memorable moment!

On top of Revelation Point

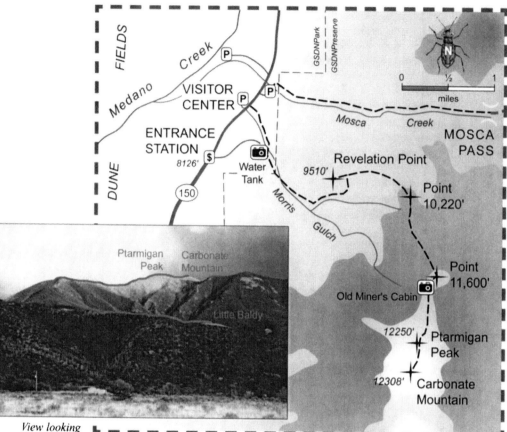

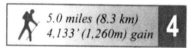

View looking
southeast from
Piñon Flats Campground
showing the route to
Carbonate Mountain

5.0 miles (8.3 km)
4,133' (1,260m) gain

4

CARBONATE MOUNTAIN
VIA REVELATION POINT

This hike is a continuation of the **Revelation Point** hike described above. Continuing on from this point requires the knowledge and use of a map and compass, and/or GPS, as well as good physical conditioning. You should be an experienced **off-trail hiker**, as the journey from Revelation Point to Carbonate Mountain consists of serious bushwhacking through dense stands of pine and aspen. At times your navigational skills will be put to the test due to the fact that your long range visibility will be severely limited.

However, the panoramic view from near 11,600 feet (3,536m) on the ridge makes your effort very worthwhile — you get to see the *Full Monte!* A good pair of binoculars will make the views even more striking.

GPS waypoints/landmarks for this hike:
- **Elevation 9,510'**: *UTM 456380mE, 4174795mN (summit of Little Baldy)*
- **Elevation 10,220'**: *UTM 457527mE, 4174530mN*
- **Elevation 11,200'**: *UTM 457845mE, 4173565mN*
- **Elevation 11,600'**: *UTM 457965mE, 4173250mN (ridge of Carbonate)*
- **Elevation 12,308'**: *UTM 457630mE, 4171760mN (summit of Carbonate Mtn.)*

Ball cactus in bloom

From the summit of Revelation Point, head back east and down to the saddle below Revelation Point, then hike uphill on open grassy slopes toward the 10,220-foot (3,115m) high point ahead. This point is identified by a clearing on its lower southwest side. If you are observant as you hike up the hill, you should be able to identify some **mountain ball cactus**. These are small, solitary cacti about the size of a baseball, with tiny pink blooms in the spring and red/brown coloring.

Continue up and over **Point 9,800** (2,987m), staying above any drainages which lead off to the southwest. This area is approximately a two hour hike from the Visitor Center and makes an excellent out-of-the-way spot for a picnic. You'll be rewarded with outstanding views, shade, peace and quiet. If it just had a water source this would be the perfect spot!

Hike uphill along the southwest flank of **Point 10,220**, keeping to the right of the tree areas as long as possible. This area is characterized by thick tufts of grasses, which glisten golden yellow in the early morning light.

Once you reach Point 10,220, the fun really begins! You can tell if you're at the correct location, as you should find another of those pesky mine prospect holes on the northeast end of the highpoint, next to a stately pine tree. Move out into the open and study your route. You'll be heading south from where you now stand, and hiking up the densely forested hillside to 11,200 feet (3,414) on the ridge. Take a compass bearing on this point, or if you're using a GPS receiver, compute its UTM coordinates from your map.

Hike south through the open area along the ridge crest and quickly lose 125 feet (38m) as you drop down to the saddle south of Point 10,220. This area is crisscrossed with aspen trees which have been blown down over the years. A cursory examination of the direction in which the trees have fallen gives us a strong clue of the direction of the prevailing winds. Exercise extreme caution when stepping over these trees, as a broken leg or twisted ankle at this juncture would be a major problem. We hate it when that happens!

Notice the **claw marks** on the still-living aspen trees. Undoubtedly this area is used by the local bear community as a training ground for ripping open coolers and car doors of the unwary camper!

Having negotiated the minefield of fallen trees, you're ready to set off on an adventure of another kind — penetration into the depths of the mountain forest. Your task is not without clues, as you should immediately encounter a well-traveled **game trail** which leads you ever so steeply up the slope toward ridge **Point 11,200**. If your calves are begging for mercy you might try counting backward from 11,200 by sevens to distract yourself from your discomfort. Just keep in mind how enjoyable it will be descending back to the saddle.

Keep checking your compass bearing, or GPS *GOTO* reading, to insure that you haven't wandered too far to the left (east) or right (west), as you ascend through this dense forest. Just when you think you'll never live to see your family and friends again, you'll pop out into the open on the rocky nose of the ridge at 11,200 feet. All is revealed. This is a great spot to take a well deserved break and enjoy the outstanding views. See if you can identify the entire Sand Ramp Trail, from its beginning in the campground, to its termination at Sand Creek. Binoculars can make this task far easier.

View of the dunes and Mt. Herard

This is an ideal time to evaluate weather conditions, stamina, snack and water supplies and the remaining daylight. You can see most of the rest of your route from this point. You're got a good two hours of effort from here to the

summit of Carbonate Mountain, and back to this point. The high point on the ridge to the south, which you can see, is a 12,250 feet (3,734m) bump on the ridge, informally called **Ptarmigan Peak**. Carbonate Mountain lies 0.2 mile (0.3 km) south along the ridge, and is hidden from view.

Depart your rest spot and hike uphill over small talus, and through a couple of easy rock outcrops, on your way up to the north-south Carbonate Mountain ridge, located 400 feet (122m) above you at 11,600 feet (3,536m). Off to your left (north), you should have an unobstructed view of the **Mosca Pass Trail** and **Mosca Pass**.

Old cabin on the ridge to Carbonate Mtn.

A pleasant surprise awaits you once you reach the 11,600-foot point. Turn right (south) and follow the ridge as it heads over toward Carbonate Mountain. In just a very few minutes you'll encounter the remnants of an old **miner's cabin**. The views would have been great but the living conditions would have left a lot to be desired — sure would have been a long way to go for a glass of water!

At this point, you intersect the hiking route to Carbonate Mountain coming up from Mosca Pass (see page 155). From here the hike is all above treeline, so evaluate weather conditions prior to heading for the summit. Traverse south along the ridge, passing over or near Ptarmigan Peak's false summit. The top of **Carbonate Mountain**, 12,308 feet (3,751m), is a bit over 1.0 mile (1.6km) from the miner's cabin.

Ptarmigan Peak's false summit

Hikes in the Park: From Dunes Parking Lot

EXPLORING THE DUNES

What would a visit to the Great Sand Dunes National Park be without actually getting out there on the dunes? Hiking on the dunes is a unique and special activity. In many National Parks and Monuments, rangers must remind visitors not to touch

5 | 2.5 miles (4.2 km)
400' (122m) gain

this, or walk on that, feature of the area. When you hike onto the dunes, however, you can draw your name in the sand in 18-foot high letters if you like, because you won't be doing any harm. The winds will erase your artwork in a few hours, or a few days. These ancient sand dunes will continue to wonder and amaze visitors for many, many years to come.

Rent a copy of **Woman in the Dunes** *(Suna no Onna)*, a Japanese film about life in a sand pit in Japan. This interesting and provocative story is based on the novel by Kobo Abe. The film is subtitled in Japanese and is a real classic — nominated for an academy award for best foreign film in 1964. The ending will keep you guessing! *(Warning: this movie contains mature themes and adult content.)*

There are many ways to access the dunes. The primary access is from the **Dunes Parking Lot**, just north and west of the Visitor Center. If you are camping, perhaps you should visit the dunes via the **Dunes/Piñon Flats Trail**, which starts near campsite #52 in Loop #2, and drops down through Loop #1 near campsite #34. This trail is also accessible off of the main road, just north of the entrance to the Medano Pass Primitive Road. Or, if the main Visitor Center parking lot is open following construction in 2002-2004, follow the **Visitor Center Interpretative Trail** until you see a

TRAIL TO THE DUNES

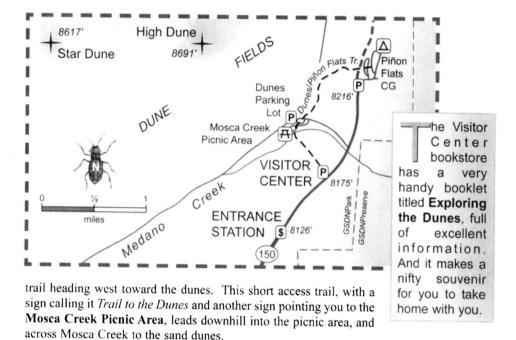

Map labels: 8617' Star Dune; High Dune 8691'; FIELDS; DUNE; Dunes/Piñon Flats Tr.; Piñon Flats CG; Dunes Parking Lot; 8216'; P; Mosca Creek Picnic Area; Creek; VISITOR CENTER 8175'; P; GSDNPark; GSDNPreserve; ENTRANCE STATION 8126'; Medano; 150; 0 ½ 1 miles

The Visitor Center bookstore has a very handy booklet titled **Exploring the Dunes**, full of excellent information. And it makes a nifty souvenir for you to take home with you.

trail heading west toward the dunes. This short access trail, with a sign calling it *Trail to the Dunes* and another sign pointing you to the **Mosca Creek Picnic Area**, leads downhill into the picnic area, and across Mosca Creek to the sand dunes.

Hikes onto the dunes vary in distance due to the uniqueness and magnitude of the terrain. Any exploring you do in this area will have its *ups and downs*. Hikes can easily be both strenuous and exhausting. Make your own path to whatever destination your energy level and spirit dictate.

Two popular destinations are **High Dune** and **Star Dune**. High Dune is the dune which has the highest elevation above sea level, while Star Dune is the *tallest.* Confused? Let's explain. High Dune, rising 650 feet (198 m) above the valley floor, is at an elevation of 8,691' (2,649 m) and lies about one mile (1.6 km) west from the Dunes Parking Lot. Star Dune rises 750 feet (228 m) to an elevation of 8,617' (2,26m) and sits about 1.5 miles (2.4 km) off to the left of High Dune, when viewed from CO 160 as you drive into the Park. Star Dune has the highest *relief*, or distance above where the dune ridge meets the surrounding valley floor. So even though it is the *tallest* dune, it is not the *highest* dune (elevation above sea level.)

Distances in the dune field are somewhat deceptive, with plenty of hiking up one dune and then down the other side. Points of interest may be a certain distance away as the crow flies, but much further away as the human walks. You'll almost certainly underestimate the amount of effort and time it takes to go to High Dune, and especially on over to Star Dune. You should allow two to three hours for a leisurely round trip to High Dune and back to the parking lot.

Star Dune is so called because it has three or more connecting ridges that merge to the center of the dune. **Star dunes** sort of resemble a starfish. There are several star dune complexes in the Park.

It's best to keep those shoes handy; surface sand temperatures can reach 140° F (60° C) — talk about your basic *hotfoot!* During the summer, go hiking early in the day to avoid the debilitating heat. Heat exhaustion can be dangerous! Be prepared, take plenty of water, sunscreen, sunglasses, and a nice, wide-brimmed hat to keep the sun from cooking your brains.

View from Star Dune, with the Crestones on the far left and Mount Herard on the right

You will find the hike over to Star Dune from High Dune to be very rewarding. The panoramic views are simply spectacular. To the west, you have the San Luis Valley and in the distance, the San Juan Mountains. To the north, you will see the dramatic northern Sangre de Cristo Mountains, including a few of the tougher 14,000-foot (4,267m) peaks, **Crestone Peak** and **Crestone Needle**. The looming peak on the right is **Mount Herard**. To the south, you will see the stark ruggedness of the Blanca massif which contains such high peaks as **Blanca Peak** and **Little Bear Peak**.

If Medano Creek is flowing, as it usually is in the spring, carry your shoes and be a kid again as you run, jump and rush into the **surge flow** of the water. Be careful you don't get washed *out to sea!*

Next to the Dunes Parking Lot, you can take advantage of the outdoor **foot wash** that the Park Service has installed for your convenience. You will find these exciting devices located beside the parking area, as you head toward the restroom, as well as located just to the right of the restroom doors. During busy times of the day the foot wash area is easily located by following the screams of *"It's cold!"* If sand covers more than just your feet, there's a higher spigot to let you spray cold water over your entire body! After you rinse, take advantage of the new changing rooms nearby, to get out of your wet togs and into your picnic attire.

Adventurous spirits might consider staying overnight on the dunes. Sunset and sunrise can be exceptionally memorable times to spend some quality time with that special someone. Sleeping on the dunes requires a free permit, obtainable at the Visitor Center (see page 93).

Playing in the surge flow

ESCAPE DUNES/GHOST FOREST TO CASTLE CREEK

We wouldn't take this hike alone! The names *escape* and *ghost* bring back dark, dark images from the story of *Ichabod Crane and the Headless Horseman.* Don't believe us for

> 2.5 miles (4.2 km)
> minimal elev. gain
>
> **6**

a moment; actually this hike is a wonderful lesson in geology at work.

This particular hike does not have an established trail. You will encounter many informal use trails made by animals and other visitors. The more adventurous Park visitor will find this to be a very interesting hike. From your path, you will be able to enjoy the unique area between the dunes and Medano Pass Primitive Road.

Start this hike from the north end of the **Dunes Parking Lot**, just past the RV parking area. Proceed down to the creek bed and then parallel **Medano Creek** upstream, as it winds back and forth between the main and escape dunes, on to your ultimate destination, **Castle Creek**. You will quickly realize that the walking is less strenuous if you walk on sand which is still damp. Depending upon the time of the year, you may find that minor detours are necessary to avoid actually walking in the creek. During dry periods, you can actually walk up Medano Creek, sans water.

Look off to your right as you walk along the creek and you will see what appear to be very large *sand traps* like those you would see at a golf course. This would certainly be the golf course from Hell — par must be at least 85!

Soon you will begin to notice that you are walking predominately on **escape dunes**. Remember that all dunes on the east side of Medano Creek have somehow *escaped* the main dune complex. As you encounter some of the larger escape dunes, you will notice an area of trees which have become entrapped in the sand and succumbed to its allure. This is the dreaded **ghost forest**. How long does this process take, and will it continue into perpetuity? We leave that question for you to ponder, as we continue our journey.

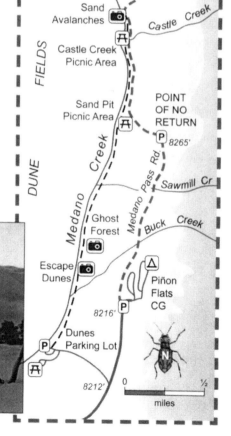

Ghost forest

The trees here have been smothered, and subsequently died as a result of their source of moisture being terminated. Why did trees die, when there is obviously an adequate source of moisture not far below the surface? Scientists are still pondering this question.

This is the best example of a ghost forest to be found in the area. If you explore just to the north of the main ghost forest area, you will see an example of *ghosting* in action. Some **ponderosa pine** trees are silently being buried, even as you watch. Take a photograph of the trees which are being buried, and then come back in a few months, or a year, and get an idea of just how long it takes for the dunes to complete their dirty deed.

Pines being buried by encroaching dunes

As you continue on past the ghost forest, the amount and variety of vegetation becomes more abundant. That's not the only thing which becomes more abundant in this area. Where you have water and vegetation, you can usually count on voracious mosquitoes, and various other *no see 'ems*. Application of bug repellant will go a long way toward making this a more enjoyable hike.

The local deer population makes this section of the Park one of their main watering areas. Deer tracks become more plentiful, closer to Castle Creek.

Watch your step a little more closely as you continue to negotiate your way upstream. It's easy to become distracted and trip over one of the increasing number of larger rocks. Your path will merge into the Medano Pass Primitive Road, as you reach Castle Creek. You will notice that the Park has a gate here, usually locked during the winter months, when the road above this point becomes impassable for travel. This event can also occur sometimes during the spring, when excessive water can erode the road bed, making travel dangerous.

Well, you have reached your destination — *almost*. We have a little surprise in store for you. Continue on up the road for approximately five minutes before encountering an old road leading off to your left. Take this road for several more minutes and you will come to the remains of an old structure. This was the headquarters of one of the prior Park concessionaires. Careful here, there are still some old rusty nails in this area and one of them probably has your name on it!

The Park's system of mountains, sand dunes, wind and water are nature's giant **recycling plant**. From the mountain tops, to the streams that feed the valley floor, to the winds that return sands back to the dunes, none of the sand goes to waste here. Everything is used, recycled, and used again. Sands that are blown off the dunes end up in Medano Creek, only to be washed back down the valley floor, dried out and blown back up into the dunes complex. This cycle has repeated itself for thousands of years.

In the area near Castle Creek, you may see a dramatic portion of this process. Sand is deposited on steep **slip-faces** which creep toward the **angle of repose** — the lowest slope angle at which the sand will begin to slide, or the steepest incline

Turn left here and go down to Medano Creek. This truly is one of the more fascinating areas along the creek. Walk closer to the creek and spend some quiet time here in this mesmerizing spot. Watch the **sand avalanches**, as they suddenly slip beyond the **angle of repose**, tumble down into Medano Creek and, ever so slowly, start a journey to another place far, far away. Here again is nature recycling itself. Your hiking partners may be exclaiming, *"look at this one over here!"* and point to where a large, sand avalanche has just released, sending its contents rushing down to the creek — reminds us of being kids again, and why not!

When you're finally ready to head back, you may be tempted to walk along the Medano Pass Primitive Road all the way back to your point of origin, instead of retracing your path along the creek. This is not recommended. You'll need to be constantly alert for vehicles driving rapidly through the deep sand and around blind curves, and be ready at a moment's notice to jump out of their way.

Make your way back toward Medano Creek and downstream toward your point of origin. Now and then, you may want to climb out of the creekbed on the west side to explore the main dune mass, or climb out on the east side to take a peek at the road.

If you get a vantage point where you can see the road, you will see first-hand what a really nasty drive it is between Castle Creek and the Sand Pit area. If you're lucky, perhaps someone will come roaring by on their way up to Medano Pass. You can always identify the rookies by their *white knuckles!* This stretch of the road is only passable by robust, high-clearance, four-wheel drive vehicles.

You may spot a number of signs on the hilly slope to the east of the creek, as you continue downstream. This is the Sand Pit Picnic Area, at the terminus of the **Sand Pit Trail**. As an alternative to staying next to Medano Creek, you may elect to hike the Sand Pit Trail back to **Point of No Return**, where the trail meets the Medano Pass Primitive Road again. From Point of No Return, head uphill onto the **Sand Ramp Trail**, leading to **Piñon Flats Campground**. The trail will bring you to Loop #2 of the campground. Turn left when you reach the paved road in Loop #2, and follow the road past the first restroom building and on to the second restroom building. You'll see a sign beside the building showing the start of the **Dunes Trail**. Turn right here (west) and follow that trail down hill, through Loop #1, and across open land toward the dunes. Watch for a sign for the **Dunes Parking Lot**. Turn left (south) on the trail to the Dunes Parking Lot and proceed approximately 0.5 mile (0.8 km) to the parking area.

Obviously, this hike can be done going in either direction, or shortened by driving to Point of No Return and making it a loop trip from there.

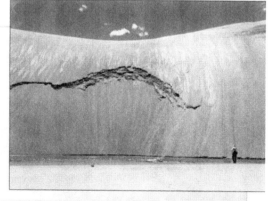

at which it will not slide. This is usually between 30° and 45° degrees, depending upon the granular nature of the sand and its moisture content. (We always thought the angle of repose was that point which occurred after you have fallen asleep in your chair watching TV, and tip too far forward!) Suddenly, it slips and deposits a load of sand into Medano Creek, to be swept down valley!

Hikes in the Park: From Piñon Flats CG

DUNES TRAIL/PINON FLATS TRAIL

The **Dunes Trail** is also known as the **Piñon Flats Trail**, when accessed from the Dunes Parking area. This path starts in Loop #2 of the **Piñon Flats**

7	0.8 miles (1.3 km) minimal elev. gain

Campground near campsite #52, makes its way down through Loop #1 near campsite #34, crosses the Medano Pass Primitive Road and then proceeds down to Medano Creek and the dunes. Shortly before reaching Medano Creek, you will encounter a sign indicating that the **Dunes Parking Lot** is 0.5 mile (0.8 km) to your left.

Piñon Flats Campground may also be accessed from the Dunes Parking Lot by going to the north end of the lot, just past the RV parking section, and taking the Piñon Flats Trail. Follow the Piñon Flats Trail until you reach the Dunes Trail and then turn right. This will take you up to Loops #1 and #2 of the campground. This path sees a lot of pedestrian traffic due to its convenient access to the dunes from the campground.

SAND RAMP TRAIL TO POINT OF NO RETURN AND/OR DUNES OVERLOOK

Begin this enjoyable hike from near campsite #62 in Loop #2 of the **Piñon Flats Campground**. Note that this point is the start of the **Sand**

8	1 to 2 miles (1.6 to 3.2) km) 400' (122m) gain

Ramp Trail. The first part of this trail was previously referred to as the Little Medano Trail. Upon intersecting the Medano Pass Primitive Road, the name changed to the Sand Creek Trail. On newer maps, the entire trail is now called the Sand Ramp Trail. You may encounter signs along the way using the older trail names.

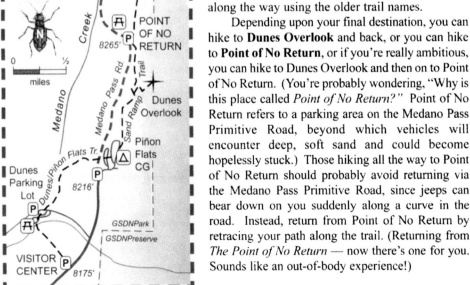

Depending upon your final destination, you can hike to **Dunes Overlook** and back, or you can hike to **Point of No Return**, or if you're really ambitious, you can hike to Dunes Overlook and then on to Point of No Return. (You're probably wondering, "Why is this place called *Point of No Return?*" Point of No Return refers to a parking area on the Medano Pass Primitive Road, beyond which vehicles will encounter deep, soft sand and could become hopelessly stuck.) Those hiking all the way to Point of No Return should probably avoid returning via the Medano Pass Primitive Road, since jeeps can bear down on you suddenly along a curve in the road. Instead, return from Point of No Return by retracing your path along the trail. (Returning from *The Point of No Return* — now there's one for you. Sounds like an out-of-body experience!)

Hiking past a grove of piñon pines on the Dunes Overlook Trail

You will find a **trail register** shortly after you begin this hike. Please register your passage. Trail registers are important environmental management tools for the Park Service. If you're lucky, there may even be a pencil to write with and something to write on. Look to see who else might have taken this journey from your hometown.

This trail gives you a little better perspective of the damage from the fire of April 2000. This area was obviously a real *hot spot*. You will gain and lose very little elevation as you walk through groves of juniper and cottonwood trees. Breathe deeply and take in that *real forest scent*. We're sure it's the same scent that merchants are always trying to sell us, to freshen up our bathrooms and vehicles. As the trail drops into drainages and climbs back up the other side, you may find yourself chanting a mantra, *"Plod, plod, plod up the sandy hill."* Ah, but it's worth it to see the lovely cottonwood trees in one drainage, and the trickling stream in another!

At the half-mile mark you will come to the **Dunes Overlook Trail** junction. Take the right fork to climb up to Dunes Overlook. The left fork stays on the Sand Ramp Trail and goes on to Point of No Return. The Dunes Overlook Trail gains 270 feet (82m) in another 0.5 mile (0.8 km). We can overwhelmingly recommend this little side journey — talk about your outstanding views! We hope you remembered to bring your camera!

Rustic bench

Let's head to the overlook. The trail winds its way through various types of resident conifers, yucca and cactus. After a short period of time, you will come to another trail junction going off to the left. This spur goes over to the ridge point, where a **rustic bench** has been provided for your viewing pleasure. Check it out and then return to the main Dunes Overlook Trail to complete your journey to the top.

Proceed uphill, past another rustic bench, to the top of the ridge, which is the Dunes Overlook. The views don't get much better than this. Up north you'll see **Mount Herard**, to the west is the dunes complex and the San Juan Mountains and to the south is the **San Luis Valley**. This viewpoint gives you a better perspective of how far back the dunes really go. You don't realize the full magnitude of the dunes complex from the Visitor Center.

Return to the main branch of the Sand Ramp Trail. Turn right to proceed to Point of No Return or turn left to return to Piñon Flats Campground — the choice is yours. Turning to the right will lead you downhill through groves of very mature **ponderosa pines**. Some of these trees have been around for more than 400 years! We spotted one huge pine whose top was probably destroyed by lightning years ago. It has a massive trunk that abruptly changes into a number of smaller, new branches, growing from it's broken top. Inspired by this tree's will to live, one of the authors did her tree-hugging demonstration. She declared that this was a *2 ½ tree-hugger*, meaning it would have taken two adults and a small child to hug the entire trunk.

This is another of those trails which would be spectacular in the fall, when the aspen trees are changing colors. The spring season isn't half bad either, as you have the added ambiance of Medano Creek surging and flowing down from the mountains.

Once you are at the parking area for Point of No Return, retrace your steps via your original route to the Piñon Flats Campground. (Walking back along the Medano Pass Primitive Road is risky and ill-advised.) Shortly after passing the campground, you will pass under some power lines and encounter the **Dunes Trail** on your left. The Dunes Trail leads up through Loop #1 and terminates in Loop #2, near campsite #52.

This is a good hike to make after dinner, or before breakfast — or if you're looking to lose a little of that spare tire, *instead* of breakfast! Don't forget to take your water along.

Views of the dune fields and the San Juan Mountains from Dunes Overlook

The tree dubbed "Papa Piñon"

PAPA PINON

There are many old, lovely **piñon pines** along this part of the Sand Ramp Trail, with wide-spreading branches. One particularly symmetrical and enormous piñon pine caught our eye. We dubbed it "Papa Piñon." What a lovely spot! Seeing these hardy specimens, it is hard to imagine that if present conditions continue, the state could lose most of its piñon pines in just a few short years.

The culprit is a tiny insect, the **ips beetle**, sometimes known as the "engraver beetle." Helped by a four-year drought which has weakened the resistance of the trees, ips beetle infestation has exploded over the past two years. In some areas of southwestern and southern Colorado, losses have been put at 50% of piñon pines. About 40% of the state's 1.7 million acres of piñon pines are now infested, with the bugs spreading rapidly throughout the tree's range.

Adult beetles bore beneath the tree's bark to mate and lay eggs. The resulting larvae burrow into the tree's nutrient-rich cambium layer and feed; eventually girdling the tree and killing it. New generations of beetles over-winter beneath the bark and then emerge in the spring, flying off to infest new trees. The bugs are highly dependent on weak trees; only a return to normal rainfall patterns will end the plague.

Piñon pines are common in the dry, rocky soils of the Sangre de Cristo Mountains up to elevations of about 9,000' (2744m). While they show up occasionally in pure stands as shown above, more often they exist in open woodlands, mixed in with junipers. The trees don't grow much taller than 20 feet and are sprawling in nature. Historically, the tasty **piñon nuts** have been a very important food source for native people and animals. To a lessor extent, these seeds are still collected by people throughout the southwest. You may see the distinctive **piñon jay** close by, named for its preference for nesting in these pines.

Hikes in the Park: From Point of No Return

SAND PIT TRAIL

This short walk starts at **Point of No Return** on the **Medano Pass Primitive Road**. This parking area is accessible by normal passenger car via the Medano

9	0.5 miles (0.8 km)
	minimal elev. gain

Pass Primitive Road, which starts across from the amphitheater and recycling

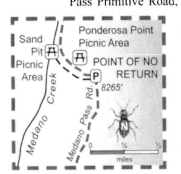

collection bins. Allow yourself an hour for this hike and you'll probably have a few minutes left over when you're done.

Cross the road and follow the signed path as it heads downhill, over to the **Sand Pit Picnic Area**. As you come over the first rise, you'll be treated to an outstanding view of the dunes complex. Off to your right is one of the many beautiful stands of **ponderosa pines** found in the Park. As you walk, scan the areas on either side of the trail for the various types of cactus and bushes indigenous to this area. And, as always, be on the lookout for trash which you can collect and deposit in the proper place.

Give some thought to the environment which you are visiting. It's amazing that such diverse plant life can exist in such a sandy area. Notice how the wind and grasses have combined to sculpt exquisite patterns in the sand.

As the path works its way down toward the Sand Pit area, you'll be able to view an encroaching dune off to your left. Just past this point, the Medano Pass Primitive Road comes into view from your right.

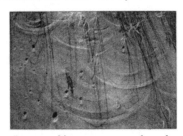

Patterns, blowout grass and sand

View along the Sand Pit Trail

After you arrive at the picnic area, walk out to the Medano Pass Primitive Road and you will understand why this area is named the Sand Pit. Wait a few minutes and perhaps someone will come past in their 4WD vehicle. You can witness the classic *man versus nature* challenge.

For those who are brave (or foolish) enough to attempt to drive their vehicle to this point, take a few minutes to stop and enjoy the shade and outstanding view of Mt. Herard from the **Ponderosa Point Picnic Area**. This picnic site is located about half-way between Point of No Return and the Sand Pit. We think that Ponderosa Point offers a much better choice of picnic locations over the Sand Pit, due to the spectacular views and the beauty of the large ponderosa pines which shade that spot.

While you're hiking along the sandy trail, note the variety of animal tracks. You should be able to see evidence of deer, coyote, rabbit and mice.

SAND RAMP TRAIL TO SAND CREEK TRAILHEAD

This interesting and informative hike has two potential starting points, and several ways of reaching each of them. You may begin the hike from near campsite #62 in Loop #2 at

🚶 3.4 miles (5.5km)
300' (91m) gain

10

Piñon Flats Campground or from the parking area at **Point of No Return**, located on the Medano Pass Primitive Road. If you chose to start hiking from Piñon Flats Campground, you will need to add 1.0 mile (1.6 km) each way to the hiking distance. Refer to Hike #8 on page 136 for directions about the first mile of the trail, if you choose that option.

Be advised that this is a multi-use trail, shared by both pedestrians and horses. Pedestrians must always yield the right-of-way to horses by stepping off of the trail a safe distance. This behavior will keep the horse from becoming frightened.

Due to the extremely sandy nature of the trail, you will find that the **Sand Ramp Trail** requires more energy than many of the other trails that we have described in this book. You should allow approximately four hours to complete this hike. Bring at least two quarts/liters of water, and drink it. The trail starts out in a firm, somewhat rocky area, just above the parking area at Point of No Return. Don't be fooled by the footing — classic *Great Sand Dunes* hiking conditions are just over the next rise!

Vegetation in the early part of the hike consists of an abundant array of cactus, yuccas and various types of grasses. In 0.2 mile (0.3 km) you'll encounter a very stately **ponderosa pine**, silently standing guard over the trail. What a fine example of a tree — definitely one of our favorites! (Brings to mind the poem, *Trees* by Joyce Kilmer — *"I think that I shall never see, a poem as lovely as a tree."* If you've never read this poem, you're missing one of the really great ones.)

The Sand Ramp Trail (Little Medano Trail) goes to the right from this spot at Point of No Return

The **Sand Ramp Trail** (formerly called the Little Medano Trail and the Sand Creek Trail) is your key to six of the designated backcountry campsites within the Park and Preserve, as well as to scenic and culturally significant sites along the eastern edge of the dunes. Hikes #8, #10 and #11 combined cover the extent of the Sand Ramp Trail. It begins near campsite #62 in Loop #2 at **Piñon Flats Campground**, and can be used to access the **Dunes Overlook Trail**, as well as to reach **Point of No Return** and the **Sand Pit Trail**. Ghost forests, escape dunes and peeled trees can be seen along the trail.

You can also access the Sand Ramp Trail by driving or walking along the Medano Pass Primitive Road to Point of No Return. The trail intersects the road again at the **Sand Creek Trailhead**.

The trail continues on through a mixture of piñon pines, mountain juniper and sage, as it makes it way toward **Castle Creek**. This is a very hardy ecosystem. Notice, however, the absence of aspen trees, which require a more abundant source of moisture than is available here.

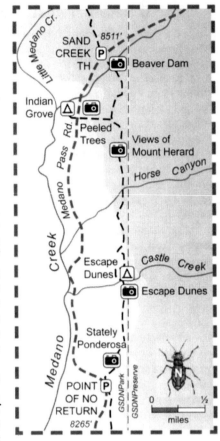

Shortly, you will encounter what are technically called **escape dunes**. We wonder if they shouldn't be called *suburban* dunes, as they are out and away from the main dune complex. These are dunes which have jumped east across Medano Creek, when the creekbed was dry. If you look around this area, you will notice that some of the dunes have buried trees sticking out of them. This area is referred to as a **ghost forest**. The trees have become buried and smothered by the sand. Some of these trees look like driftwood which has washed up on the shore of a lake or ocean.

The Castle Creek drainage is located just past the escape dune area. Depending on the amount of precipitation received during the winter months in the surrounding mountains, Castle Creek will normally flow during the spring and early summer months. It's interesting to see this volume of water in such a high-desert, sandy environment.

The footing starts to get a little more solid after you come up out of the Castle Creek drainage and start into the ponderosa forest. Stop at this point and take in the views. You'll get a better perspective of how the escape dunes are formed.

Shortly after you cross Castle Creek, you will encounter a trail going off to the right. This is a short trail which goes over to the **Escape Dunes Campsite**,

a designated backcountry site, 1.4 miles (2.2 km) from Point of No Return.

Backcountry permits are required to camp in any of the authorized backcountry camping areas in the Park. See page 94 for details on using backcountry sites. For those of you who are camping out, check with the Park staff ahead of time to find out if there's water at Castle Creek for cooking and drinking. Water shoud be boiled, treated or filtered.

Sand Ramp Trail, near Escape Dunes Campsite

Continue on down the trail and you will drop into the Horse Canyon drainage, among several types of conifers. Take a few minutes while you are walking to study the various tracks left by the many creatures that inhabit this area. There are small tracks, large tracks, tail drag markings and various other unrecognizable tracks. If you're lucky, you'll see some of the small critters that make these tracks. The **blowout grass** makes some interesting designs in the sand, so keep your eyes on the sandy areas, just off the trail. All of these little things co-exist, to make a truly magical kingdom.

The looming peak on the skyline is **Mount Herard**. At approximately the 2.5 mile (4.0 km) mark you will encounter a signed trail going off to your left; this is the trail to the **Indian Grove Campsite**. As you walk along this trail, observe the ponderosa pine trees around you. The bark on the lower portion of many trees has been removed. Welcome to the convenience store of the **Ute Indians**. The Utes removed the bark for food, medicine and various other household uses. You will see many of these scarred trees on the way to Indian Grove Campsite, as well as along the Sand Ramp Trail.

A side journey to view the Indian Grove Campsite is well worth the effort, and can easily be a destination in itself. Follow the trail to the campground as it heads over toward the Medano Pass Primitive Road. Along the way, you will see other areas where native people, and other early visitors, made their campsites. One more recent site appears to contain a small garbage dump. How long does it take before *litter* becomes a part of history and an archeological treasure?

After the path crosses the road, it drops down into a sheltered area surrounded by pines and cottonwood trees. You can see why the Native Americans chose such a useful spot for their campground. The Park Service has

Mount Herard looms ahead on the Sand Ramp Trail

recently added a new **composting toilet**, off to the side of the camping area. Note to overnight campers — check with the Park personnel on availability of water from Medano Creek. Take the usual precautions for treating drinking water!

Return to the junction with the Sand Ramp Trail. The terrain starts to flatten out as you continue north along the Sand Ramp Trail. This is an open area of fewer trees, predominately inhabited by sage and grasses. You should be able to get a good view of Mt. Herard from this vantage point. Off in the distance, you can see a line of trees which delineate **Little Medano Creek**. These trees, along with Little Medano Creek, provide sanctuary for a variety of bird life. If you brought along your binoculars, you can scan the horizon to discover what the naked eye has missed. Turn farther to the left and see if you can spot anyone hiking on the dunes.

Follow the trail as it drifts to the right and gradually heads uphill, before dropping into a drainage by some ponderosa trees. Here you will find another fine example of **peeled trees**.

Crossing the bridge at Medano Creek

The scenery continues to change dramatically as you approach Medano Creek. As the trail turns to the left, your surroundings suddenly change from high desert to the lush vegetation of Medano Creek. What a significant difference water can make to the environment (and for humans). But be sure to treat or filter water taken from this stream.

Stop for a few minutes as you cross the creek on the **log bridge**. Look at the **beaver dam** which has been built upstream. Did you know that some beaver dams can exist for 100 years? Generations of beavers continue adding on to, and improving, the original structure. Of course, nature can change the course of history in an instant by sending flood waters down to destroy decades of hard work.

When you're ready, make a short hike uphill for more beautiful scenery off to your right. This has to be one of the most scenic areas of the Park. (We know, we say that about every place we've described, but they are all true!) Off to the left you will notice the Medano Pass Primitive Road. In just a few short minutes the trail will drop down to join the road at the junction with the **Sand Creek Trailhead**.

Once you've arrived back at Point of No Return, take a few minutes to examine your clothing for any **ticks** which may have hitched a ride along the way. We've actually seen them dropping from tree limbs onto people's heads! Ticks can burrow into your skin and make you very sick, so be extra careful.

To return, we don't recommend walking along the Medano Pass Primitive Road due to hazards from vehicle traffic, not to mention the billowing dust. As you retrace your footsteps on the Sand Ramp Trail to Point of No Return, notice how massive the dune complex appears. We're always amazed at the number of things we see on the return trip that originally went unnoticed. This is an enjoyable excursion; take along plenty of water, a hardy lunch and make a day of it.

Hikes in the Park: From Sand Creek TH

SAND RAMP TRAIL TO SAND CREEK CAMPSITE

This trail, formerly known as the Sand Creek Trail, is a continuation of the **Sand Ramp Trail**. The hike starts from the **Sand Creek Trailhead** parking area at the junction of the Sand Ramp Trail with the Medano Pass

> 6.4 miles (10.2km)
> 600' (183m) gain
> 1,150' (351m) gain (return)
>
> **11**

Primitive Road. To access the Sand Creek Trailhead you must either have hiked the Sand Ramp Trail from Piñon Flats Campground or from Point of No Return, or have negotiated the four-wheel drive Medano Pass Primitive Road to this point. Sorry, dropping in by parachute is not allowed!

If you decide to hike all the way to **Sand Creek Campsite**, you will have a journey of 6.4 miles (10.2 km) each way, or a round trip of 12.8 miles (20.4 km). It's important to note that you will have nearly twice the elevation gain on the return from Sand Creek Campsite, than on the walk out there. Given that you are hiking in sand most of the way, and there are some long, steep hills to ascend, this can be a full day's adventure. You may decide to make this trip an overnight ––– there are several designated backcountry campsites along the trail. A parking/camping permit is required for overnight use of the campsites, available free of charge at the Park Visitor Center.

Leave the Sand Creek Trailhead and hike uphill through aspen and ponderosa pine to your first objective ––– **Little Medano Campsite**. This point is 0.6 miles (1.0 km) from the trailhead. After departing Little Medano Campsite, the rolling terrain passes among thinly spaced ponderosa pines until it makes a right turn and drops down to meet **Little Medano Creek** in 0.3 miles (0.5 km). At this time, you need to evaluate your water supply and decide what your requirements will be, since this might be the last available water on the trail. From here on, it is mostly hiking in the sand with sparse vegetation, and even sparser shade.

Here are a few hints which might make your journey easier and more successful. Don't attempt this hike during the hottest part of the day; the heat will wear you out. **Hiking sticks** or **trekking poles** are extremely useful when hiking this section of the trail. Bring along a couple of empty, gallon water jugs with good lids, that you can use to hold your water supply.

Carry plenty of water (one gallon per person per day), or have a **water filter** with you and know where along the trail water will be available. It's important that you check with the Park Service, prior to undertaking this hike, for the latest information on availability of water in the streams along the way. Most of these hold water only seasonally, and in dryer years, may not run at all. Don't underestimate the amount of effort required for this hike; you will be in a very remote area of the Park!

Struggling out of the Little Medano creekbed

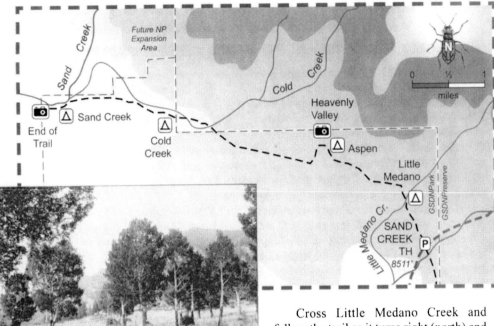

Tent at Aspen Campsite

Cross Little Medano Creek and follow the trail as it turns right (north) and then back to the left (west), skirting the northern end of the dune complex. You will find that the trail has a tendency to disappear in some areas, due to drifting sand. Just stay to the right of the main dune field and keep your eyes peeled for the occasional trail sign.

You will gradually gain elevation as you head up to **Aspen Campsite**, which is the highest campsite along the trail. Aspen Campsite is 2.3 miles (3.7 km) from the Sand Creek Trailhead. *"Hiking uphill in the sand is fun!"* — just keep repeating that mantra to yourself, and you'll be there before you know it! The final hill up to Aspen Campsite seems to go on forever, but the real giveaway is the small grove of aspen trees awaiting your arrival. This is a great spot to take a rest if you're day-hiking, and it's simply the best backcountry campsite on the entire Sand Ramp Trail. The views of the dunes to the south, and **Heavenly Valley** to the north, are just a couple of the outstanding features of this site.

No shade along the Sand Ramp Trail.

The next authorized campsite, **Cold Creek**, is an additional 2.5 miles (4.0 km) west along the Sand Ramp Trail, again skirting the dune field. This section of the trail has its ups and downs, as it continues to traverse along the northern edge of the dunes, before dropping down approximately 600 feet (183 m) into Cold Creek. We think Cold Creek is a misnomer; not a lot of breeze gets down into this area and hiking back out can be a real religious experience.

View of dunes from near the high point of Sand Ramp Trail

Once you are down in the Cold Creek drainage, the foliage and vegetation change dramatically. This is a typical creek bottom environment, complete with heavy underbrush, a goodly supply of large ponderosa and cottonwood trees, and a large variety of flying insects, which are either incessantly buzzing your ears or attempting to bite you wherever there is exposed flesh. The actual campsite is at the far end of this drainage.

This campsite lacks any significant views of the dunes and is remarkable only for the large ponderosa pines around the site. If you want to *get away from it all* or *find your space,* then this is the ideal spot for you. It is extremely doubtful that you will see another human being while you are here. Your friends will be of the four-legged variety.

Next stop is **Sand Creek Campsite**, approximately 1.6 miles (2.6 km) due west. There is very little elevation gain on the way to Sand Creek Campsite, the current end of the Sand Ramp Trail. Evaluate your stamina and water supply before continuing on from this point.

Hike along the trail, with increasing views of the peaks and valleys to the north and the dunes complex to the south. There are very few trees along this section of the trail. Take advantage of any shade you find, if it's a hot day. The good news is that you will be able to see the trees lining Sand Creek in the distance; the bad news is that they never seem to get any closer.

Once you drop down into the Sand Creek drainage, you may be surprised to see the difference in terrain. This area is a classic river bottom with dense stands of cottonwood trees — what a change from just a few minutes ago when you were walking primarily in a desert environment.

Walk through the cottonwoods for about ten minutes more until you arrive at a sign proclaiming *End of Trail.* You've done it! It's an enjoyable journey for sure, but Aspen Campsite still gets our vote as best backcountry place to spend the night.

While the Sand Ramp Trail currently ends at Sand Creek Campsite, there are plans to link up with the **Sand Creek Trail** in the National Preserve at a future date. Until the Park expands north into the lands of the old **Baca Grant #4**, backpackers intent on reaching the Sand Creek Trail must bushwack over the ridge north of **Cold Creek**. Check with the Park personnel for directions on this option.

Hikes in the Park: From Montville Trailhead

MONTVILLE NATURE TRAIL

This trailhead is located approximately 0.25 miles (0.4 km) north of the Visitor Center. Parking is available in the lot at the trailhead. From this

12 *0.5 miles (0.8 km) minimal elev. gain*

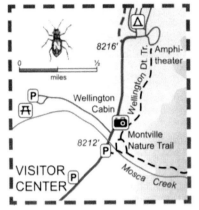

parking area, you have a number of choices for enjoyable hikes. The **Montville Nature Trail** loop links to the **Wellington Ditch Trail**, the **Montville-Visitor Center Trail** and the **Mosca Pass Trail**. In turn, the Mosca Pass Trail links to the **Carbonate Mountain Trail**, for those who want a more ambitious hike.

Sorry, bicycles are not allowed on this trail. Equestrians must lead their horse, until reaching the Mosca Pass Trail. Also, camping is not allowed at this site. Obtain a copy of the very informative booklet, *Montville Nature Trail, A Step Into the Past,* available for purchase at both the trailhead and the Visitor Center. Your 0.5 mile (0.8 km) walk around this loop will be greatly enhanced by this booklet, as it references **numbered posts** that are keyed to information about the trail — another nice souvenir to help you remember what you saw on your visit to the Park!

Pioneers operated a toll gate here for those traveling over Mosca Pass. The booklet brings alive the cultural and natural history of the Mosca Pass area, as you stroll along this outstanding nature trail. At the start of the trail you will be observing the effects of the **wildfire** in April of 2000 that swept through this area. In the past, this area has been burned over, cut down by man and devastated by flood. Take a few minutes to visualize the people and events that occured here, slightly over a hundred years ago. Don't get run over by those wagons coming down from the pass! Take your camera and allow a little extra time, as this trail is bursting with history.

Hikers enjoying the Montville Nature Trail

WELLINGTON DITCH TRAIL

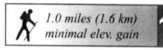

1.0 miles (1.6 km) minimal elev. gain **13**

This enjoyable walk is one of our favorites! If you don't have much time to spend in the Park, we suggest that you hike the Montville Nature Trail to the **Wellington Ditch Trail**. Either one, or both of these hikes, makes an ideal after-dinner stroll with the family. Horses and bicycles are not allowed on these trails.

Follow the **Montville Nature Trail** and proceed to the bridge which crosses **Mosca Creek**, just past the *Point of Interest reference post #9*. Bear right here; you are now on the Wellington Ditch Trail. You may also start the Wellington Ditch Trail hike from the end of the loop in **Piñon Flats Group Campground**. This location is south of group site A in Loop #3. Both entrances to the trail are signed.

You will hike through groves of aspens, conifers and many varieties of bushes. See which ones you can identify. The Montville end of the trail still has some significant damage from the recent fire. It will be interesting to see how long it takes to regenerate this area. The aspen trees are already beginning to make their presence known.

Look down in the trees toward the dunes, at about the half-way point, and you'll see the remains of an **old cabin**. This is the original Wellington family homestead. It can be visited via a faint path from the Visitor Center road.

Some portions of the trail follow the original ditch, hand dug by the Wellington family in 1927 for irrigation purposes. Today, we would need to conduct an environmental impact study to undertake a project of this type!

The Wellington Ditch Trail affords the visitor easy walking with memorable panoramas of the dunes. There is a good view of the Montville Nature Trail and the Visitor Center from the south end of the Wellington Ditch Trail. Be sure to bring your camera to capture the moment.

WELLINGTON CABIN

The home of the very hard-working Wellington family can be seen from the Wellington Ditch Trail, or if you keep a sharp lookout, from the main Park road. From the intersection of the main road with the road to the Dunes Parking Lot, park in the small paved pull-out just north of the intersection. Look for a culvert and drainage ditch across the road, and about 65 yards north of your parking spot. A very faint trail follows the drainage ditch east, for a walk of about 200 yards to the historic remains of the **Wellington Cabin**.

Homesteaders **Frank Wellington** and family dug irrigation ditches near their cabin, as well as in other parts of the valley, including the Zapata Falls area. Take care when you visit this old home. For your own safety, do not go inside the structure. Just peek through the windows. Imagine preparing meals in that old kitchen, or picture yourself sitting in front of the cabin on a summer evening, relaxing after a hard day's work (digging ditches!) and enjoying the view of the dunes in the dwindling light.

The Wellington cabin

MOSCA PASS TRAIL (FOREST SERVICE TRAIL #883)

And a fine adventure it is! The **Mosca Pass Trail** climbs up to **Mosca Pass** at 9,750 feet (2,972 m) through Mosca Canyon. You're not in Kansas

14 *3.5 miles (5.6 km)*
1,540' (470m) gain

anymore; you're hiking up into the **Sangre de Cristo Mountains**! Don't forget to take an adequate amount of water and some snacks for your journey — the mountain air is dry and you will be perspiring.

Access this trail from *Point of Interest reference post #8* on the **Montville Nature Trail**, just past the Mosca Creek bridge. Horses are allowed on the Mosca Pass Trail but riders may walk their horses along the Montville Nature Trail to reach the start of the Mosca Pass Trail. Bicycles are not allowed on either the Montville Nature Trail or the Mosca Pass Trail.

Sign the trail register, located on your right at the beginning of the trail. It's fun to review the list of prior hikers' names and states to see where everyone hiking the trail comes from. We found mostly Colorado residents — guess they know a good thing when they see it! Note that you will also find a trail register at the Mosca Pass end of the trail. There is no need to register at both locations.

Be aware that this area is home to mountain lions, bears and other wildlife, so it doesn't hurt to make a little noise to let them know you want to pass through their territory!

The trail starts to climb immediately and most of your elevation gain occurs in the first half of the hike. So just about the time you're beginning to drag a little, the trail will level out and give you some breathing room. Follow the trail as it traverses along the hillside on the north side of **Mosca Creek**, sometimes high above the creek, and at other times dropping down to the creek level.

Notice how the terrain and vegetation change as you ascend up the mountain. Hike through groves of aspen, cottonwood, juniper, piñon, ponderosa, spruce and fir trees. You will also see currant and chokecherry bushes along the path. And look at those gnarly rocks on the left side of the trail — not a good place to be during an earthquake!

There are also plenty of colorful butterflies and birdies for your enjoyment. Where there are butterflies and birds, there must be flowers. This is one of the premier flower hikes within the Park and Preserve during the summer.

Notice how the **aspen trees** have been defaced by persons unknown who have carved their initials and statements of undying love into the tree bark. We suspect these trees will endure much longer than most of the relationships described thereon. One tree had a date on it which was nearly a century old. Leave your pocket knife at home and just send your sweetie a nice card. The Native Americans referred to aspens as *the trees with eyes.*

As you are hiking along, try to imagine where the old toll road must have come down the drainage. You can see by the "U" shaped nature of this drainage how heavy rains upstream could unleash a flash flood, like the one in 1912 that finally spelled the end for the tiny settlement of Montville. Cleanse your lungs of those exhaust fumes and breathe in some of that fresh Colorado mountain air.

Keep your eyes on the trail and maybe you'll be lucky enough to spot one of nature's little creatures of the wild, a real *snake in the grass*. We saw a **garter snake**, as we crossed a small stream at approximately 9,475' (2,880m). We had previously observed snakes as high as 10,000' (3,048m) in California, but this was our first sighting in Colorado. On visiting with ranger Patrick Myers at the Visitor Center, he noted that garter snakes can live as high as 12,000' (3,658m) — guess you can learn something new every day!

As you leave the forest, you will encounter an area of open meadows. This section of the trail is easy hiking. You are now approaching the eastern end of the Mosca Pass Trail. A short hike along this area brings you to the **wilderness boundary** fence, which just happens to be a very nice place for a picnic lunch. The Mosca Pass Trail continues on up the hill, a short distance past the wilderness boundary, and joins up with Forest Service Road 583, subsequently becoming Huerfano County Road 583 (also known as the Mosca Pass Road) which comes up from Gardner in the Wet Mountain Valley.

Once at the pass, other hiking options are available. Those who still have a lot of enthusiasm and energy can opt to hike generally south for 3.3 miles (5.3 km) to reach 12,308 (3,752m) **Carbonate Mountain.** There is a well defined trail leading to the summit ridge (see Hike #15). Don't overextend your time or capabilities, as your journey is only half-completed. You will still need to return to your vehicle. Colorado weather in the high country can turn nasty very quickly; be prepared and descend immediately if threatening weather occurs.

This is also an outstanding fall hike when the aspens are changing color!

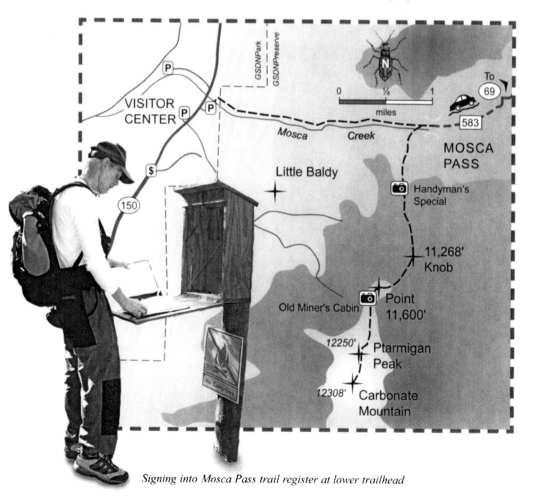

Signing into Mosca Pass trail register at lower trailhead

MOSCA PASS TO CARBONATE SUMMIT

The trailhead for **Carbonate Mountain** can be reached from the upper end of the **Mosca Pass Trail**. You may either follow the driving directions for

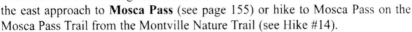

15 *3.3 miles (5.3 km)*
2,680' (817m) gain

the east approach to **Mosca Pass** (see page 155) or hike to Mosca Pass on the Mosca Pass Trail from the Montville Nature Trail (see Hike #14).

The **Carbonate Mountain Trail** begins approximately 350 yards from Mosca Pass. Proceed west and downhill from the trailhead register, until you see a distinct trail heading off to your left. Follow the trail as it goes briefly downhill and then bends around to the left. Very shortly you will encounter the ruins of an **old cabin** off to your left — *a handyman's special.* The trail crosses the meadow and continues into the trees, while paralleling the small stream on your right. Follow the trail along the stream for approximately 0.5 mile (0.8 km), when it will start to gradually climb up and to the left. The trail is well-defined and easy to follow.

In approximately 1.0 mile (1.6 km), the trail gains the ridge to the southwest, which marks the boundary between Alamosa and Huerfano counties. Follow this ridge for approximately 1.5 miles (2.4 km) until it comes out of the trees at about 11,268 feet. Once you get above tree line, this hike is a *no brainer.* From this vantage point you will be able to look generally southwest and see a false summit

Old cabin near Mosca Pass

(also known as Ptarmigan Peak) at 12,250 feet (3,734m), in front of **Carbonate Mountain**. While it appears that it is an easy walk over a couple of hills to the summit of Carbonate Mountain, this is deceptive. A study of your map will indicate that there is a deep drainage between the hill in front of you and the hill going up to the summit.

Your route leaves the 11,268' knob and drops approximately 100 feet (30m) into a saddle and then climbs rather steeply up the hill. Keep to the left as you ascend this hill, as you will need to make a rather sharp left turn at the top, in order to traverse over to the ridge connecting it with Carbonate Mountain.

As you start to traverse the Carbonate Mountain ridge, you should encounter an old **miner's shelter**. This is the spot where the **Revelation Point** route (Hike

GPS waypoints/landmarks for this hike:
 ▌ **Elevation 9,630':** *UTM 495500mE, 4175820mN (trailhead)*
 ▌ **Elevation 11,268':** *UTM 458580mE, 4173700mN (treeline)*
 ▌ **Elevation 12,308':** *UTM 457630mE, 4171760mN (summit of Carbonate Mtn.)*

View north from near summit of Carbonate Mtn.

#4) intersects your route. We suggest that you traverse along the east, or left side, of the ridge, keeping just below some rock outcroppings. Be cautious, as there is at least one abandoned mine shaft along this route. While it does not appear deep, it should be avoided. The distance from the miner's shelter to the top of Carbonate Mountain is slightly over 1.0 mile (1.6 km). Allow approximately 1.5 hours of steady hiking time from the 11,268' knob to the summit, and approximately 45 minutes for your return trip. This area of the hike is all above treeline, so evaluate the weather conditions prior to heading for the summit.

BRISTLECONE PINE

Timberline on Carbonate Mountain is a dramatic place. Trees make their last stand here against the forces of nature, before giving way higher up the slope, to alpine meadows. One of the most distinctive trees adapted to this harsh environment, especially in the dry, rocky soils of the Sangre de Cristo Mountains, is the **Bristlecone Pine**. Their knarled trunks, at times impossibly twisted, are favorites as photographic subjects; and the many dead trees, lying about, testify to the struggle to survive, as treeline rises and falls over the centuries.

Bristlecones are so-named for the distinctive prickles on their cones. Their other common name, **Foxtail Pine**, comes from the dense clusters of forward-pointing needles that resemble bushy tails. In Colorado, these long-lived pines have been dated to over 1,000 years old in places; while 4,000 year old specimens in California's White Mountains are considered the oldest living things on earth.

Bristlecone Pine at treeline on the route to Carbonate Mtn.

Eastern Access Hikes: The 3Ms

The major geologic features of the Sangre de Cristo Mountains that contribute to the formation of the Great Sand Dunes are the three low passes situated directly behind the dunes. These affect the wind patterns and cause sand to be deposited at the base of the range. We fondly refer to these three passes as the *3Ms*: **Mosca Pass**, **Medano Pass** and **Music Pass**. Several good hikes orignate from the 3Ms — most of which visit the high, alpine reaches of the **National Preserve**. This is a very different experience from the hikes within the **National Park** (see pages 122-153), most of which are centered around the main dune complex. Here, high in the mountains of the Sangre de Cristos, you'll encounter different plants and animals, marvel at the abundant water in lakes and streams and perhaps, even frolic on snow in the middle of the summer! Unparalled natural diversity — that's what makes the Great Sand Dunes National Park and Preserve so unique.

To get to hikes accessed from the eastern side of the Sangre de Cristo Mountains, visit the beautiful **Wet Mountain Valley**. All three passes are best accessed from CO 69, the main north-south highway in the valley. As you drive along CO 69, you'll encounter secondary roads that lead to each pass. We suggest that these roads should be named *The Good*, *The Bad*, and *The Ugly*.

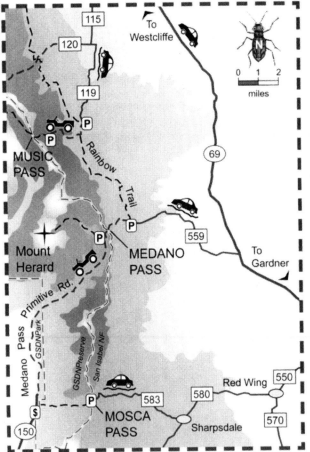

The Good *(Tip: Use your own vehicle):* The road to the Mosca Pass Trailhead is gravel, very well maintained, and with a gentle grade. A passenger car will have no trouble.

The Bad *(Tip: Use your friend's vehicle!):* The road to Medano Pass, including the trailhead to Medano Lake and Mount Herard, starts off fine, but as it makes the final climb to the pass, it becomes a steep, 4WD-only road. Our mini-SUV made the trip, but there were many tense moments.

The Ugly *(Tip: Rent a Hummer H2!!):* A passenger car will do fine, until the final 1.75 miles of road to the Music Pass Trailhead. Our mini-SUV bumped and bounced, as we ventured beyond the place where most passenger cars chose to park, but we soon reached a section of road that was clearly impassable for our vehicle. A handful of heavy-duty trucks and big SUVs were parked at the Music Pass Trailhead.

Eastern Access Hikes: From Mosca Pass

The **Mosca Pass Trail** can be accessed from within the National Park starting at the trailhead for the **Montville Nature Trail**, located about 0.25 miles (0.40 km) north of the Visitor Center (see Hike #14, page 150 for details.)

Alternatively, you can drive to **Mosca Pass**, and hike the Mosca Pass Trail down into the National Park.

The upper trailhead for the Mosca Pass Trail

The trailhead for **Carbonate Mountain** is also accessed from the Mosca Pass Trail. From Mosca Pass, proceed west and downhill from the trailhead register until you see a distinct trail heading off to your left (see Hike #15, page 152 for details.)

If you're trying to drive to Mosca Pass from the **Great Sand Dunes National Park**, drive south from the park entrance on CO 150. At the intersection with US 160, turn left (east) toward La Veta Pass. Before reaching the pass, about 29 miles (46.7 km) after turning onto US 160 and just after *Mile Marker 276*, turn left onto the first side road you see. There won't be a left turn lane here, so take care. This is CR 572, although the only signs you'll probably see here are for *Rd. 29* and a development called *Paradise Acres.* Cross the cattle guard. A little-used road to *Paradise Acres* goes straight ahead, while a much better gravel road (CR 572) turns left immediately after the cattle guard and curves uphill. Turn left onto this road, and follow it for about 12 miles (19.3 km) through beautiful ranchland and rocky canyons to the little town of **Red Wing** at the junction of CR 570 and CR 550. 9.2 miles (14.8 km) after turning off US 160, you'll reach an unsigned intersection with CR 570. We suggest turning right here for the more direct route to CR 550 (which leads to Mosca Pass). However, you can also reach CR 550 by turning left, since CR 570 is a loop road. Once you reach CR 550, turn left (west) to continue to Mosca Pass.

Follow CR 550 for 18.2 (29.1 km) to the pass, as it changes from blacktop to gravel (and is renamed as CR 580, and then again as CR 583). There are numerous parking/camping spots located in this area. This road is suitable for normal passenger cars.

You can also reach CR 550 from CO 69. From the south, take CO 69 to the town of **Gardner** and turn left onto CR 550. To reach Mosca Pass from the north, take CO 69 from **Westcliffe**, going south for 32.7 miles (52.3 km) to Gardner. Turn right onto CR 550.

Eastern Access Hikes: From Medano Pass

The moderate, 2.5-hour hike to **Medano Lake** is one of the most enjoyable trips in the Park and Preserve. The terrain is varied and the trail is generally gradual, with only a couple of steeper sections, nearing the lake. You can extend your outing to include a strenuous hike to the summit of **Mount Herard**, which offers wonderful views of the entire sand dune complex, the Sangre de Cristo Mountains, the San Luis Valley and the San Juan Mountains in the distance — *no admission charged!*

From the intersection of CO 96 and CO 69 in Westcliffe, head south on CO 69, proceeding approximately 24.2 miles (38.7 km) to CR 559, the **Medano Pass Road**. Turn right and follow this gravel road for 7.0 miles (11.2 km) to the National Forest boundary where it become FSR 559. The road is suitable for normal passenger cars. The property on both sides of this road is private and belongs to the **Wolf Springs Ranch** — no camping or trespassing is allowed! Keep your eyes open for views of their **bison herd**.

Approximately 0.5 miles (0.8 km) after entering the National Forest, you will reach the junction with FSR 412. There you will see a sign indicating the distance to Medano Pass as 2.5 miles (4.0 km) — 4WD ONLY. Don't even think about proceeding beyond this point with anything other than a four-wheel drive vehicle. This road is very steep, and a 2WD car wouldn't have the traction to make it up some of the hills, nor the clearance to make it over some of the rocks and ruts.

Once at **Medano Pass**, you will encounter yet another sign indicating 6.0 miles (9.6 km) to the Great Sand Dunes. The **Great Sand Dunes National Preserve** boundary starts at Medano Pass. Beyond the pass, this road is known as the **Medano Pass Primitive Road**. If your intention is to continue beyond the trailhead for Medano Lake, and to drop into the National Park, you should read the cautions on page 103. However, if you've made it this far, you can probably drive down to the trailhead (and make it back up again when you are ready to leave.) From Medano Pass, proceed 0.5 mile (0.8 km) down a very steep hill to the trailhead sign, located at a "T" intersection. Turn right at this intersection and drive 0.1 miles (0.2 km) to the trailhead parking area. There are several good campsites along this road and at its termination. Water is usually available from **Medano Creek**. Remember to treat or boil all water prior to drinking. The southern approach to the Medano Lake Trailhead, along the Medano Pass Primitive Road, requires either a very long hike on sandy roads (9.5 miles (15.2 km)) or a very rough drive up the road — again see the cautions on page 103 before attempting that.

Spur road leading to Medano Lake Trailhead

MEDANO LAKE TRAIL

3.3 miles (5.3 km)
1,920' (585m) gain
16

The hike to **Medano Lake** (and optionally to Mount Herard) begins just after you cross Medano Creek at elevation 9,600 feet (2,926m). Sign in at the trail register and follow this enjoyable trail, as it climbs gradually up through dense stands of evergreens and aspens. The trail crosses Medano Creek several times on its journey up to the lake. You will pass through clearings surrounded by beautiful stands of aspen — some groves growing as dense as we've ever seen. There are also outstanding examples of rock formations composed of **Crestone conglomerate**, higher up on the trail. As you approach the lake, enjoy the views of the sheer cliff faces off to your left and of the cirque that surrounds the lake. Mount Herard lies directly ahead; it's the rounded mountain behind those jagged walls.

Elevation at the lake is approximately 11,520' (3,511m). There's great picnicing and fishing. Set up your tent at one of the nice camp spots located near the outlet of the lake, and enjoy this scenic place for another day or so! For those with a more adventurous spirit, and if the weather gods are smiling on you, you may choose to invest an additional three hours for an energetic, round-trip hike up to Mount Herard (see Hike #17.)

Dense stands of aspen in fall colors along the trail

At the outlet for Medano Lake

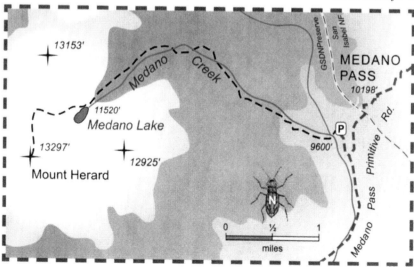

MOUNT HERARD TRAIL

We feel that **Mount Herard** offers one of the most outstanding panoramic views of the Great Sand Dunes complex.

17 *4.7 miles (7.6 km)*
3,700' (1128m) gain

But get ready to work hard for such a beautiful reward, as this is a very strenuous hike/climb up steep, grassy slopes and rocky paths above **Medano Lake**. You will find a trail which takes off to the right (northwest) from the trail that brought you to Medano Lake (see Hike #16.) Start hiking diagonally up the grassy slopes on a faint trail that becomes more distinct the higher you climb. Follow this trail as it climbs steeply, traversing beside the rock faces north of the lake. Be alert for spontaneous rock fall from the cliffs above and to your right.

The trail then becomes fainter as it climbs, reaching a flat area at about 12,000 feet (3,658m). From this point, you will be able to assess the final portion of your hike. Your objective is to gain the ridge in front of you that runs up and to your left. You can access this ridge by heading to the left of the low saddle in front of you, while staying on the grassy areas as you climb. Once on the ridge, turn left and climb over steep but easy ground, toward an obvious notch on the skyline. Allow yourself about 1.5 hours to reach the notch from the lake.

Once at the notch, sit down and take a break, enjoying the scenery. The hardest part of the hike is behind you. When you've caught your breath and checked the weather again, climb through the notch and head right, for an easy stroll of 20 minutes or so on a faint trail, following the ridgeline on your left to the obvious summit of Mount Herard, 13,297' (4,053m), *UTM 456550mE, 4188990mN.* Be sure to take along your camera and plenty of film, especially in the fall when the colors are changing. Allow about an hour or so for your return to the lake.

Now here's one for *Ripley's Believe It or Not.* While hiking up the steep slope below the notch, we found a new golf ball. Someone had probably carried their 9-iron all the way up to the ridge and shot some balls down toward the lake. We guess the par for this hole must be around 12,550!

Mount Herard could be called the *Sentinel of the Dunes,* for it seems to stand sentinel over the entire sand dunes complex!

Eastern Access Hikes: From Music Pass TH

Music Pass is a fine destination in itself for a short and easy hike; but it also lies on the boundary for the **Great Sand Dunes National Preserve** and is a major gateway to the Preserve's remote and spectacular alpine wilderness, popular with hikers, fisherman, backpackers, equestrians and climbers.

From the intersection of CO 96 and CO 69 in **Westcliffe**, head south on CO 69, proceeding 4.5 miles (7.2 km) to CR 119, also called **Colfax Lane**. Turn right at this signed intersection. CR 119 starts out as blacktop, changes to gravel and finally to dirt. Just past the turn, a Forest Service sign will be

Music Pass is a popular entry point for the Preserve

on your right, indicating that the distance to **Music Pass Trailhead** is 13.5 miles (21.6 km) and that it's 9.5 miles (15.2 km) to the junction with the **Rainbow Trail**.

Proceed on CR 119 for 5.5 miles (8.8 km), arriving at a "T" intersection with CR 120. CR 120 goes off to your right, leading up South Colony Road. Continue on CR 119, making a left turn at this intersection. A sign at this intersection indicates that it is 8.0 miles (12.8 km) to Music Pass. Reset your vehicle's trip odometer at this point.

As you follow CR 119, you will encounter a road heading off to your left to **Music Meadows**. Keep right at this junction; do NOT go to Music Meadows. After 5.0 miles (8.0 km), you will reach the San Isabel National Forest boundary (and the end of decent roads). In another 0.5 miles (0.8 km), you will encounter the junction with the Rainbow Trail, FST 1336, and Medano Pass FDR 559, which goes off to your left. These are both hiking trails. You are now 2.5 miles (4.0 km) from the Music Pass Trailhead. Two-wheel drive passenger vehicles should park at this location!

Keep to the right when you reach the junction with FST 1337, which continues on to Music Pass. The trail to the left is the continuation of the Rainbow Trail (FST 1336), closed to all motorized traffic.

The remaining distance to the Music Pass Trailhead is definitely for 4WD ONLY! The first mile of this road is especially bad, consisting of deep dips and large, tilted rocks with deep gouges from prior visitors. This is not the place for your sissy, *city-slicker* mini-SUV. Only high-clearance, low-geared vehicles need apply. It's a long, long way here from road service

For those of you whose vehicle made it this far, park in the area located at the end of the road. The Music Pass Trailhead is the first trail to the right, as you enter the parking area. You may see a sign that reads *Music Pass.* This is not actually Music Pass. Perhaps this sign formerly pointed to the trailhead for Music Pass. At any rate, FST 1337 begins to the right of the sign and is recognizable by a large dirt berm, blocking vehicles from proceeding beyond this point.

MUSIC PASS TRAIL

Register at the trailhead and start your journey to Music Pass. This easy-to-follow trail gradually gains elevation, rising through different varieties of pine forests

18	*1.0 miles (1.6 km)* *700' (213m) gain*

which gradually thin out as you approach the pass. Some of the last pines you will encounter are the famous **bristlecone pines**, a long-lived species (nearly 5,000 year old specimens in California are believed to be the oldest living things on earth.) Examine the arrangement and density of the pine needles, compared to some of the other varieties. As you begin to leave the trees behind you, take a minute to turn around and enjoy the views back to the east. Can you spot the road you took from the highway to get to this spot?

Just below the pass, you'll encounter a very pleasant, semi-secluded rest spot in amongst the trees. It's hard to leave such a lovely place when the time comes, but there's a lot more to be discovered just over the hill. A few minutes more of hiking will bring you to the top of the pass.

Looking out and west from Music Pass, you will have outstanding views of **Tijeras Peak** to your left, with **Music Mountain**, **Pico Asilado** and **Milwaukee Peak** straight ahead. Looking back east, you have a panoramic view of the **Wet Mountain Valley** with the **Wet Mountains** beyond. Look hard enough and you can even spot **Pikes Peak** off in the distance. That will be **Beck Mountain** on the north side of the Music Pass saddle. *Ah, so many mountains, so little time!*

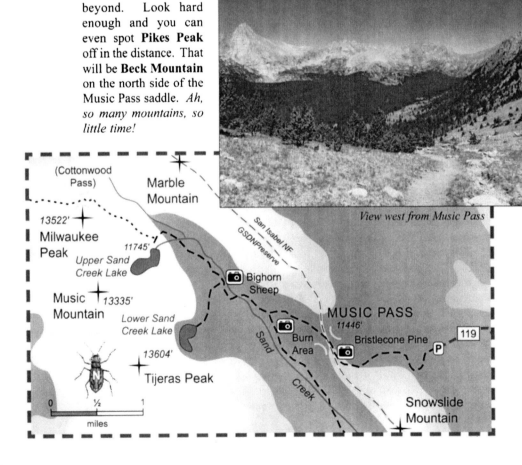

View west from Music Pass

LOWER SAND CREEK LAKE TRAIL

Follow the trail to **Music Pass**, described under Hike #18. From your vantage point at Music Pass, you can see most of your possible hiking/fishing

2.7 miles (4.3 km)
1,100' (335m) gain

19

destinations. Follow the trail as it drops 460 feet (140m) into the Sand Creek basin. Dead trees off to your left are the result of a **forest fire**, long since past. The sparse vegetation is being replaced with succulent mountain grasses and willows. Before you know it, you will be walking in a lush, high alpine meadow. In normal moisture years, this area will hold pockets of snow until mid-June. During most of late spring and summer, this area is ablaze with numerous varieties of wildflowers. Bring along your flower identification book and see how many flowers you can find. You'll have to admit that this is one of the premier areas in Colorado for wildflowers.

In 0.7 mile (1.1 km) you will reach the junction with the **Sand Creek Trail**. The sign post indicates that the trail to the left is FST 903, but most maps show it as FST 743. This is a trail for more adventurous hikers and backpackers. (Follow this trail south for 3.5 miles (5.6 km) to connect with the **Little Sand Creek Lake Trail**, FST 863. See page 174 for more information about the Sand Creek Trail at its western access.)

Fire ravaged trees near treeline

Continue right, past this trail junction, for another 0.3 miles (0.5 km) to intersect with the signed **Lower Sand Creek Lake Trail**. This trail junction is a very popular spot for a herd of **bighorn sheep** living in the area. It is not uncommon to see them grazing as you walk along the trail. Take a few minutes to rest, sit quietly here and you'll undoubtedly be rewarded with some outstanding sheep photos. (Remember, one of the *Leave No Trace* principles is that you not harass wildlife.)

Follow the signed trail, FST 877, as it quickly drops down to cross **Sand Creek** and then heads back up the other side of the drainage, amidst thick timber. Look off to either side of the trail and observe the vast amount of deadfall littering the forest floor. It's easy to understand why some of the recent forest fires have been so devastating.

Tijeras Peak behind the lake

The trail meanders through thick pine forests, as it reaches an area of switchbacks and begins gaining elevation on its way up to Lower Sand Creek Lake. Once there, the views of the lake and surrounding peaks will make you wish you had brought an extra roll of film. That is **Tijeras Peak**, elevation 13,604' (4,146m), across the lake. Take some time to enjoy the serenity of your surroundings and walk around the perimeter of the lake. *Now, if only we had brought along our tent and stove!*

UPPER SAND CREEK LAKE TRAIL

Follow the trail to **Music Pass**, described under Hike #18, and drop west off the pass to the intersection with the **Sand Creek Trail**. To the left, that trail

| 20 | *3.0 miles (4.8 km)* *1,445' (440m) gain* |

descends Sand Creek. Instead, go right on FST 743 and on past the turn-off for Lower Sand Creek Lake (see Hike #19), traversing alpine meadows and rising above a marshy area. The trail in this area has recently been rerouted to avoid the worst portion of the marshy area. The old trail has been blocked off with rocks and should not be used.

The re-routed trail begins at the sign for **Upper Sand Creek Lake**, FST 862. Follow the trail as it switchbacks through pine forests, crossing the outlet stream for the lake. Continue following the trail as it makes one final switchback, again crossing the outlet, winding its way up toward the lake itself.

On your way up, you'll pass a faint, spur trail which leaves the Upper Sand Creek Lake Trail and climbs steeply to the

Crossing the outlet stream

northwest, passing over a saddle on the north shoulder of **Milwaukee Peak**. At over 13,000' feet, this unnamed pass (informally known as *Beer Pass* or *Cottonwood Pass*) gives adventurous backpackers access to the **Cottonwood Creek Trail** on the west side of the range (see page 172).

Arriving at the lake, as you might imagine, there are numerous trails to choose among. Follow whichever trail looks like it might take you to where you wish to go. The views are well worth the effort it takes to get here. **Music Mountain**, 13,335'(4,065m), stands off to your left with Milwaukee Peak, 13,522' (4,122m), to your right. There is great fishing for **Rio Grande cutthroat** and **rainbow trout** in both Lower and Upper Sand Creek Lakes. The lakes are also destinations for climbers wishing to summit the various high peaks in the area.

A picnic with Milwaukee Peak behind

Eastern Access Hikes: From Music Pass Rd.

The pleasant, easy-to-follow **Rainbow Trail** contours the east slope of the Sangre de Cristo Range for 85 miles (136.8km). The **Music Pass Road**, (FSR 119), crosses the Rainbow Trail at a point 2.5 miles (4.0 km) before the Music Pass Trailhead. On some maps this point is labeled as the **Grape Creek Trailhead**, on others it is, somewhat confusingly, called the **Marble Mountain Trailhead**. Strictly speaking, the hikes on the Rainbow Trail at this point are entirely outside the National Park and Preserve; however, they afford interesting hiking alternatives, especially for those who lack a 4WD vehicle and can't reach the Music Pass Trailhead. We offer three hikes here, at different levels of difficulty — an enjoyable hike with outstanding views of the **Wet Mountain Valley** which can be shared with the entire family, an unusual hike to the highest natural caves in the U.S., and a summit hike/climb with unsurpassed views into the alpine heart of the National Preserve. A fourth hike (Hike #24) offers a more direct route to the same summit from a closer trailhead.

The hikes along the Rainbow Trail, described here, are clearly visible as you travel on FSR 119, providing a great opportunity to study the **Marble Caves** area, as well as **Marble Mountain**. FSR 119, also called **Colfax Lane**, departs CO 69, 4.5 miles (7.2 km) south of **Westcliffe**. The trailhead for the first three hikes is located 11.0 miles (17.7 km) south of CO 69, and it has camping, a parking area and an outhouse. It can be reached in a normal passenger vehicle.

Hikes on Marble Mountain viewed from FSR 119

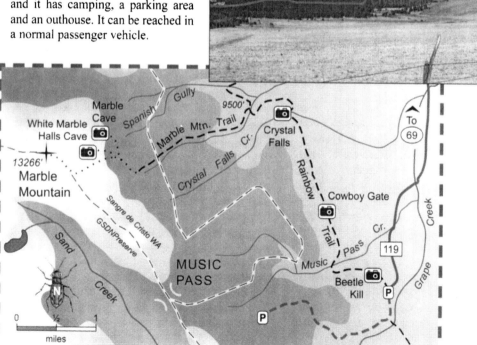

RAINBOW TRAIL TO CRYSTAL FALLS

Proceed to the outhouse and turn right to view the trailhead sign. You will not find **Crystal Falls** on this sign; instead it erroneously indicates that it is 2.5 miles (4.0 km) to the **Marble Mountain Trail**. Actually the start of the Marble Mountain Trail is beyond Crystal Falls, 3.9 miles (6.3km) from the trailhead sign (see Hike #22). Be aware (or beware) that the Rainbow Trail is open to motorcycle, ATV, bicycle and horse traffic, as well as to hikers, but not to trucks, jeeps or SUVs. As the trail is relatively narrow in spots, this mixture of traffic can add a bit of interesting adventure to your journey, especially if all these conveyances just happen to converge at the same time and place!

3.1 miles (5.1 km)
745' (227m) gain

Step aside for ATVs on Rainbow Trail

As you leave the aroma of the outhouse behind, you are greeted by an interesting spectacle. Numerous trees have been cut down along both sides of the trail. This pruning of the forest was needed because of an attack by the dreaded **mountain pine beetle**. These beetles

infect a tree and effectively cut off the water supply by leaving a fungus around the perimeter of the tree. Evidence of active beetle infestation can be detected by observing *cream to dark-red masses of resin mixed with boring dust* on the bark of the tree. Mountain pine beetles can destroy thousands of trees in just a single season, leaving the area highly susceptible to forest fire. Pass through the devastated tree area and then enter a forest which is the way it should be — with mixed stands of aspen, along with various pines and flowers. *Life is good!*

If you're energetic and adventurous, an alternative to *hiking* to **Crystal Falls** or the **Marble Mountain Trail** exists. The section of the Rainbow Trail over to Crystal Falls Creek, and beyond, is *mountain bike friendly*. The trail contains extended stretches of level, open terrain, with good visibility, making it ideal for a quick bike trip over to the falls. Be alert for large rocks on the trail and hang on tight to those handle bars!

Quite soon the trail makes an abrupt right turn as it crosses **Music Pass Creek**, and climbs gradually on its journey toward **Crystal Falls Creek**. Ah, how nice the shade can be on a stifling, hot summer's day. All too soon you'll find yourself lusting after the shade as it's left behind. But all is not lost. Without a thick forest to obstruct your view, you will be treated to vistas unmatched elsewhere in this part of Colorado. Look in the drainage below the trail for a magnificent stand of aspen, which in their fall colors are simply spectacular and not to be missed. Only a master painter could duplicate the scene!

In less time than you can imagine (actually, about an hour into the hike) you will encounter a **cowboy gate** — in layperson's terms, a gate made of barbed wire. At the gate, look down and to the

A hiker along the Rainbow Trail

right of your feet, and you will find a metal *Township and Range* marker. These are also referred to as *permanent range markers*. If you open a gate, be sure to close it behind you.

The scenery along this section of the trail is characterized by wide open spaces, great views and grassy slopes, mixed with various scrub bushes. Follow the trail as it descends down into the Crystal Falls Creek drainage. Once you arrive at the creek, take a few minutes to rest and enjoy this idyllic setting. The falls are just a short, five-minute hike up the *use trail* to the right of the creek. Exercise care when approaching the falls, as some of the terrain may be slick.

You'll find abundant photographic opportunities in and around the falls area. There is a small cave located on your left, as you face the base of the falls. We hope that your hike to the falls has been a memorable event. If this was your destination, you should return using the same trail back to the trailhead. If, as we hope, you have a more adventurous spirit (and are in good physical condition), then read on about Hike #22, a journey to what are quite possibly the highest natural caves in all of North America, the **Marble Cave** complex.

RAINBOW TRAIL/MARBLE MOUNTAIN TRAIL
TO MARBLE CAVES

There are numerous caves within the limestone cliffs and rock outcroppings, high on the slopes of Marble Mountain. The largest of these, and probably the most popular to visit, are called **Marble Cave** and **White Marble Halls Cave**.

6.4 miles (10.3 km)
2,510' (765m) gain
22

Many stories and legends surround these caves. Some people say *Spanish Conquistadors* mined here, using Native Americans as slave labor. Marble Cave is sometimes called *Caverna del Oro* (Cave of Gold). Another story, related to us by Hobey Dixon of the **Friends of the Dunes** organization, is that if you throw a blanket into the shaft, it comes blowing back out. This seems quite possible at the entrance to Marble Cave! Wait until you feel that icy-cold air,

GPS waypoints/landmarks for this hike:
■ **Elevation** 11,710': *UTM 454335mE, 4200440mN (entrance to Marble Cave)*
■ **Elevation** 11,760': *UTM 454445mE, 4200100mN (entrance to White Marble Halls Cave)*

blowing out of the cave! Another story is that wind blowing from the caves whines and howls, giving **Music Pass** its name. Only the *Shadow* knows for sure! Let's go locate the entrances to these legendary caves.

The **Marble Mountain Trail** leaves the **Rainbow Trail** at 3.9 miles (6.3km) from the trailhead on the Music Pass Road. The sign at this trailhead incorrectly lists the distance as only 2.5 miles (4.0 km). Follow the Rainbow Trail to **Crystal Falls Creek** (see Hike #21). Leave Crystal Falls Creek and hike gradually uphill, following the trail as it turns left into a clearing. Stop here for a moment and look around. The mountain you see off to the northwest is Marble Mountain, another 4,000' above you.

Continue along the trail and pass through a **cowboy gate**, just prior to **Hudson Creek**. After crossing the creek, make a short uphill hike and you will encounter a sign for **Marble Caves**. The sign indicates that it is 2.25 miles (3.6 km) to the caves (left) and 2.5 miles (4.0 km) to **South Colony Road** (straight ahead). The distance from this spot to South Colony Road (FSR 120) is actually only 1.5 miles (2.4 km). Turn left on to the Marble Mountain Trail (FST 1338).

The trail sign indicating the distance to the caves is a bit misleading. The distance to White Marble Halls Cave is in fact 2.2 miles (3.5 km), with a gain of 2,260' (689m). The distance to Marble Cave is 2.5 miles (4.0 km), with a gain of 2,210' (673m). These caves are located 0.4 mile (0.6 km) apart, so if you want to visit both cave formations, you must add another 350' (107m) of gain, either by ascending to easier ground above Marble Cave or by descending down into the valley and traversing south around the nose of the rock buttress, regaining lost elevation as you climb back up to the White Marble Halls Cave.

Leave the Rainbow Trail and begin hiking west on the Marble Mountain Trail, as it starts to climb up along the north side of the Hudson Creek drainage. Shortly you will encounter a trail register. If you rode your mountain bike to this point, this would be a good area to secure it to a tree. It is not possible to take your bicycle up the Marble Mountain Trail, as there is an abundance of downed timber crossing the trail and the trail enters a wilderness area in about 0.75 miles (1.2 km), where bicycles are prohibited. If you are on horseback, your trusty steed may be able to make its way over or around the trail obstacles.

The Marble Mountain Trail is much narrower than the Rainbow Trail, but is still well-defined at this point. Hike up through a mixture of aspen and pine for a short period, until you leave the trees and enter a level meadow area. The trail is somewhat faint here, but if you continue straight ahead into the trees, you will easily find the trail again. There is an established campsite off to the right and up in the trees. Water is usually available from Hudson Creek.

From this point on, the trail steadily gains elevation as it climbs through the pine forest and enters into the **Sangre de Cristo Wilderness Area**. As you reach treeline, the trail begins to level out somewhat and enters a classic, high mountain meadow. Here you'll get an unobstructed view of Marble Mountain, the upper Hudson Creek drainage and the caves area. White Marble Halls Cave is located in the drainage directly above you, along the left side of the rock buttress. Marble Cave is located in the next major drainage to the right, called **Spanish Gully**, that divides the rock buttress.

A hiker on the Marble Mountain Trail

The hike up Spanish Gully to Marble Cave involves some steep, rocky terrain, and may involve a little rock scrambling. The cave entrance is small, and a non-technical explorer can only visit the first 30-40 feet of this cave. The hike to the entrance of White Marble Halls Cave is also a bit steep, but the terrain offers much easier footing. White Marble Halls Cave can be explored to much greater lengths, by non-technical means. If you think you only have the time and energy to visit one cave, we recommend White Marble Halls Cave.

To reach Marble Cave from the mountain meadow, begin traversing diagonally up toward the drainage, keeping low on the slope, but to the left of the trees. After you reach the Spanish Gully drainage, you will need to decide how far up on the left side you can easily continue walking, before it will become necessary to cross over to the right (north) side. You need to avoid the steep, rocky area on the left (south) side of the drainage. After you do cross over to the right side of the drainage, it is generally easier to hike a short distance away from the drainage itself. Once you are in the upper drainage, it will be necessary to hike close to the right (north) wall to enable you to discover Marble Cave. There is a very faint, red marking above the cave's entrance. You may also feel a rush of cold air coming out of the rocks, indicating that you are walking past the cave entrance.

Pointing to White Marble Halls Cave (left) and Marble Cave (right)

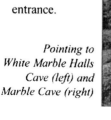

In White Marble Hall Cave

DANGER!! The Marble Mountain Caves are dangerous and should only be entered by properly equipped persons, experienced in cave exploration. There is serious risk of injury, hypothermia or even death. NEVER enter these caves alone!

Most of the cave entrance may be blocked by snow until late summer. Even after the snow melts, you'll only be able to crawl a short distance into the cave before reaching a icy, snowy spot, by a steep drop-off. If you aren't an experienced caver with proper equipment and training, it's time to retrace your steps (make that *retrace your crawl.*)

Marble Cave extends for several thousand feet, and moves through about 700 feet of elevation, making it one of the deepest (and highest elevation) caves in the U.S. It is also the most dangerous cave on Marble Mountain, and possibly the most dangerous in all of Colorado.

To reach White Marble Halls Cave from the meadow near treeline, continue straight ahead, setting a course that will take you just to the left (south) of the major rock formation located above you. You will notice a major rock buttress, separated from the rocks above it by a gap. Another major landmark is the presence of several dead trees, standing among the rocks. The entrance to White Marble Halls Cave is located approximately 100 feet (30m) above the rock gap. There are several caves in this area. The correct cave can readily be identified by writing that is on the wall, indicating it is *400 feet to White Marble Halls* and by the number *3,* painted in red beside the entrance.

If you don't mind crawling, crouching, stooping, with a little bit of squeezing thrown in now and then, you can explore quite a distance into White Marble Halls Cave. After about 400 feet of such modes of travel, you'll arrive at **King's Chamber**, with its lovely white walls rising to a height of about 30 feet. **Queen's Chamber** is a smaller, but similar formation, along a spur to the right of the entrance to King's Chamber. Heed the cautionary comments of *Sandy* on this page before entering this or any other cave.

The next cave, located slightly higher up on the slope, is identified by the numeral *1,* painted above the entrance. It is also worth looking into, so to speak. Another cave entrance, *#2,* can be found downhill from cave entrance #3.

The entrances to Marble Cave and White Marble Halls Cave are difficult to spot, unless you are nearly standing in front of, or above, them. Early in the season (spring or early summer), it may be nearly impossible to locate the caves due to

Entrance to Marble Cave

snow which can accumulate and hide the entrances.

If you do decide to explore any of these caves, you should plan on carrying warm clothing, including hat and gloves. Knee pads might be a welcome addition for crawling through low and narrow openings. A headlamp with a bright light and extra batteries is essential. Bring along a backup headlamp in the event your primary source of light fails. By all means, don't go alone and let someone know where you intend to go. There are probably a dozen caves of various configurations in this area. It might take

Lingering snow may hinder finding cave entrances

several days for rescuers to find you, in the event you become lost or stuck!

RAINBOW TRAIL/MARBLE MOUNTAIN TRAIL TO MARBLE MOUNTAIN

Marble Mountain, 13,266' (4044m), may be hiked to the summit by way of the **Marble Mountain Trail**. Follow the directions for Hike #22, as far as the area

> 7.5 miles (12.1 km)
> 4,020' (1226m) gain **23**

of the caves. Depart the Marble Caves area by continuing carefully up the drainage, gaining the grassy slopes above. Once clear of the rocky drainage, you will be presented with two choices. You may either continue straight ahead to the low point on the ridge or traverse right over easy ground, intersecting the ridge in a more northerly direction. While either choice will take you to Marble's south-facing ridge, we suggest the traverse, as you can avoid a series of small rock outcroppings along the way.

Given luck with the weather, and intestinal fortitude, you should arrive at the summit within the hour, as you have approximately 0.75 mile (1.2 km) and 1,000 feet (305m) remaining to travel. Take along your camera, as you will get some outstanding views of the **Sand Creek** basin and surrounding mountains, including a couple of Colorado's most notorious *Fourteeners,* **Crestone Needle** and **Crestone Peak**, off to the northwest. To the north is another Fourteener, **Humboldt Peak**. To the southwest in the National Preserve is **Milwaukee Peak**, with **Pico Asilado** poking up behind it, and finally off to the south, you'll find **Music Mountain** and **Tijeras Peak**. Back to the east lie the **Wet Mountains** and **Wet Mountain Valley**. This is certainly one of the finest mountain views in the state!

View southwest from the summit into Sand Creek basin

RAINBOW TRAIL/MARBLE MOUNTAIN DIRECT TRAIL TO MARBLE MOUNTAIN

24 5.2 miles (8.4 km)
4,150' (1265m) gain

This hike is for those who wish to forego visiting the **Marble Caves** (see Hike #23) and are only interested in hiking to the top of **Marble Mountain** by the shortest route. The hike begins from the **South Colony Road** (FSR 120), a spur off the **Music Pass Road** (FSR 119). Turn off CO 69 onto **Colfax Lane** and follow FSR 119 south for 5.5 miles (8.8 km), arriving at a "T" intersection. Turn right onto FSR 120 and proceed for 1.5 miles (2.4 km) to a signed parking area. Passenger cars and non-high clearance vehicles should stop here. Be aware that the next 1.5 miles (2.4 km) of road are private property. You are NOT allowed to park or camp anywhere along this section of road. Begin hiking up the road, west and then southwest, for 2.0 miles (3.2 km) to the junction with the **Rainbow Trail**, FST 1336.

High clearance, 4WD vehicles may continue along the road to the junction with the Rainbow Trail. There is room to park vehicles on both sides of the road. But be warned that the South Colony Road has a deserved reputation as one of the nastiest roads in the state. It is NOT a road for *city-slicker* SUVs, and even a heavy-duty vehicle will be reduced to crawling at speeds that any hiker could easily match.

Leave the trailhead and proceed left (south) on the Rainbow Trail (FST 1336). The trail sign incorrectly indicates that it is 2.5 miles to the **Marble Mountain Trail**. The actual distance to that trailhead is 1.5 miles (2.4 km). Proceed along the trail for 0.2 mile (0.3 km), which should take about five minutes of

Cairns mark the turn for the Direct Route

hiking. There is a *use trail* heading to your right. This trail is commonly referred to as the **Marble Mountain Direct Route**, as it heads directly up the ridge to the summit. This trail is suitable for pedestrian traffic only. Even though this turnoff is marked with **cairns** on either side of the trail, it is very easy to miss, as it is not well defined for the first 20 or 30 feet. In addition to the cairns, an aspen tree on the right side of the trail has been carved with an arrow, pointing uphill, as well as the name "Joe." Perhaps the Forest Service (or some other kind soul) will install a sign at the correct location, to mark the beginning of this fine trail. Do not confuse this *use trail* with the Marble Mountain Trail, FST 1338, located 1.5 miles (2.4 km) further south along the Rainbow Trail.

Follow the Marble Mountain Direct Route as it steadily ascends up the northeast ridge to the summit of Marble Mountain. Initially, the trail passes through dense pine and aspen forests, breaking into open areas near treeline where the elevation allows only stunted growth. The Direct Route is well defined and easy to follow, until you start to approach treeline. At this point the trail seems to disappear. When in doubt always maintain a course which keeps you on the ridge crest.

Once at treeline, you will encounter a large **talus field**, composed of rock with a pinkish tint. The talus affords easy and steady walking to the alpine tundra above. Follow the ridge crest to the top. When you reach the summit, your hard work will be rewarded as you look down into the **Sand Creek** drainage, or look around at the majestic views of three of Colorado's *Fourteeners* — **Crestone Needle**, **Crestone Peak**, and **Humboldt Peak**. Marble Mountain sits on the boundary of the Great Sand Dunes National Preserve. Looking south and southwest, you'll easily spot **Music Mountain**, the dramatic **Tijeras Peak**, **Milwaukee Peak** — all also on the Preserve's boundary — and **Pico Asilado**. Look back east at the **Wet Mountain Range** and the **Wet Mountain Valley**, your starting point for this enjoyable hike.

The **Marble Mountain Direct Route** makes a fine winter hike, relatively free from avalanche hazard. Drive to the 2WD parking area as described. Ski up to the junction with the Rainbow Trail (where there is an excellent winter campsite). Trade your skis for a pair of snowshoes at this point and go for the summit. Try it, you'll like it!

Always use good judgment and test for avalanche conditions prior to ascending any snow slope.

Hiking up Marble Mountain, with Humboldt Peak behind

Western Access Hikes

Several trails lead into the Sangre de Cristo Mountains from the town of **Crestone**, the **Baca Grande Subdivision**, and through the historic **Luis Maria Baca Grant #4**. However only two, the Cottonwood Creek Trail and the Sand Creek Trail, afford access into the **Great Sand Dunes National Park and Preserve**. The Baca Grant land is crisscrossed with old jeep roads, some of which lead to trails east and up to interesting destinations within the **Sangre de Cristo Wilderness**. But for now, no public access is permitted up Cedar, Deadman or Pole Creek canyons— hopefully, soon these historic and scenic trails will reopen as part of the Park and Preserve's future expansion.

While the Cottonwood Creek Trail could conceivably be done as a long day-hike, both of these lightly-traveled trails make more sense as backpacking trips. You may enjoy a multi-day trip that takes you over high passes, linking with trails leading to the dunes or to trails on the east side of the Sangre de Cristos. Climbers may also use these trails to get to challenging peaks in and around the Preserve (see the *Climbing* section on page 192.) Two other trails that we describe in this section, the Cottonwood Lake Trail and the Little Sand Creek Lake Trail, are side trails to be explored from the two main access trails.

The change that takes place — from desert and dunes to alpine tundra — will make you appreciate the incredible natural diversity of the Park and Preserve.

COTTONWOOD CREEK TRAIL

The **Cottonwood Creek Trail**, FST 743, provides access to the alpine interior of the the old land grant. You can also climb over a saddle north of **Milwaukee**

| 25 | 5.8 miles (9.3 km) 4,900 (1494m) gain | 🚶 |

Peak and pass into the National Preserve's Sand Creek basin, with its popular lakes and adventurous descent down the Sand Creek Trail to the National Park. Or you can continue over **Music Pass** for a complete crossing of the range.

The **Cottonwood Creek Trailhead** is located at the south end of the Baca Grande Subdivision, south of Crestone. Leave CO 17 at **Moffat** and go east on **County Road T** to the intersection with **Camino Baca Grande**. Turn south (right) at this point and drive approximately 5 miles (3.0 km), crossing the signed South Crestone, Willow and Spanish Creeks. Your ultimate destination is the intersection of Camino Baca Grande with **Cottonwood Creek**, elevation 8,400' (2560m). Park your vehicle in the area west of the light-colored water tank.

From the trailhead, proceed along the road toward the water tank. When you get to Cottonwood Creek, turn left on a trail that starts heading uphill. Do NOT follow the road around to the right. This is private property and is posted — please respect their privacy. Hike along the north (left) side of Cottonwood Creek, along an old road bed. You will encounter low-angle rock in approximately 3.0 miles (4.8 km). Look around and behind you, as you enter this section, as it will look different when you are heading back this way, which could make route finding a little tricky. We sometimes tie pieces of surveyor tape to tree limbs along the way, and then retrieve them when we retrace our steps.

Shortly after reaching this rock section, look to the left (north) for a side canyon and the junction with FST 861, the **Cottonwood Lake Trail** (see Hike # 28). If you hike about 2.0 miles (3.2 km) an hour, you will reach this spot about 1.5 hours after leaving the trailhead. The Cottonwood Creek Trail continues ahead and shortly crosses Cottonwood Creek twice. The trail can be sketchy — if in doubt, stay on the north side of the creek. Around treeline, you enter a flat basin with fine views of rugged **Pico Asilado** ahead.

This is the start of a very steep, 1500' (457m) climb due east, up the headwall of the cirque in long switchbacks, to the

COTTONWOOD LAKE TRAIL

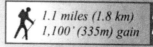

1.1 miles (1.8 km)
1,100' (335m) gain

26

This enjoyable trail (FST 861) is a spur off the Cottonwood Creek Trail, offering a less traveled approach for climbers intent on reaching the magnificent **Crestones**. From just past 3.0 miles (4.8km) into the Cottonwood Creek Trail, turn left and hike up through aspen and pine. Follow closely along the tumbling creek to the high lake above treeline in about 1.0 mile (1.6 km). *Great camping, inspiring views!*

13,300' (4055m) pass (informally known as *Beer Pass* or *Cottonwood Pass*) between Milwaukee Peak's north and south summits. While a grunt, the trail is in good shape here and easy to follow. If you make it, you'll be rewarded with exceptional views into the National Preserve's northern limits. Those who dare to venture on into the Preserve itself, should read about the **Sand Creek Trail** (Hike # 29).

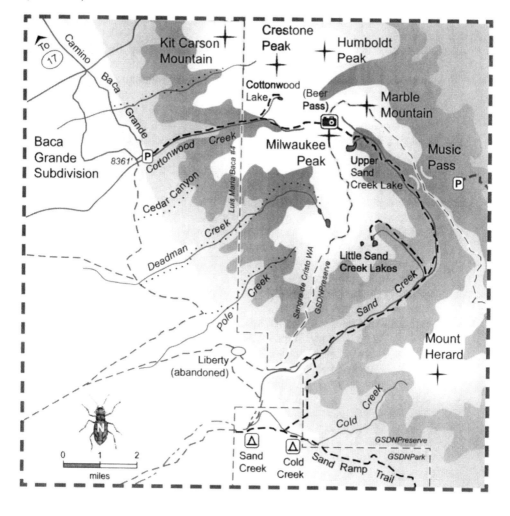

SAND CREEK TRAIL

The **Sand Creek Trail** is the longest trail in the Park and Preserve and provides the adventurous backpacker with a magnificent journey, gradually unfolding from dunes to tundra. The Sand Creek basin is the largest in the Sangre de Cristo Range, and is unusual in that it runs in a northwest to southeast direction, *parallel* to the range, before assuming a more normal exit to the southwest, where its waters sink into the sand of the San Luis Valley.

27 *12.5 miles (20.1 km) 6,500 (1494m) gain*

The upper end of the trail is easily accessed from **Music Pass** and is popular with visitors. But the lower valley is lightly visited — if you are seeking solitude, you will find it here.

Historically, the Sand Creek Trail exited the canyon at the now defunct settlement of **Liberty**. At that point, it hooked up with the network of jeep roads on the old land grant. One branch went south to cross Sand Creek and connect up with the "Lower" Sand Creek Trail (now renamed the **Sand Ramp Trail**) in the vicinity of **Sand Creek Campsite**. At least for the time being, this route is off limits until transfer of the old land grant to the federal government is completed. Instead, hikers must negotiate a short, but difficult, bushwack that hugs the boundary of the Park and Preserve, in order to reach the Sand Creek Trail from the Sand Ramp Trail.

Follow the directions in Hike #11 for the Sand Ramp Trail until reaching **Cold Creek Campsite**. If it's late in the day, then this would be the logical place to camp (but make sure you secured a backcountry camping permit beforehand from the Park personnel at the Visitor Center.) Your goal from here is to climb over the **forested ridge** to the north, separating Cold Creek and Sand Creek. Stay west on the Sand Ramp Trail for another 0.25 mile (0.4 km), heading downhill from the campsite. Leave the trail, cross Cold Creek and head northeast up an obvious drainage. Stay in the drainage as best you can, gaining 600' (183m) in about 0.75 mile (1.2 km). At this point the drainage briefly turns due east, and you have crossed from the Park into the Preserve. Leave the drainage and go due north by your compass, climbing a steep slope to top out at last on the crest of the ridge, at an elevation of about 10,000' (3045m). Contour around the nose of the ridge and then drop east into a drainage. Turn left (northwest) and follow this steep drainage down to intersect the Sand Creek Trail.

If everything went as planned, you will meet the trail where it briefly travels on the south side of Sand Creek. But if the trail is nowhere in sight, your trajectory probably was off a bit — just cross to the north side of the creek, turn right and you should run into the trail shortly. Don't underestimate this bushwack; it's steep and hard going, on only a vague suggestion of a trail. Check with the rangers at the Visitor Center before heading out, as they may have additional navigation suggestions.

If you made it this far, then the Sand Creek Trail is a breeze, as it gently passes up the valley on the north side of Sand Creek, with plenty of good camping. At mile 3.0 (4.8 km) after leaving the Sand Ramp Trail, the trail crosses to the south side of the creek and climbs a few hundred feet above the streambed. It crosses the creek twice more in the next 0.75mile (1.2 km), before a short, steep hill. After several more crossings, the trail meets the **Little Sand Creek Lakes Trail** (see Hike #28), about 6.0 miles (9.7 km) after leaving the Sand Ramp Trail. This would be a good spot to camp, especially if you wish to spend a day visiting **Little Sand Creek Lakes** on a side trip. There's water in nearby Sand Creek, but be sure to treat or filter it.

It's another 3.5 miles (5.6 km) to the intersection with the **Music Pass Trail** (see Hike #18, page 160) on a gentle grade; the trail curving around to the northwest with views unfolding of the splendid alpine peaks in the upper basin. Here you may decide your final destination —

LITTLE SAND CREEK LAKES TRAIL

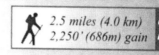

These two lakes are about as remote a spot as you can find in the

2.5 miles (4.0 km)
2,250' (686m) gain

28

Preserve. Leave the Sand Creek Trail at about 6.0 miles (9.7 km) after the start from the Sand Ramp Trail. Turn left (northwest) up the Little Sand Creek Trail through aspen and pine. Shortly after treeline, the trail crosses an outlet stream from a tarn above you, then curves west and then south to reach the first lake on its 12,000' (3658m) bench. There's good camping here, better than at the other lake, due west and 400' (122m) higher.

An alternate, and slightly shorter, approach to these lakes is to come down the Sand Creek Trail from over Music Pass (see Hike #20).

turn right and cross **Music Pass** to complete your adventure at the Music Pass Trailhead or investigate the beautiful alpine lakes, just a short distance ahead? There's great camping and fishing at either one. To visit **Lower Sand Creek Lake**, turn to Hike #19 on page 161, and follow the directions from the point where the Music Pass Trail intersects the Sand Creek Trail. **Upper Sand Creek Lake** is also close-by (read about Hike #20). That's also the way to go if your ambitious goal is to cross from the Sand Creek basin into the **Cottonwood Creek** drainage, hooking up with Hike #25.

Follow the directions for Upper Sand Creek Lake, but turn off on a faint trail near the end of the switchbacks, just before the lake. Your objective is to climb up the drainage that lies to the left of the southeast ridge which drops off **Milwaukee Peak**'s north summit. After you pass beneath the east-facing cliffs of Milwaukee's main, south summit, turn west and climb very steeply up a gully to the saddle between the two summits. You'll be forced to the right as you scramble up this last bit.

Whew! It's a 1500' (457m) climb from the lake to this spectacular, 13,300' (4055m) pass (informally known as *Beer Pass* or *Cottonwood Pass*.) Don't undertake it if the weather is threatening.

The route climbs up from near Upper Sand Creek Lake and then passes behind Milwaukee's main summit

Hikes in Zapata Falls Recreation Area

Welcome to **Zapata Falls**, established for your pleasure, circa 2,000,000 B.C! Okay, so this area isn't in the Park or Preserve. Even so, the trip to close-by Zapata Falls is a must for every visitor to the Park. Don't miss it. If you decide you've just got to go into the cavern, don't forget to bring your towel! (*Oops!* We almost gave away the secret of this unique area.)

Some two million years ago, a huge lake of glacier meltwater broke through a rock dike, gouging out the cavern that today is Zapata Falls. The Bureau of Land Management administers the site with emphasis on recreation, including **hiking, mountain biking, picnicing** and **bird watching.** Zapata Falls is also a gateway for hikes into the Sangre de Cristo Wilderness Area (see Hike #30).

Access to the **Zapata Falls Recreation Area** is approximately 11.0 miles (17.6 km) north of the US 160/CO 150 junction, or 8.0 miles (12.8 km) south on CO 150 from the Park entrance station. If coming from the south, turn right onto a good gravel road, following it for approximately 3.5 miles (5.6 km) to the Zapata Falls parking area. You will gain approximately 1,500 feet (457 m) along the way! This gravel road is suitable for normal passenger vehicles. There are modern restrooms, as well as wheelchair-accessible picnic tables and barbecue facilities, located at the parking area.

Park your vehicle at the established parking area, across from the restrooms. Take a few minutes to enjoy the views! The mountains that you can see off to the north, towering above the Great Sand Dunes complex, are (from left to right) **Challenger Point** (named to honor the crew on the *Challenger* space shuttle disaster), **Kit Carson Peak, Crestone Peak, Crestone Needle, Cleveland Peak** and **Mount Herard.** Out to the west, you should be able to view the expanse of the **San Luis Valley,** 100 miles long and 50 miles wide!

BLACK SWIFT

Zapata Falls is one of only 50 known spots in the state to be identified as a breeding site for the elusive **black swift**. These very specialized birds nest on precipitous cliffs, near or behind **high waterfalls**. Nest sites typically have a commanding view over surrounding terrain, enabling swifts to fly straight out from the nest and very quickly be hundreds of feet above the valley floor. In their search for insects on the wing, these birds are sometimes spotted from the access road and in the parking lot below the falls area.

Black swifts exist only in scattered colonies in Colorado with perhaps only a few hundred breeding pair. Yet their continued protection is a high priority, as at least 20% of all black swifts breed in Colorado. Hikers, rock climbers or ice climbers visiting Zapata Falls must take care not to disturb nest sites.

The area just below where you are standing encompasses the **Zapata Loops** trail system, comprised of a series of four, short interlocking loops. Unless you head down hill toward CO 150, these trails will always return to your starting point or your vehicle. Information signs, describing the trail system, are located at the individual trailheads. The Zapata Loops are a **mountain bike friendly** trail system — you'll find more information about it in the *mountain biking* section on page 113 of this guide. Horses are not allowed on this trail system.

ZAPATA FALLS TRAIL

**0.25 miles (0.4 km)
200' (61m) gain**

29

From the parking area, the trail to **Zapata Falls** is easy to follow, as it climbs east from the trailhead information sign, gaining approximately 200 feet in one-quarter mile (0.4 km). The trail then makes a short drop down to **Zapata Creek**. You will encounter several park benches, which have been placed along the way to allow you the opportunity to take some time out, just relax, and enjoy the scenery. There is also a bench nestled in the trees next to Zapata Creek, at the bottom of the trail. It's fun to sit on this bench and watch all of the folks that wade in the stream. This trail is not wheelchair accessible.

Visit the falls in the spring to experience their full grandeur. The roaring of the water, back in the cavern, draws one in like a moth to flame. But be prepared, as even on a warm day the water can be very cold and

Descending Zapata Creek

swift and the rocks can be extremely slippery. Unsuspecting waders could be injured by a fall in the stream. Do not, under any circumstances, allow young children to wade alone in the stream, as they could easily be swept away.

In order to actually see the falls, you will need to hike up the stream a short distance and then back into the cavern. The waterfall itself is approximately 50 feet (15 m) high. We have seen many visitors scramble up the informal paths next to the falls, in order to get to the top. This practice is dangerous, due to loose rocks, and it causes destructive erosion. An easier and more scenic way to the top of the falls is to take the easy walking trail, located a short distance back toward the parking area. Follow this trail, the **South Zapata Lake Trail** (Hike #30), as it makes a few switchbacks and heads back over to the top of the falls. Be careful when viewing the falls from above, as a fall would likely be fatal and don't throw objects over the edge.

Winter at Zapata Falls

The snow and ice of winter make the short hike to Zapata Falls an enjoyable and scenic off-season trip.

For your return to CO 150, follow the one-way loop from the parking area toward the main road. Several **picnic areas** are located on both sides of the road. Zapata Falls Recreation Area is for day use only. Overnight camping is not allowed.

SOUTH ZAPATA LAKE TRAIL

The hike into the **Sangre de Cristo Wilderness Area** and up to **South Zapata Lake**, along FST 852, makes a pleasant extension of your visit to Zapata Falls. We

30 | *4.5 miles (7.2 km)*
2,600' (793m) gain

think that this hike has something for everyone to enjoy. You can either make this a shorter hike, 1.2 miles (1.9 km), to a **rustic cabin** where you can have a lunch stop, or you can continue on up to the lake itself. Be advised that the hiking becomes more strenuous after you depart the cabin site — opt for the shorter hike if you're out of shape or coming from a low elevation.

The South Zapata Lake Trailhead is located to the right of the information sign at Zapata Falls. You will notice two distinct paths heading off to the right in this area. These paths connect in a very short distance. In approximately 100 feet, you will encounter yet another set of paths. The path on the left heads steeply up hill to the top of Zapata Falls. The path on the right is the **South Zapata Lake Trail**. Follow this path to the right, as it traverses west and then back east, gradually gaining the plateau above the falls. For just this little bit of effort, you will be rewarded with outstanding views to the north of **Mt. Herard**, **Crestone Peak** and **Crestone Needle**. Off to the west is **San Luis Lakes State Park** and surrounding San Luis Valley scenery.

During the summer months, it would be advisable to get an early morning start if you're going to hike all the way to the lake, thus avoiding the debilitating heat which might be encountered at mid-day, lower down on the hike. An added bonus for an early start is the spectacular shading on the dunes, enhancing their photographic appeal.

Views to the north of the dunes and Sangre de Cristo peaks

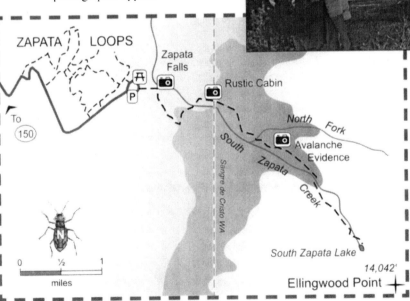

Shortly after the first switchback, when the trail heads back east, you will encounter a trail junction. Take the right fork at this point; the left fork leads to the top of Zapata Falls. In a short period of time, you will come to a trail sign and register. When we visited this site, the register was missing. Stop here for a moment and look around; you'll be treated to some nice alpine vistas. From this vantage point, you will notice scattered aspens, growing in places where the ponderosa pines have thinned, and framed by the skyline peaks, snow covered in the spring. Springtime produces a plethora of **golden banner**, lavender and yellow **mountain daisies** and various kinds of blooming **cactus**. You'll achieve a sense of solitude, as you make your way up the mountain, listening only to the sounds of wind and birdsong through the trees. This is a pleasant trail that everyone can enjoy!

After approximately 1.1 miles (1.8 km), you will cross **South Zapata Creek**, on your way up to the cabin area that we mentioned earlier. After crossing the creek, you will enter a nicely shaded area, complete with a fine carpet of decaying leaves. We've always enjoyed the scent that this type of environment gives off; there's just something basic about the feeling you get.

The trail starts to steadily gain elevation at this point, as it heads up toward the cabin. The cabin is a place to rest and decide if you wish to continue on up to the lake. Either way, take some time and look around the cabin area. Think you could live here for a couple of years? Inside the cabin, we were surprised to find several items of interest — a pint of tequila (empty), a fifth of whiskey (empty), and an old tin box, labeld *Milk Chocolates.* And yes, someone had eaten all the chocolates. Guess we missed a lively party but avoided a dandy hangover!

Rustic cabin along the South Zapata Lake Trail

After leaving the cabin area, enjoy the ever changing views as the trail steadily gains elevation, switchbacking up and over into the South Zapata Lake drainage. If you're continuing on to the lake, there is a nice spot after the switchbacks to take a few minutes rest. The trail temporarily levels out at this point and allows you an unobstructed view up the valley. With all of those aspens around, you're not going to want to miss taking this hike when the colors change to brilliant yellow. This hike in simply spectacular in mid-September to early-October. Trust us on this one!

As you continue, your journey takes you around and through some **talus fields**. Talus is a field of larger-sized rock debris. Another rock description which you should become familiar with is **scree**. Scree consists of much smaller-sized rocks, like those that litter the trail in some places. Scree is what we usually slip on; talus is what we usually trip over. As we walk nonchalantly through these talus areas, we should be saying a little *thank you* to the trail crews who obviously worked so hard to make our travel day carefree. It must have really been a *blast* creating a path through all of these rocks!

Summer snow banks along South Zapata Creek trail

Snow in June? Throw a pair of **gaiters** in your pack if you are hiking in the spring or early summer, as it is not uncommon to encounter residual snow in the shaded areas of the trail. **Bread bags**, with the ends cut off and secured with a couple of rubber bands, also work quite nicely to keep the snow out of your boots.

Some areas have impressive cliff faces located high above the trail. Notice all of those large rocks just sitting there? Well, now look off to your right and observe the scars on many of the trees downhill from the trail. Danger can lurk above, from falling rock. You may also notice an abundance of **claw marks** on the aspens. (Perhaps you *bearly* noticed them.) These are left by the local black bear population.

In approximately 2.4 miles (3.8 km), the trail drops down to cross the **North Fork** of Zapata Creek and then climbs up to where it joins with the **North Fork Trail** (FSR 868) which heads off to your left. Continue straight ahead, following the South Fork Trail, as it descends down to the stream bed.

The South Zapata Lake Trail meanders uphill as it travels through a mixed forest of aspen and various pines. Here you will encounter past evidence of the forces of nature. Take a few minutes to evaluate the evidence left behind by this event. On your left, you will notice that a large number of trees have been knocked down and are pointing downhill. Off to your right are tree stumps which have been broken off about 2 feet (0.61m) above the ground. What you are seeing here is the result of a **snow avalanche**, which roared down the valley sometime in the past.

Snow had accumulated and then consolidated to a depth as high as the stumps you see. Then more snow fell, did not bond with the underlying layers, and subsequently slid down the slopes from above, breaking off the trees at the height you have observed. The trees lying on the ground to the left were likely knocked down by the **wind blast** from that, or another, avalanche.

Finally leaving the trees behind, the trail passes through a classic example of a high alpine meadow, complete with the remnants of an **old miner's cabin** off to the left; or perhaps this was someone's *summer home?*

Note how the area to the left of the trail, at one point, is comprised of a large talus field, while to the right

Hiker on the trail with views up the valley

of the trail, the ground has been reclaimed by grasses. Here's nature at work again, probably as the result of water running down the valley floor and subsidizing the flatter area with the silt and minerals required for grasses to exist.

The final distance to the lake consists of mixed rock formations with a multitude of streams flowing in various directions. This is usually a sure indication that you are close to a major water source, in this case South Zapata Lake. Just kick back and enjoy the views. You will usually encounter some cool breezes coming down from the surrounding high peaks, so make sure you keep warm while enjoying yourself.

The largest peak across the lake to the southeast is **Ellingwood Point**, 14,042' (4,280m). It is over 2,000 feet above where you stand. Ellingwood Point is officially classified as one of Colorado's *Fourteeners* — peaks over 14,000'. (Just in case you wondered, there are sixty-eight officially recognized peaks in the lower-48 States which rise to over 14,000'. We have 54 here in Colorado, there are 13 in California, and Mount Rainier is in Washington.)

The trail back contains as many adventures and things to be discovered as on the way up, so keep a sharp eye out. Lower down on the trail, you get an outstanding view of **San Luis Lakes State Park**, as well as the entire **San Luis Valley**. On your descent, you'll be amazed at the amount of elevation you gained on this hike. Before you know it you'll be back at Zapata Falls! We hope you didn't forget to throw in your towel and sandals for some cool wading in the stream below the falls!

South Zapata Lake with Ellingwood Point behind

CLIMBING

Rock climbers on the summit of Kit Carson Mountain, with Crestone Peak behind

W hile the sand dunes and surrounding backcountry are alluring to hikers and backpackers, experienced mountain climbers may be surprised by the challenges that can be discovered in the high country of the **National Preserve**. Here tower rugged and remote peaks with idyllic campsites, beside cool, mountain lakes — scenes to lighten the heart of any mountaineer. This chapter is divided into three climbing areas. The first covers climbing opportunities within the Preserve itself, centered around the headwaters of Sand Creek. Oddly enough, little of the high alpine region of the Preserve can be seen from the dunes, as most remains hidden behind the bulk of Mount Herard. What the visitor does catch a glimpse of are two spectacular areas containing some of Colorado's most famous peaks, the **Fourteeners**. To the south is the **Blanca massif** and to the north is the **Crestone group**. While both of these groups are just outside the present boundaries of the Park and Preserve, we include sections on them because of their great interest to climbers and close proximity. A visit to either could easily be part of a trip to the Great Sand Dunes. They contain some of the most challenging mountaineering in Colorado.

All of the climbs detailed in this guide are multi-day trips, requiring a backpack to a suggested **basecamp**. This camp may serve simply as an overnight for a two-day trip or may be utilized for several days in the case of several peaks targeted in the area. With each climb, there is an **information box** that lists the *one-way distance* and *elevation gain* for

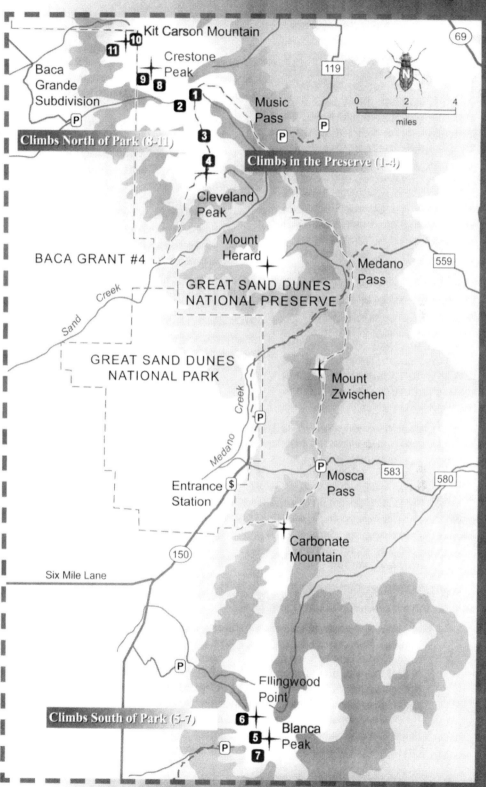

Kit Carson Mountain

11 **10**

Crestone
Peak

9 **8**

Baca
Grande
Subdivision

2 **1**

Music
Pass

P

Climbs North of Park (8-11)

3

Climbs in the Preserve (1-4)

4

Cleveland
Peak

119

69

0   2   4
miles

N

P

Mount
Herard

BACA GRANT #4

Medano
Pass

559

GREAT SAND DUNES
NATIONAL PRESERVE

Creek

Sand

Mount
Zwischen

GREAT SAND DUNES
NATIONAL PARK

Creek

P

Medano

P

Mosca
Pass

583

580

Entrance $
Station

150

Carbonate
Mountain

Six Mile Lane

P

Fllingwood
Point

Climbs South of Park (5-7)

6

Blanca
Peak

5

7

P

WARNING! Do not take the sport of mountaineering or the difficulty of climbing in Colorado lightly. The elevation, the terrain and the weather associated with mountains of this height make for potentially dangerous situations.

Thunderstorms are a common summer phenomenon, usually building early and rapidly. Get an early start and plan to be heading down from any exposed ridges or summits prior to noon, or earlier if the weather looks threatening.

All of the climbs described in this section require previous climbing experience and proper equipment. None of these climbs would be considered suitable for beginners. Check with one of the organizations and clubs listed in the *Resource Guide* section to climb with experienced leaders while you make some new friends.

that climb. Note that these are calculated from the suggested basecamp, not from the initial trailhead. To get the total mileage and gain for a trip, you'll have to add distances and gains for the access trails. In several cases, the access trails are ones that have already been detailed in the *Hiking* section of this guide. If not, then you'll find the access trail description detailed with each climb.

Also note that we offer no ratings on the relative difficulty of these climbs. They range from simple *walk-ups,* to scrambles, to a classic alpine rock climb. But none are for inexperienced or ill-equipped climbers.

Climbers are always interested in the quality of the rock before attempting a climb. The area around the Crestones is made up of the famous **crestone conglomerate**, which is generally reliable and fun to climb on. Rock climbers enjoy this quirky, but mostly solid, rock. Once south of there, the rock is not as appealing. While here and there you'll find good rock, more often you'll scramble shattered ridges or hike on extensive talus slopes. The danger of rock fall increases south of the Crestones. Climbers visiting these areas will encounter snow, especially in couloirs and on north slopes, well into late-June, or even late-July in heavy snow years. In that case, crampons and ice axe may be required.

Mountaineering usually involves a greater amount of route finding expertise. You should obtain and know how to read a **USGS 7.5 min Quad** map before undertaking mountaineering activities. The maps provided in this guide for each climb should be used for general navigating purposes only.

The Sangre de Cristo Mountains have accounted for numerous injuries and deaths over the years, involving both the novice and experienced mountaineer. Lose your concentration for just a moment while climbing these peaks and you may lose your life.

Climbs in the Preserve

The high peaks tucked away in the northern reaches of the Great Sand Dunes National Preserve are a well-kept secret. Few climbers venture into this alpine wilderness where you are more likely to encounter fisherman and backpackers. In fact, a few of these peaks didn't record first official ascents until the 1960s — perhaps some of the last high peaks in Colorado to be climbed. These beautiful peaks are quite challenging, requiring scrambling ability and good route-finding.

The suggested base camps for climbs in the National Preserve are at **Upper Sand Creek Lake** and **Lower Sand Creek Lake**, which can be reached from three different trails and directions. While two approaches — up the Sand Creek

Trail from the south (see Hike #27) or the Cottonwood Creek Trail from the west and over so-called *Beer Pass* (see Hike# 25) — would be interesting epics, both are too long and involved for most parties. The practical route for most climbers will be from the east over **Music Pass**.

Follow the directions in the *Hiking* section for reaching Upper Sand Creek Lake (Hike #20) or Lower Sand Creek Lake (Hike #19). You'll want to pause along the way, at the top of Music Pass, to take in the alpine panorama before you. Looking to the west, you'll be able to study many of the routes on (from right to left) **Milwaukee Peak** (13,522' (4123m)), Music Mountain (13,355' (4072m)), **Tijeras Peak** (13,604' (4148m)) and **Cleveland Peak** (13,414' (4090m)). These peaks make up the western boundary of the Preserve and are the four highest points in the Park and Preserve. **Pico Asilado** is hidden behind Milwaukee from this viewpoint, and is actually slightly west, and outside, of the Preserve.

You'll also see your final destination, either of the two lakes. Note that it is a short hike between lakes, making it easy to shift camps on an extended climbing adventure. There is excellent camping on the east side of both lakes, with the peaks close at hand. As always, keep a clean camp that doesn't attract animals, and treat or filter water from the lakes. Backcountry permits are not currently required for camping in the Preserve.

MILWAUKEE PEAK

Milwaukee Peak is the large, blocky ridge directly northwest of Upper Sand Creek Lake. The ascent is short and straight-forward but not without some brief difficulties and exposure.

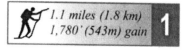
1.1 miles (1.8 km)
1,780' (543m) gain **1**

From the outlet of the lake, work your way up the obvious drainage that lies to the left of the southeast ridge of Milwaukee's north summit. You should eventually meet the faint **Sand Creek Trail** as it climbs up to an unnamed pass north of Milwaukee's south summit (see Hike #27). From this high pass at about 13,300' (4055m), climb south onto a narrow, exposed ramp that contours along the east side. When that ends, scramble right and up to the ridge crest and finish up ledges to the top. It's only a couple hundred feet to the summit from the pass and not too difficult, but on very exposed ground.

PICO ASILADO

The shortest way to reach **Pico Asilado** from Upper Sand Creek Lake is via the west ridge of Milwaukee Peak. Asilado is the highest of the group, although it is too far west to be the highest peak in the National

1.6 miles (2.6 km)
2,180' (665m) gain **2**
320' (98m) gain (return)

Preserve. Climb Milwaukee Peak by the route described (see Climb #1). Scramble down Milwaukee's west ridge to the 13,200' (4024') saddle between the peaks. Climb southwest, up the ridge towards Asilado, passing minor obstacles on the south side of the ridge, to a notch about 200' (61m) below the summit block. Scramble south and down 30 yards to meet a series of small, steep gullys and ledges on the southeast face. Pick the best line and ascend these to meet the ridge, just a few yards east of the summit. Take care to note your line for the return.

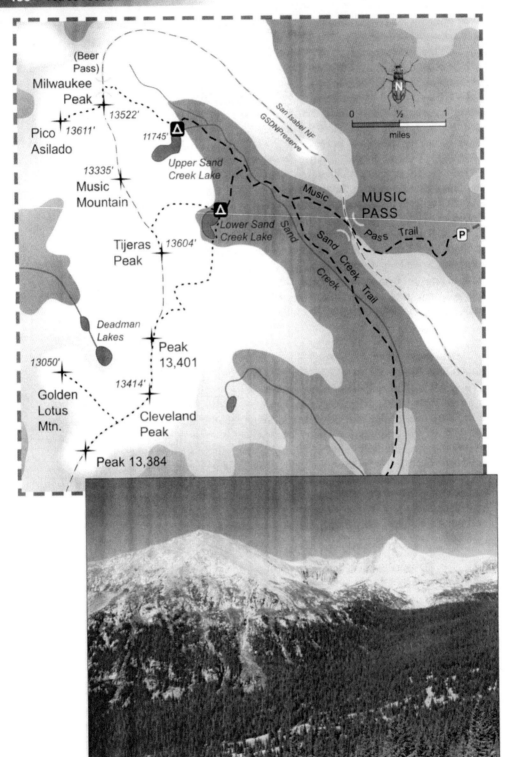

(Beer Pass)

Milwaukee Peak
13522'

Pico Asilado
13611'

11745'

Upper Sand Creek Lake

13335'

Music Mountain

San Isabel NF
GSDNPreserve

Music

MUSIC PASS

Tijeras Peak
13604'

Lower Sand Creek Lake

Sand

Pass

Trail

P

Sand Creek Trail

Creek

Deadman Lakes

Peak 13,401

13050'

13414'

Golden Lotus Mtn.

Cleveland Peak

Peak 13,384

N

0   ½   1
miles

Cleveland and Tijeras Peaks from Music Pass

TIJERAS PEAK

Tijeras Peak is an impressive summit, sitting directly west of Lower Sand Creek Lake. From your camp at the lake, go north and then northwest on game trails to timberline,

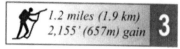

1.2 miles (1.9 km)
2,155' (657m) gain **3**

climbing up to the prominent, 200' (61m) tall, cliff band that crosses the broad northeast face of the peak. Look for a rocky ramp that splits the center of the steep cliff band. Enjoy the fun scramble up this on good rock. Note the location of this ramp for your return. Easy slopes above lead to the northwest ridge of the peak. Scramble up this on decent rock for 200' (61m) to the summit.

CLEVELAND PEAK & UNNAMED PEAKS

There are several remote summits, south of Lower Sand Creek Lake, that are difficult to get to and that see few ascents. **Cleveland Peak** gets the most traffic, likely because it is named, but three other unnamed summits are

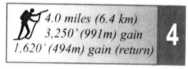

4.0 miles (6.4 km)
3,250' (991m) gain **4**
1,620' (494m) gain (return)

nearly equal in height. All can be done in one long day of fun ridge-running. But keep in mind that there is no practical, alternative way to return to camp, other then to run the ridge back. Setting a goal for Cleveland Peak shortens it to a two-summit day.

Contour around the south shore of Little Sand Creek Lake and follow game trails south through timber for 0.5 miles (0.8km), and up to a small basin under Tijeras Peak's impressive south face. The basin looks like it has no easy way up and out. Climb west into the back of the basin and you'll find a grassy ramp leading left (south) and up to a ridge that runs east off the main crest. Once atop this ridge, turn west and then contour around the south side of a small ridge point, and into the saddle directly northeast of **Peak 13,401**.

You are now on a *knife-edge* ridge that runs for 2.0 miles (3.km) more, with opportunites to nab four summits along the way. The Class 3 scrambling is never hard (one party reports that their eager *Golden Retriever* had no problems.) But you should keep a close eye on the weather as the ridge is just hard enough that getting off it, in the face of an approaching thunderstorm, would be difficult.

From the saddle beneath Peak 13,401, aim south and clamber up shortly to its summit. You'll drop about 350' (107m), as you continue south into another saddle between Peak 13,401 and Cleveland Peak. The ridge sharpens as you pass over the summit of Cleveland, where the ridge makes a dog-leg to the west. Continue another 0.3m (0.5km) to a tri-cornered, flat spot on the ridge at about 13,300' (4055m).

This is a good spot to rest and contemplate your choices. Either continue southwest on the main ridge, losing 300' (91m) to the next saddle, before climbing up to the ridge's end point, **Peak 13,384**, or head north into a saddle, twice as deep, and scramble up to **Peak 13,050** on a spur ridge. This appealing little summit has the unofficial name of *Golden Lotus Mountain* and has a perfect, pyramidal shape, with a lovely lake nestled beneath each of its three identical faces. If you do both peaks, keep in mind that there is a lot of climbing to do to get back to camp!

Climbs South of the Park and Preserve

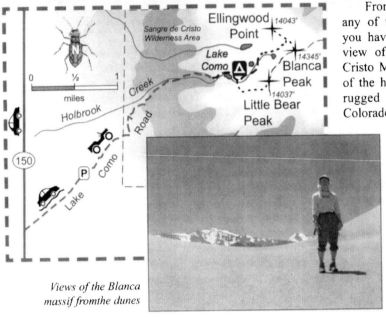

Sangre de Cristo Wilderness Area

Ellingwood Point 14043'

Lake Como

Blanca Peak 14345'

14037' Little Bear Peak

N

0   ½   1
miles

Holbrook

Creek

Como Road

150

P

Lake Como

From a viewpoint on any of the high dunes, you have a magnificent view of the Sangre de Cristo Mountains. Some of the highest and most rugged peaks in Colorado surround you. To the south are located four of Colorado's 54 **Fourteeners**; peaks over 14,000' (4,267m) in elevation. This group of peaks is called the **Blanca massif** and is

Views of the Blanca massif from the dunes

composed of **Blanca Peak** 14,345' (4,372m), **Ellingwood Point** 14,043' (4,280m), Mount Lindsey 14,042' (4,280m) and **Little Bear Peak** 14,037' (4,278m). Mount Lindsey is tucked out of sight behind Blanca Peak.

Here's a good example that size isn't everything. Blanca Peak has the distinction of having the highest elevation of the group and dominates the skyline. But it's quite straight-forward to climb. Little Bear Peak, with the lowest elevation of the group, is the most difficult to climb. Little Bear appears on most climbers' list of the ten hardest Fourteeners to climb.

There's an elevation gain of 6,695 feet (2,041m) from the valley floor. So, most folks decide to climb these peaks as overnight backpacks; and a good decision it is. While Blanca and Ellingwood are easier Fourteeners and an enjoyable overnight trip, Little Bear is a serious climb for experienced mountaineers with the right equipment.

Drive south from the Park entrance on CO 150 for about 15.5 miles (25.0 km) to the signed, 4WD road to **Lake Como**. Turn left (east) and continue uphill until your nerve, or vehicle, expire. Recently, there was a fatality on this hazardous road. You can expect large boulders, steep slanting curves, deep holes and every other driving obstacle you might imagine.

Most hikers drive about 2.0 miles (3.2 km) up the road to the 8,000' (2,438m) level and park there. This proves to be both wise and efficient, as you can walk the remaining distance to camp faster than you can drive! Get an early start, as during the summer months this can be one of the most withering hikes you'll ever experience.

Leaving your vehicle, follow the road as it twists and turns up the hillside for 5.0 miles (8.0 km) to your probable basecamp, east of Lake Como at 11,800' (3,597m). You'll gain 3,900' (1,189m) of elevation along the way. The cabins surrounding the lake are located on private property. Do not camp in their vicinity.

Get an early start from camp the next morning and follow the trail as it winds past the east side of Blue Lakes and on up to Crater Lake, passing it on the north. **Blanca Peak** will be in front of you as you stand at the lake. Zig-zag up the steep west face of the cirque to the saddle between Blanca and Ellingwood Point. Turn right and follow the north ridge of Blanca Peak to the summit. Expect some easy scrambling along the way.

BLANCA PEAK

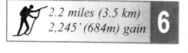

2.2 miles (3.5 km)
2,545' (776m) gain

5

Ellingwood Point (left) and Blanca Peak (right) from Como Lake

ELLINGWOOD POINT

2.2 miles (3.5 km)
2,245' (684m) gain

6

Ellingwood Point was one of the last peaks to be deemed a separate Fourteener, and to this day, it is seemingly dominated by its big brother, Blanca Peak. However, it was considered to be important enough to commemorate Albert Ellingwood, Colorado's premier climber in the early part of the 20th Century. To climb it, follow the description above to the saddle between Blanca and Ellingwood. Once there, turn left and hike northwest about 350' (107m) up to the summit.

LITTLE BEAR PEAK

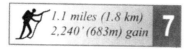

1.1 miles (1.8 km)
2,240' (683m) gain

7

Little Bear Peak is southwest of Blanca on the massif, with the two separated by one of the ruggedest ridges in Colorado. That ridge is beyond the scope of this guide. Instead, the most common route is via the **West Ridge** — a short route made dangerous by potential rock fall. Bring a helmet and a rope for a possible rappel. From your camp on the east side of Lake Como, head for the obvious, south-facing gully leading to a prominent notch in the West Ridge. Early in the season, this gully will have snow in it, possibly requiring crampons. Once in the notch, head east along the ridge, over a small intermediate point and into a small saddle. You'll have to leave the ridge here and contour along a **use trail** on the southwest face, to the base of an large, obvious gully. This is the famous **Hourglass**, the scene of several accidents from rock fall.

Be very careful from this point, especially if there are parties above you. Wear your helmet! Scramble up the gully until you arrive at a water-polished section. This is the crux, especially if there is some water running down. Carefully scramble up for 200' (61m), leaving the gully occasionally for the rock on either side. Finish the climb to the summit by scrambling up easier ledges, littered with rubble. Usually, there are several rappel slings above the crux for your return.

Climbs North of the Park and Preserve

Crestone group on far left

A group of **Fourteeners** north of the dunes provides a dramatic backdrop for visitors to the Park and Preserve. There you will find **Crestone Peak** 14,294' (4,357m), **Crestone Needle** 14,197' (4,372m), Humboldt Peak 14,064' (4,287m), **Kit Carson Mountain** 14,165' (4,317m) and the last named Colorado Fourteener, **Challenger Point** 14,080' (4,292m). (Challenger Point is not yet officially recognized as a separate Fourteener.) Humboldt Peak is hidden fom view and not accessible from the San Luis Valley.

All of these peaks are just outside the present boundaries of the National Preserve. Several are in the **Sangre de Cristo Wilderness Area**. Kit Carson Mountain is one of only a handful of Fourteeners that are contained in private land — in this case, the old Baca Land Grant #4. It is scheduled to become part of the new Baca National Wildlife Refuge once the proposed federal purchase of the ranch is completed.

Among climbers in Colorado, the Crestones are legendary. They were the last of the Fourteeners to be conquered, by larger-than-life climber Albert Ellingwood in 1916. They were so hard to survey, that the first detailed map of them didn't appear until 1968. Today's climbers still thrill at their sheer ruggedness, considering Crestone Needle and Crestone Peak to be among the most challenging of the Fourteeners to scale.

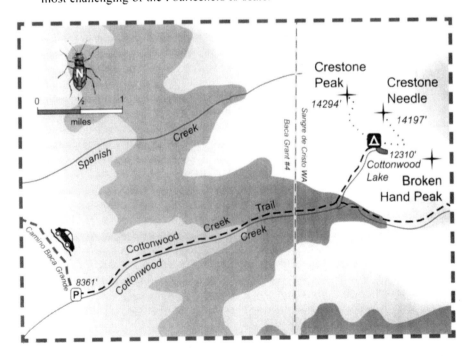

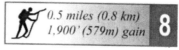

CRESTONE NEEDLE

To tackle both Crestone Needle and Crestone Peak from the San Luis Valley, follow the directions for the Cottonwood Creek Trail (Hike #25) to the Cottonwood Lake Trail (Hike #26), in the *Western Access Hikes* section of this guide, to arrive at the beautiful alpine setting of **Cottonwood Lake**. It's a long, arduous approach to Cottonwood Lake. But once there, a basecamp at this high lake actually provides the shortest and technically easiest route for climbing either peak. We will describe them as separate climbs, although they are often done together in a day with a thrilling ridge traverse between them. However, most people will want a rope on this traverse for an airy pitch just beyond the Needle's summit. By climbing them separately, no rope is needed, as the climbing level never rises above steep scrambling.

Contour around the north shore of the lake. From there, it's a short, easy hike east and up into the saddle separating **Crestone Needle** on the left from Broken Hand Peak on the right. Turn left and follow the obvious **use trail**, staying to the left (west) of difficulties as you pass through some small cliff bands. You will come to a pair of couloirs that penetrate the steep, upper face of the climb. Take the right-hand one, then angle over to the left as necessary. Both lead up to easy scrambling, close to the summit.

*Looking at Crestone Needle
from the saddle*

The rock in these couloirs is the famous **crestone conglomerate**, noted for being solid, with plenty of knobby holds. However, there have been at least two fatalities here from rock fall. Wear your helmet and use caution, especially if there are parties above you. There is not a lot of room to move out of the way in a hurry.

CRESTONE PEAK

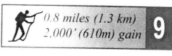

The climb up **Crestone Peak**'s south face from Cottonwood Lake is probably the easiest route on the mountain, but seldom done due to its remoteness. Leave the west shore of the lake, and begin a rising contour around and underneath the west face of Crestone Needle. Your objective is to get into the basin beneath Crestone Peak's south face. Head for the main couloir in the center of this face. Scramble up on the right side of the couloir for several hundred feet. Move out into the couloir where it broadens, climbing to the notch at the top. Early in the season, this will be a snow climb. From the top of the notch, turn left and scramble northwest, up a few hundred feet to the summit.

Congratulations, you have climbed the highest of the Crestone group! You will have fine views of the other Fourteeners in this group. To the northwest, you will see Kit Carson Mountain, to the east is Humboldt Peak and to the southeast is Crestone Needle.

KIT CARSON PEAK

The recommended trailhead for **Kit Carson Peak** is the **South Crestone Trailhead** located near the town of Crestone.

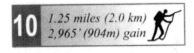

10   *1.25 miles (2.0 km)*   *2,965' (904m) gain*

From the small town of Moffat, located 42 miles north of Alamosa on CO 17, turn right onto **County Road T**. Follow County Road T as it heads east (with a short jog around one stretch of farmland) for 12 miles to a stop sign and information kiosk. Turn left, following the signs into Crestone, and then follow signs directing you to the South Crestone Trailhead. As you go along through town, you'll pass a new Post Office on Alder Street. Turn right at the intersection of Alder and Galena. Shortly after this turn, the road changes to gravel, and then to a steep, rough dirt road marked as FSR 949. If the road is dry, you'll probably be able to drive the 2.3 miles (3.7 km) from the Alder/Galena intersection to the trailhead parking area in a normal passenger car. However, four-wheel drive will make this much easier, especially if there has been any recent rain or snow.

Park your car in the parking area, and begin your hike by heading up the trail for about 100 yards to a trail junction. Turn right at this junction, following the sign that points to FST 865, leading to **Willow Lakes**. This trail crosses a stream almost immediately. If you miss this junction and continue straight, you'll be on FST 860 which leads to South Crestone Lake — NOT your destination!

The Willow Lakes Trail generally consists of switchbacks, followed by level terrain and then more switchbacks. If you're counting, you have a total of 63 switchbacks to negotiate before your final pull to Willow Lake. It is approximately 3.25 miles (5.2 km) from the trailhead to Willow Lake, with an elevation gain of approximately 3,000 feet (914m).

Follow the Willow Lakes Trail as it crosses to the south (right) of **Crestone Creek** at elevation 8,880' (2,761m). Shortly after crossing the stream, you will encounter a fork in the trail. Stay to the left at this fork and hike up to the Forest Service information sign. Register your destination and number of participants here.

Follow the trail as it begins to climb steadily up the Willow Creek drainage, passing 11 of those 63 switchbacks along the way. At approximately 9,880 feet (3,011m), you'll come to a pleasant resting spot, just before the trail drops

slightly and then starts to level out, passing above **Willow Creek Park**. For the next 1.0 mile (1.6 km), it gains only a couple of hundred feet (61m) in elevation. Along the way, the trail crosses rocky slabs below a small, photogenic waterfall.

Just past the rocky slab area, you will notice a tree off to your right which has sustained a major blunt trauma event, inflicted by a very large boulder bounding down the slope to your left. Imagine the amount of force it would take to inflict the same amount of damage to this tree with your vehicle. Imagine the amount of damage this would have caused to your vehicle. Finally, imagine how your body would have looked after this kind of impact! *Ouch!* The damage to this tree graphically illustrates how devastating and dangerous rock fall can be. Stay alert.

As you approach Willow Creek you will see an apparent fork in the trail. Keep to the right at this point and cross the creek. The trail continues through a major talus field, as it switchbacks up the final sustained section on your journey to Willow Lake.

Most of the hard work is over, as you finally level out above the talus field. From here on, the trail re-enters the trees and gradually gains elevation up to the designated camping area at 11,500' (3,505m), just below the lake. Be advised that camping is prohibited within 300 feet (91m) of Willow Lake. A basecamp at Willow Lake makes for a nice, reasonable two-day round trip, accompanied by spectacular scenery. Be sure to take in the enchanting beauty of the lake and falls as the sun sets. Challenger Point and Kit Carson Peak are slightly southeast of your current position. Both are on a single ridge known as Kit Carson Mountain.

Good morning! We hope that if you are planning to climb Challenger Point, and perhaps continue on to Kit Carson Peak, you begin with an early start! Well then, let's be on our way.

From the campsites at the west end of Willow Lake, follow the **use trail** through the willows, as it climbs up and along a cliff area northeast and above the lake, and then crosses above a waterfall. This area has always been one of our favorites and makes for an outstanding photographic opportunity.

Everyone has a different idea of what the best route is up any peak. We have chosen an approach that offers the least technical difficulty. This and other routes on these two mountains have claimed lives over the years, so don't get too complacent — pay attention to what you're doing while climbing!

The trail levels out, just past the waterfall. Follow the Willow Creek drainage for approximately 1.0 mile (1.6 km), until you see a prominent slope off to your right (south) that heads up to the main Challenger ridge. This is the north slope of Challenger Point. Take a few minutes here to study the terrain you will be climbing.

Hike over to the slope and proceed to work your way up to the ridge that leads over to Challenger Point, performing some easy scrambling along the way. The ascent to the Challenger Point ridge is the major elevation gain of the climb. Once on the ridge, turn left (southeast) and hike up the ridge to the summit. Challenger Point is

The route ascends the lefthand ridge, behind Willow lake

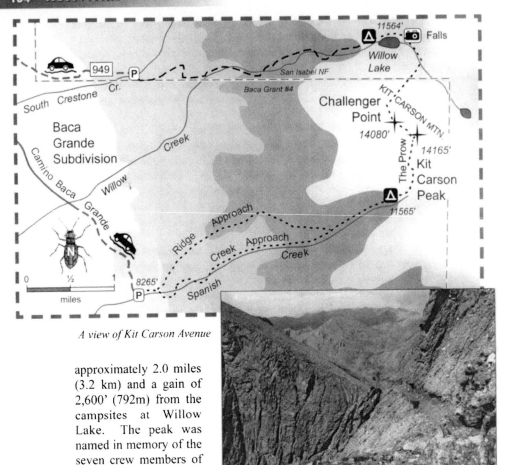

A view of Kit Carson Avenue

approximately 2.0 miles (3.2 km) and a gain of 2,600' (792m) from the campsites at Willow Lake. The peak was named in memory of the seven crew members of the ill-fated, space shuttle **Challenger**, which exploded in flight at 11:38 AM on January 28, 1986. You will find a memorial plaque at the summit of Challenger Point.

From Challenger Point, proceed east along the ridge crest to a saddle that drops approximately 300' (91m) between Challenger Point and Kit Carson Peak. Follow the well trodden path (commonly called **Kit Carson Avenue**), which gains and loses elevation as it contours generally southeast along, and around, the prow of Kit Carson Peak. After rounding this feature, the trail actually starts heading downhill. Don't panic. Very shortly you will encounter a wide gully heading left (northeast), up to the summit. This gully is actually past (east of) Kit Carson's summit. Turn left at the gully and gain approximately 400' (122m), as you climb to the top of the mountain. Keep alert for **cairns** (*ducks* to our California friends) along the traverse and up the gully. Kit Carson Avenue is very easy to follow, and the gully that you ascend to the summit is easy to identify.

We like to take along a few pieces of surveyor tape to mark our ascent; we collect these markers during our descent. It's not a good idea to walk off some cliff on your way down, because you weren't paying enough attention on the way up! The majority of accidents seem to occur on the descent. Retrace your route carefully when descending.

KIT CARSON PEAK, THE PROW

If you like alpine rock climbs, The Prow is a route not to be missed. It's challenging, it's fun and it's a classic! The views aren't too bad either! But do NOT

0.8 miles (1.3 km)
2,600' (793m) gain
11

underestimate the serious and committing nature of this alpine rock climb. Climbers must be competent on 5.8 rated rock, in an alpine setting. Both the altitude (14,000' (4,593m)) and the exposed nature of the climb further complicate matters. Having a good weather forecast is essential.

The approach to the climb also involves a stiff bushwhack, through downed timber, brush and across interminable talus, to reach the basecamp. But for the experienced climber, this two-day adventure can be an exciting experience. Despite the lack of great protection, **crestone conglomerate**, with its curious, imbedded knobs, is a pleasant surprise to climb on.

The trailhead to get to basecamp for The Prow is 3.6 miles (5.8 km) south of the intersection of **County Road T** and **Camino Baca Grande**, immediately southwest of the information kiosk at the entrance to the town of Crestone. The road begins as asphalt, changing over to gravel in 2.3 miles (3.7 km). The road continues on for an additional 1.3 miles (2.1 km) to the trailhead at **Spanish Creek**. Normal passenger vehicles are fine on this road, and there is off-road parking for multiple vehicles near the trailhead.

From your start at 8,265' (2519m) to basecamp at 11,565' (3525m) is a gain of either 4,070' (1241m) or 3,300' (1006m), depending on which of two possible routes are taken, the *Ridge Approach* or the *Creek Approach*. Most parties opt to head up the ridge, to the north of the creek, returning via Spanish Creek, which is easier to follow on the descent. Either way it's nasty, and you will earn every foot of elevation you gain! But the views of The Prow from either approach are simply spectacular. For both approaches, you'll find a trail sign on the north side of Spanish Creek, reading *HUA Foot Path*. You are traveling on private property at this point. Take care to make your presence as unobtrusive as possible.

For the **Creek Approach**, cross to the south side of the creek in 0.4 mile (0.6 km) on a wooden plank bridge. This is where the fun begins. Parallel the south side of the creek through dense underbrush, bashing your way up hill. The trail appears and disappears, as it meanders along the lower reaches of Spanish Creek, with several crossings along the way. As the trail begins to climb up the valley, it becomes more defined.

Hike along the easy-to-follow trail as it gains elevation through stands of aspen and pines, finally entering the upper reaches of the drainage. At this point, you will encounter the *dreaded* burn area; countless trees which have burned and collapsed into a hopeless jumble of obstacles. If you were a high hurdler in school, you'll be right at home, making those high steps over downed trees. Try to keep close to the stream, following the faint trail marked with cairns usually perched upon fallen

The dreaded burn area

trees. Take care not to fall over some of these toppled monsters. The folks who chose the Ridge Approach are probably laughing at you from above, but you'll have the last laugh.

Continue fighting through the fallen trees until you reach the non-burned area at the upper end of the drainage. Shortly, you'll encounter a good trail marked with cairns, leading to a very comfortable campsite near the creek in the vicinity of *UTM 446808mE, 4202339mN* at 11,565 feet (3525m). This basecamp is about six to eight hours and 3.25 miles (5.2 km)) from the trailhead.

For the alternate route, the **Ridge Approach**, the main objective is to follow the creek upstream, avoiding as much difficult terrain as possible. This is best accomplished by staying above the creek, on the north side, as you make your way up the valley. Follow the creek upstream for 0.4 miles (0.6 km) to where you encounter a wooden plank bridge, which crosses to the south side of the creek. Do not cross here. Instead, stay on the north side, following a faint trail heading steeply up the hillside. As you gain the ridge, the terrain is rocky with loose footing and the occasional cairn. Bushwack up the ridge, climbing out of the Spanish Creek drainage. Take care not to drift too far to the left (north). Most obstacles, like rock outcroppings, can easily be bypassed on the left.

Follow the ridge until you encounter a talus field near the 11,800' (3597m) level. Your pain and suffering are about to end. Shortly, you'll crest out on the ridge at 11,883' (3622m). Take a well deserved rest here and survey the terrain below you, in the drainage to the southeast. This is the burn area described above. Your task now is to find a route down to creek level through all of this debris. As you descend, keep traversing and following the creek toward the non-burned trees.

Shortly after reaching the non-burn area, you'll find a good trail, marked with cairns. This leads to a very comfortable campsite, located in the vicinity of *UTM 446808mE, 4202339mN* at 11,565 feet (3525m), near the creek. This basecamp is located about six to eight hours and 3.8 miles (6.1 km) from the trailhead.

Get an early start the next morning. From your camp, follow the well-defined trail as it winds its way up through the trees to the upper end of the

Spanish Creek drainage. As you leave the trees you'll have a clear view of The Prow. Contour on the right hand side, below The Prow, up easy slabs until you cross beneath its base. Follow a line to a small saddle, below and to the left of the start of the climbing route.

As you approach the base of The Prow, hike around to the left (west) where you will encounter a 50 foot (15m) wall of challenging Class 4 rock. This is a good place to break out the rope, helmet and associated climbing gear. Put on your rock climbing shoes, if you brought them, and have someone lead up through this area. While not extremely difficult, this section can be dangerous and time consuming. Belaying this pitch will make the climb go faster, and everyone will feel more relaxed when they get to the real climb, which starts in the notch directly above you.

A climber leading a pitch on The Prow

Be forewarned: From this point on, retreat from the route becomes very difficult due to the shortage of natural features for setting up rappels. Down-climbing would be very tedious and time consuming. Being caught mid-route during a Sangre de Cristo thunderstorm would be an experience you would not soon forget. Check the weather and your estimated climbing time for the route, to insure a safe and fun experience. You have at least six pitches of climbing ahead of you.

Once past the *warm up* climb described above, you'll find yourself standing in a notch, looking up at the hardest moves on the climb — the 5.8 rated, slightly overhanging, somewhat awkward, start of the climb. After climbing through the 5.8 section, the route becomes more reasonable (5.6) and provides a few more opportunities for placing protection. The second pitch, while somewhat steep, allows the leader to take almost any line they feel comfortable with. Protection placements on this, and subsequent pitches, are few and far between. Don't bother taking a #3 or #4 camming device; you'll never get an opportunity to use them!

Although exposed, the climbing on the remaining pitches is much more relaxed. Take some time to look at the surrounding scenery. There's a great view of the famous **red couloir** on Crestone Peak, from a point higher up on the route. Experienced parties will find that *simul-climbing* these pitches, while the leader places protection, is very efficient and time saving.

Once arrived at **Kit Carson Avenue**, you'll have good views of the standard route for **Kit Carson Mountain**, coming over **Challenger Point** (on your left) and down into the notch between Challenger and Kit Carson. It then climbs up the well-beaten path, which goes around The Prow, and continues on down toward the couloir which accesses the summit of Kit Carson. At this point, you have the option of climbing the final pitch in front of you to the summit or simply walking down and to the right (north), toward the south couloir.

A climber high on The Prow

If you choose to descend the south couloir and down into the Spanish Creek drainage, be well advised that it might still contain snow during heavy snow years. Be sure to check out your descent route beforehand, as you approach the start of the climb.

ATTRACTIONS

Valley Adventures
Near the Park 199
San Luis Lakes 200
    State Park
Medano-Zapata 202
    Ranch
Attractions in 203
    Alamosa
Alamosa National . .204
    Wildlife Refuge
Colorado Alligator . .205
    Farm
Attractions Near . . .206
    Ft. Garland/Blanca
Attractions Near . . .207
    Crestone/Moffat
Hot Springs 207
Valley Events
Ongoing Events . . .208
Calendar of Events .210

Medano-Zapata Ranch

Colorado Alligator Farm

Flying kites at Castles, Kites and Concert festival

VALLEY ADVENTURES

To find your way around the valley, see the map on page 35!

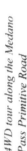

4WD tour along the Medano Pass Primitive Road

From aliens to alligators, from buffalo soldiers to buffaloes, a visit to some of the fascinating attractions in the San Luis Valley can easily be combined with your trip to the Great Sand Dunes National Park and Preserve to create a weekend, or more, of Colorado adventures! A good clearing house for information on what's happening in the valley is the **Alamosa Visitor Information Center**. Stop by from 8:00 AM to 5:00 PM Monday through Friday to check on special events in the San Luis Valley, and to pick up brochures and maps. To get to the Information Center, if you are driving west into Alamosa along US 160, take the first right turn after crossing the bridge over the Rio Grande River.

(800) BLU-SKYS (800-258-1597)
or (719) 589-4840
email: bluskys@alamosa.org

Near the Park

Just before you enter Great Sand Dunes National Park, you can't miss the **Great Sand Dunes Oasis** complex on your right. Stop in at the general store and sign up for a ride on their special, four-wheel drive **tour vehicle**. This is a great way to see parts of the National Park many people never get to see, and to learn some fascinating natural and human history while you're at it. Sure, you can also drive your own vehicle along the dreaded Medano Pass Primitive Road, but if you're not driving a robust 4WD, or just would rather not risk the $100-and-up towing fee, a tour is absolutely the way to go.

Tours generally start at 10:00 AM and 2:00 PM, but call or stop in to make a reservation. In 2002, the cost was **$14** for adults, **$8** for children. Tours last about two hours, with picture stops and breaks for short walks. Bring your camera!

5400 Hwy. 150 N.
Mosca, CO 81146
(719) 378-2222

San Luis Lakes State Park

An unlikely oasis in the desert, the **San Luis Lakes State Park and Wildlife Area** encompasses over 2,000 acres of recreation area in the eastern part of the San Luis Valley, southwest of the Great Sand Dunes National Park and Preserve. The lakes, pristine wetlands, and surrounding grasslands and low dunes offer such diverse activities as hiking, biking, boating, wind surfing, water skiing, fishing (summer and winter), swimming (sorry, summer only) and

FEES (as of 2002)
- **$3** day-pass per vehicle
- or **$50** for an annual *Colorado State Parks Pass*, which may be purchased at the Park entrance. Colorado residents who are 62 years of age or older are eligible to purchase a **$10** *Aspen Leaf Annual Pass*
- Camping fee, **$14** per night

wildlife viewing. The hiking and biking trails are level, with gravel surfaces, which provides excellent handicap access. Sheltered picnic tables along the lake shore let you enjoy a relaxed meal with great views of **San Luis Lake**, with the Great Sand Dunes and the peaks of the Sangre de Cristo Range as a backdrop.

Rainbow trout fishing is excellent throughout the year. The wildlife area north of San Luis Lake allows hunting of waterfowl and small game. Check with a park ranger or with the Colorado Division of Wildlife, *(303) 297-1192, web site: wildlife.state.co.us,* for license requirements and regulations.

Be sure to take advantage of the outstanding scenic photographic opportunities which are available in the park. This is an excellent area for birding, as sandhill cranes, bald eagles and waterfowl migrate through. Raptors and songbirds nest or winter here (see the section on *Birdwatching* on page 100 for more details.) You may also spot some of the 2,000 head of bison on the neighboring **Medano-Zapata Ranch**, or see mule deer, pronghorn and elk.

The **Wildlife Area** to the north of San Luis Lake is where you'll find most hiking and biking opportunities. This area contains wetlands and **Head Lake**, home to many of the nesting waterfowl and shorebirds. Be advised, however, that the Wildlife Area is closed from February 15 to July 15 of each year.

Reflections of the Sangre de Cristo Range on San Luis Lake

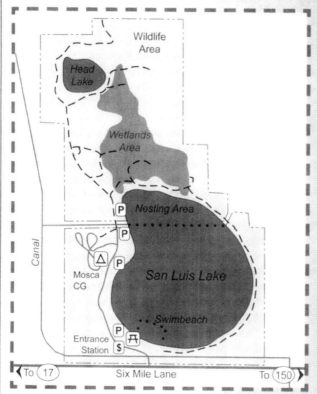

Oh to be two years old, playing by the lake, and not have a care in the world (or a stitch of clothing)

Lush wetlands attract wildlife

HOW TO GET THERE

County Lane 6 North
P.O. Box 175
Mosca, CO 81146
(719) 378-2020
email: sanluis.park@state.co.us
web site:www.coloradoparks.org/San_Luis

▪ From the entrance to the Great Sand Dunes National Park and Preserve, proceed south on CO 150 to its junction with **Six Mile Lane**. Turn right (west) on Six Mile Lane and proceed for 8.5 miles (13.6 km) to the San Luis Lakes State Park entrance.

▪ Or from the junction of US 160 and CO 150, turn north on CO 150 and proceed for 14.0 miles (22.4 km) to the signed turnoff for Six Mile Lane. Turn left (west) on Six Mile Lane and proceed for 8.5 miles (13.6 km) to the San Luis State Park entrance.

▪ Or from CO 17, drive to Mosca and turn east at the signed turnoff for Six Mile Lane and proceed for 8 miles (12.9 km) to the San Luis State Park entrance.

CAMPING

If you wish to camp on the low sand dunes near the lake, you can choose among 51 established campsites in **Mosca Campground**. Two sites are wheelchair accessible. All sites have electrical hookups, sheltered picnic tables and fire grates. Drinking water, restrooms, hot showers and laundry facilities are close by. There's even a dump station for your RVing pleasure. The campground is closed during the winter months.

Medano-Zapata Ranch

The **Medano-Zapata Ranch**, next to the Great Sand Dunes, was bought by The **Nature Conservancy** in 1999. They manage about 103,000 acres which are home to a large, free-ranging **bison herd**, plus 71 (and counting) rare

> *19667 Lane 6 North*
> *Mosca, CO 81146*
> *(719) 378-2503*
> *web site: nature.org/colorado*

and imperiled species of plants and animals. A self-guided interpretive trail is planned to open in 2003. However, there is no other open public access to the ranch — access is available by reservation only, on guided tours. See page 210 in the *Calendar of Events* for more information about tours and nature walks sponsored by The Nature Conservancy. The property entrance is a few miles southwest of the Dunes on Six Mile Lane.

This fascinating area is located mostly on what is called the **sabkha** — a plain of sand which has been hardened by its high mineral content. **Greasewood** (locals call it *chico*) grows well here, and helps to further stabilize the sand.

Bison skull

Several natural springs — very old springs — flow through the ranch, and archaeologists have made a number of discoveries here of ancient houses, tools, weapons and remains of animals, such as mammoth and super-sized bison.

Speaking of bison, did you know . . .

- they weigh close to 2,000 pounds, and some males may top that weight.

- they can jump a 6-foot fence from a standing position, or an 8-foot fence on the run.

- a bison can outrun a quarter horse in its favorite race length of ¼ mile (although it seems more likely that the bison would simply gore the horse, rather than race it.)

- this herd of about 2,000 bison is one of the largest herds in Colorado.

Bison on the ranch

Tour group at the entrance to Medano Ranch

Attractions in Alamosa

> 306 Hunt Avenue
> PO Box 1593
> Alamosa, CO 81101
> (719) 587-0667
> web site: museumtrail.org/
> SanLuisValleyHistoryMuseum.asp

The small but delightful **San Luis Valley History Center & Museum** offers displays of artifacts, antiques and photographs depicting the lives of Indian, Hispanic, and other settlers in the San Luis Valley. Models of a schoolroom and a country store

Recreation of early schoolroom

with a post office have both been recreated, and are fascinating to explore.

To get there, drive west into Alamosa on US 160. Take the first right turn (4th Street) after crossing the Rio Grande, and continue one block past the Visitor Information Center and the Public Library. Turn right on Hunt Avenue. The museum will be at the end of the block, on your right. It's open 10:00 AM - 4:00 PM daily from June 1st to October 1st. Admission is free.

Inspect a full-size narrow-gauge engine, car and depot building at the **Narrow-Gauge History Center**, located at Cole Park next to the Visitor Information Center. Engine #169 was on exhibit at the 1939 New York World's Fair and the passenger car is from the 1880s. For info, (719) 689-3681.

The **Luther E. Bean Museum**, located at Adams State College in Richardson Hall-Room 256, houses a fine arts gallery including works by local artists, as well as the Woodard Collection of artifacts from around the world. Admission is free and the museum is open Monday through Friday from 1:00 PM to 4:30 PM. Tours are offered, (719) 587-7151.

The **Chocolate Pantry & Gallery** currently displays the works of over 20 local artists in a all media including bronze, clay, oil, watercolor, wood, sculpture, photography, jewelery and handmade knives.

> 618 Main Street
> Alamosa, CO 81101
> (719) 589-4465

The **Cattails Golf Course**, an 18-hole championship course, lies beside the **Rio Grande River**, and winds through cottonwood trees (after all, *alamosa* means cottonwood grove in Spanish) and wetlands. Facilities include a restaurant, pro shop and a practice range. Check at your hotel or B&B for special golf packages. It's located just north of downtown Alamosa on State Street, beside the Rio Grande. Reservations are suggested, but not required.

> 6615 N. River Road
> Alamosa, CO 81101
> (888) 765-4653 or
> (719) 589-9515

To find your way around town, see the map on page 87!

Alamosa National Wildlife Refuge

The **Alamosa National Wildlife Refuge**, three miles southeast of the town of Alamosa, is a major stopover for tens of thousands of migrating birds each spring and fall. Take a stroll along the **Riverwalk Nature**

9383 El Rancho Lane
Alamosa, CO 81101
(719) 589-4021
web site: mountain-prairie.fws.gov/alamosanwr/

Trail (along the Rio Grande River) or drive the 3.5-mile **Auto Tour** along natural canals, oxbows and through shallow wetlands to view resident mallards, cinnamon teal, northern pintails, sandhill cranes, snowy egrets and white-faced ibis. Birds frolic and nest among the rushes, sedges, greasewood, rabbitbrush, Indian ricegrass, cattails, bulrushes and assorted native grasses on 11,169 acres. Golden and bald eagles, hawks and owls often make this their winter home. Mule deer, coyotes and beavers also frequent the refuge. The Visitor Center is open Monday through Friday, 7:30 AM to 4:00 PM. The auto tour routes and hiking trail are open from sunrise to sunset.

There is no entrance fee and the refuge is open year-round. Waterfowl numbers peak in March through May. See the section on *Birdwatching* on page 101 for more information on birding within the refuge.

To get there from the intersection of US 160 and Hwy 17 in Alamosa, drive 3.1 miles east on US 160. Turn right (south) at the sign directing you to the refuge. Follow this road 2.5 miles to the Visitor Center.

If you enjoy the Alamosa National Wildlife Refuge, you'll also like the **Monte Vista National Wildlife Refuge**. Ask at the Visitor Center for directions to this "sister" wildlife area located west of Alamosa and south of Monte Vista. The annual **Monte Vista Crane Festival** in early March provides an opportunity to view about 25,000 **sandhill cranes** at their "spring break" during migration through the San Luis Valley. For festival information, (719) 852-3552 www.cranefest.com.

Avocets are common in the marshes of the refuge

Colorado Alligator Farm

*9162 County Road 9 North
Mosca, CO 81146
(719) 378-2612
web site: www.gatorfarm.com*

Yes, they really have **alligators**. *Live* alligators! Little alligators and *huge* alligators! Also on hand are: tortoise, crocodile, snake, gecko, iguana, ostrich and an assortment of rabbits.

The **Colorado Alligator Farm** is a somewhat funky and unusual place that your kids will love. You can even rent paddle boats or a canoe, go fishing in a stocked, man-made creek and *(not to be missed)* hold a 'gator and earn a **Certificate of Bravery**. To get there, from the intersection of Hwy 17 and 6 Mile Lane at Mosca, drive north on Hwy 17 about 3 miles, following numerous *Colorado Gators* signs. It's located about a block east of Hwy 17 — you can't miss it!

Posing with a little one.

It's open daily 9:00 AM to 7:00 PM in the summer (Memorial Day to Labor Day), 9:00 AM to 5:00 PM in the winter. Admission fees are **$6 per adult**; free for kids up to age 5.

You might wonder what the heck are 'gators doing in the middle of the San Luis Valley? It all began with a fish farm using geothermal springs. In 1987, alligators were introduced to dispose of dead fish and by-products of filleted fish. Note — taking a swim in these hot springs is highly discouraged!

A large alligator basking

Attractions Near Ft. Garland/Blanca

29447 Highway 159
Fort Garland, CO 81133
(719) 379-3512

Cannon on display at Ft. Garland Museum

At the **Fort Garland Museum**, tour the adobe buildings of historic Fort Garland, established in 1858 and once commanded by Kit Carson. Displays include **dioramas** depicting life in the region during the mid-1800s, military weapons and uniforms, soldier and commandant's quarters and old wagons and stagecoaches. Another display teaches about the **Buffalo Soldiers** — African-American troops who served in Company G of the Ninth Cavalry here at Fort Garland. Admission fees are **$3 per adult**. It's open daily, 9:00 AM to 5:00 PM, from April through October and Thursday through Monday, 8:00 AM to 4:00 PM, from November through March.

As you drive west on US 160 through the town of Blanca, your eye will be drawn to the mural of a woman in a peaceful garden. In front of the building with the mural, you'll see hand-crafted wood furniture and perhaps a whimsical sculpture of a wood-nymph and a child playing musical instruments. Pull over and take some time to explore the **Forest Tango Art Works**, a gallery and gift shop, because it is even more appealing once you step inside. Browse sculpture, paintings, woven art, handmade soaps and other delights by local artists.

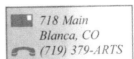

718 Main
Blanca, CO
(719) 379-ARTS

Sidewalk art in Blanca

Art gallery in Blanca

Attractions Near Crestone/Moffat

The **Challenger Golf Club** (formerly called Los Cumbres Golf Course), a nine-hole course, sits in a beautiful setting in the valley beneath the majestic Sangre de Cristo Mountains near the town of Crestone. Check at your hotel or B&B for special golf packages. No tee time is required. It's on County Road T, between Moffat and Crestone, 8 miles west of Hwy 17. *(719) 256-4856*

Hop up on a horse and experience a trail ride at **Baca Grande Stables** near Crestone. The stables also offer special rides for a higher fee, including a *botany ride* where you'll learn about local plants and ecosystems, an *architecture ride* where you'll see "alternative" building methods in the area, or visit a number of the spiritual centers which add to the character and diversity of Crestone. A *basic trail ride* costs **$15** for one hour; less for additional hours. Call for driving directions to the stables, located just outside of town, next to Willow Creek.

P.O. Box 478
Crestone, CO 81131
(719) 256-4756
www2.amigo.net/stables/
email: stables@amigo.net

Hot Springs

If you're looking for a great place to enjoy soaking in the warm waters, having a picnic, playing a little volleyball, basketball, tetherball or tossing horseshoes, this is the place to be. The **Sand Dunes Swimming Pool** includes a large pool kept at 98° to 102° degrees (depending on the season) as well as a smaller, hotter *spa* pool for soaking. The food concession offers a variety of hot or cold items, the changing rooms and showers are clean and modern, and a good time can be had by all. Regular hours are 10:00 AM to 10:00 PM. In December and January, hours are 1:00 PM to 8:00 PM. It's closed Thursdays for cleaning. *(719) 378-2807*

To get there from Alamosa, drive 20 miles north on Hwy 17, until one mile north of the town of **Hooper** (7 miles north of the intersection of 6 Mile Lane and Hwy 17), and turn east at the well-marked, *Sand Dunes Swimming Pool* sign on County Road B. After 1.5 miles, at the "T" intersection, follow the sign again by turning left. The pool is one mile north of the "T" (2.5 miles from the turn off from Hwy 17). Admission prices range from **$1** for toddlers to **$6** for adults under 65.

Come splash around at **Splashland Hot Springs** in a large, warm, geothermal pool after a hard day of playing on the sand dunes. Dressing rooms and showers are available on-site. Splashland is located one mile north of Alamosa on Hwy 17, on the west side of the road. Admission prices range from **$1** for toddlers to **$4** for adults under 60.

Splashland is open Memorial Day to Labor Day, with some extended dates depending on weather. It's closed Wednesdays for cleaning. Hours are 10:00 AM to 8:00 PM, all other weekdays and Saturdays; and Sundays from noon to 6:00 PM. There is adult lap swimming on weekdays (except Wednesday) from 6:00 AM to 9:00 AM.

5895 State Highway 17
Alamosa 81101
(719) 589-6307

VALLEY EVENTS

Sunday concert series at the Dunes

There are a number of **special events, festivals, workshops, classes** and other fun, interesting things to do in and around the Park, especially during the warmer months. Some are annual events that have been held for years; others turn up on the calendar for the first time. Here we list some of the happenings in the area, plus some resources for discovering the less predictable schedules of events at the Dunes and surrounding communities.

Ongoing Events

Young dancer at concert series

Head for the **amphitheater** by Piñon Flats Campground every Sunday evening around 7:00 PM for the **Sunday Concert Series** at the Great Sand Dunes National Park and Preserve, from late June through late August. Live music, sponsored by **Friends of the Dunes**, will entertain you. The concerts are free, and feature a range of musical styles.

See one of the largest herds of bison in North America, along with other wildlife at the **Medano-Zapata Ranch**, the 100,000-acre, historic ranch site owned and managed by The Nature Conservancy. Medano-Zapata Ranch Tours are held once per month, starting at 10:00 AM, generally from June through

19667 Lane 6 North
Mosca, CO 81146
(719) 378-2503
web site: nature.org/colorado

Nature walk at Medano-Zapata Ranch

October. You must register in advance for the tours, and we recommend that you don't wait until the last minute!

Also at the ranch, join a guide from The **Nature Conservancy** to walk around the beautiful Zapata Ranch and learn about the natural wonders of the region. **Guided nature walks** are held on most Tuesdays and Thursdays, starting at 9:00 AM, from June through October. Advance registration is required.

Ready for Alligator Wrestling 101? Contact the **Colorado Alligator Farm** in Mosca for schedules, tuition and reservations for, you got it, a hands-on workshop to learn alligator wrestling. Classes are offered during the warmer months of the year.

9162 County Road 9 North
Mosca, CO 81146
(719) 378-2612
web site: www.gatorfarm.com

Head into downtown **Alamosa** every Saturday from 7:00 AM to 2:00 PM, starting in July, for fresh produce from local growers, arts, and crafts. For info about the **Valley Farmers' Market** and other events in Alamosa sponsored by the Alamosa Uptown & River Association and the Alamosa Downtown Merchants' Association contact (719) 589-3681 x103.

The **San Luis Valley** has a rich and diverse history. **Los Caminos Antiguos** *(The Ancient Roads)* is a designated **Colorado Scenic & Historic Byway**. Drive along US 150, 6 Mile Lane, and SH 17 on a self-guided tour of Zapata Falls, Zapata Ranch, the Great Sand Dunes, Medano Ranch, San Luis Lakes State Park, the Colorado Alligator Farm, the town of Alamosa and the Alamosa National Wildlife Refuge, all discussed in

PO Box 86
Fort Garland CO 81133
(719) 379-3512
email: visitors@loscaminos.com
web site: www.loscaminos.com

more detail in this guidebook. Los Caminos Antiguos also extends south, and includes many additional sites around San Luis, Manassa, Antonito and Cumbres Pass. Contact the Visitor Information office or web site for a detailed map of the Scenic Byway and other materials.

Thunder Valley Speedway, west of Mosca, has races every Saturday during the summer. Each Saturday features a different event. For more information, contact promoters John and Linda McCormick. To find the racetrack, drive north from Alamosa on Highway 17 to Road 5 North, then head west four miles (one mile west of County Road 106).

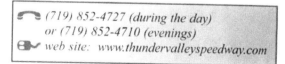

(719) 852-4727 (during the day)
or (719) 852-4710 (evenings)
web site: www.thundervalleyspeedway.com

Calendar of Events

FEBRUARY

▌Alamosa
Artwalk, a celebration of local artists, writers and performers, is an annual event in early February. Enjoy art displays at numerous locations in downtown Alamosa, and enjoy free performances. For more information, call AURA at ☎ *(719) 589-3681 x103.*

MARCH

▌Alamosa
Some places have green beer, but on Saint Patrick's Day in Alamosa, they celebrate with Green Chile! Enjoy the tastes and aromas of the **St. Patrick's Day Green Chile Cook-off**. Call ☎ *(719) 589-9483.*

APRIL

▌Alamosa
The annual celebration of **Alamosa Train Day** is held in mid to late April in Alamosa. Enjoy a tour of the **#169 steam locomotive train**, and visit the new train pavilion. Music, dance and arts are featured throughout the day. ☎ *(719) 589-3681 x103* for dates and more details.

MAY

▌Fort Garland
History buffs will enjoy the annual **Memorial Weekend Encampment** at the **Fort Garland Museum** over the Memorial Day weekend. Look for a ceremonial flag raising, followed by drills, ceremonies and re-enactment of many parts of life at Fort Garland from 1858 to 1883. For even more fun, come dressed in period costume or just stop in to enjoy the parade. ☎ *(719) 379-3512* for details.

JUNE

▌Alamosa
The annual **Summer Fest on the Rio** is held at Cole Park in Alamosa on the first weekend of June. Enjoy a crafts fair, food and live entertainment on multiple stages. Great family fun! ☎ *(719) 589-6077* for details.

Calendar of Events

Great Sand Dunes ▌

Every June, generally on the last Saturday of the month, join the fun of **Castles, Kites and Concert**. As you may have guessed, the day features sand castle building contests, kite flying and a concert. This event also kicks off the **Sunday Concert Series**, which begins the next evening (Sunday) and runs each Sunday through August.

Alamosa ▌

The annual, 6 or 7 day **Ride the Rockies** bicycle event in mid to late June follows a different route into the Rocky Mountains each year, but the route for the 2,000 cyclists included a stop in Alamosa on five different occasions from 1991-2002. See if the odds are in your favor this June by visiting 🖳 *www.ridetherockies.com* or 📞 *(303) 820-1338*.

UFO Watchtower & Campground/Hwy 17 near Hooper ▌

(Weekend festival around June 21) The annual **Summer Solstice Electronica Festival**, a.k.a. *Metaphysical Music Festival*, may be back for a future Summer Solstice. Promoters describe the festival, *"The Psychic Chakra will provide 3 screens of live visualz [sic] being preformed [sic] by some of the countries [sic] foremost visual mixing. DJ talent will be some of the most respected names in Psy-Trance . . ."* If, like us, you're not quite sure what all this means, you may prefer celebrating the Summer Solstice by star-gazing from a pretty spot on the Sand Dunes. For ticket information (**$40** and up) and other details, 📞 *(888) 270-3383*, or visit 🖳 *www.spacedub.org/psychic.html*.

Alamosa ▌

(Late June or early July weekend) *Yee-hah!* Come to the Alamosa County fairgrounds for the **Alamosa Rodeo and Demolition Derby**. Generally the fun is kicked off with a BBQ on Friday night. Over the weekend — from team roping, to bull riding, to a demolition derby — there is excitement everywhere you turn! 📞 *(719) 589-9444* for details.

JULY

Alamosa ▌

A variety of **Down Home Adventure Days** events usually begin a few days before the 4th of July, and continue for a few days afterwards.

At the annual Independence Day celebration (on July 4, of course) in Alamosa, the **Kiwanis Kowboy Breakfast** gets runners and their audience ready for the **5K Run/Walk** and a parade. After all that, move over to Cole Park for food, crafts and live entertainment. Check out the skateboarding and the **mud volleyball** and lots of other family fun. Once the sun goes down, watch the skies for the **fireworks display**.

Crestone ▌

July 4: The day begins with a **pancake breakfast** and a **5K Creep, Crawl, Run**. A parade and festival featuring live music, food, and a

Calendar of Events

variety of booths fill in the day. Finally, top off the evening with a dance at the Crestone Fire Station.

Mosca ▮

Colorado Alligator Farm holds its annual **Eggfest** on a weekend close to July 4. Come celebrate the alligators' egg-laying season by participating in an egg toss, egg races, and egg hunts in the alligator pen! We assume the eggs used for this "eggs-hibition" are just common chicken eggs.

Alamosa ▮

Look to the skies during the annual **Fly-In and Air Show**. Spot classic World War II *war birds,* modern military aircraft, and wonder at experimental and home-built planes. *"Oooo and aaah"* at acrobatic exhibitions. A **pancake breakfast** is served during the show. It's free. ☎ *(719) 852-9860.*

A UGUST

▮ Crestone

The **Crestone Music Festival** is held on a weekend in August, featuring multiple stages, and other things Crestone is famous for: artisans and "healers," food and drink, and general fun. Music styles range from blues to rock, bluegrass to celtic, salsa to country. There are clowns, contests and games for kids and adults, and even another 5K run. For details on events in Crestone, visit ☷ *www.crestone.org* or ☎ *(719) 256-4110.*

▮ Mosca

Gatorfest/Gator Olympics at the **Colorado Gator Farm** is held the first weekend in August. Watch competitors wrestle, canoe, run and jump among the alligators.

▮ Fort Garland

Fort Garland Military Re-enactments are featured at the Fort Garland Museum on a weekend in late August. Colorado volunteers conduct infantry drills and ceremonies, and also give "living history" demonstrations. ☎ *(719) 379-3512 or (970) 785-2832* for details.

▮ San Luis Lakes

Enroll to compete in a **triathlon** (perhaps your first one!), or just come by to watch. The date for **Tri The San Luis Valley** is likely to be in late August or early September. In 2002, the race featured a **1k swim** in San Luis Lakes (wetsuits strongly recommended), **20k bike race** on the very-flat 6 Mile Lane and a **5k run** along the same paved road.

☷ *golddust@amigo.net* for details, or ☎ *(719) 658-2100* (they can't return long-distance phone calls).

Calendar of Events

SEPTEMBER

Alamosa ▮

Labor Day weekend is the time to attend the **Early Iron Festival**, a celebration of antique cars, classic cars, street rods and other modes of transportation. Eat, listen to music and wander among the hundreds of very cool vehicles on display in Cole Park. For information, ☎ *(719) 589-0300 or (800) 258-7597.*

OCTOBER

Alamosa ▮

As the growing season starts to wind down in late September and early October, the **Valley Farmers' Market** gets just a little crazy as it sponsors such special events as the **Ugliest Potato Contest** and the **Longest Chili Pepper Contest**. The market is open every Saturday during warmer months from 7:00 AM to 2:00 PM in downtown Alamosa. ☎ *(719) 589-3681 x103.*

Crestone ▮

Get creative and dress up in a Halloween costume for the **Firefighters' Halloween Ball.** This annual event is a fundraiser for the local firefighters, and is fun for all. Enjoy the music and the costumes; maybe you can dress up as *Sandy the Tiger Beetle* and win a prize!

NOVEMBER

Alamosa ▮

It's the day after Thanksgiving, and time to turn on the **holiday lights**. Alamosa has a special tradition of decorating the historic **#169 Steam Locomotive**, and encouraging children to bring along a stocking to be stuffed at local merchant shops. ☎ *(719) 589-3681 x103* for more information.

Fort Garland ▮

Christmas at the Fort is held at the Fort Garland Museum in late November. Enjoy refreshments, costumes, music and story-telling. ☎ *(719) 379-3512* for details.

DECEMBER

Alamosa ▮

Join the fun of the annual **Teddy Bear Parade**. Kids bring their teddy bears to march and enjoy treats from merchants. ☎ *(719) 589-3681 x103.*

214

Notes

Notes

RESOURCE GUIDE

Information charts

Mileage Guide to . . .217
   Medano Pass
   Primitive Road
Hikes by Destination 218
Hikes by Difficulty . .219
Hikes by Distance . .220
Hikes by Duration . .221

Additional Reading 222

Organizations 224

Equipment List 225

GPS Use 226

Trail Snacks 227

Index 228

Meet the Authors 238

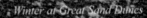

Winter at Great Sand Dunes

Air station at Point of No Return

MILEAGE GUIDE TO MEDANO PASS PRIMITIVE ROAD

Location	Uphill Mileage	Downhill Mileage	Comments	Campsites
End of paved road in Park	0.0	11.2	Start of Primitive Road	
Garden Creek	0.2	11.0	Usually flows until mid-summer, runs through Pinon Flats Campground	
Buck Creek	0.5	10.7	Intermittent Stream (may be icey in winter)	
Sawmill Creek	1.0	10.2	Usually flows until mid-summer. Accessible campsite available	
Point of No Return	1.1	10.1	4WD, high clearance vehicles only beyond this point (uphill)	
Ponderosa Point	1.4	9.8	Picnic area; nice view of Mt. Herard and Dunes	
Sand Pit	1.8	9.4	Picnic area; popular day use area for hiking	
Horse Canyon	3.3	7.9	Picnic area; views of northern dunes and foothills	
Shockey's Crossing	4.5	6.7	May have high water	
Old Fire Road	4.6	6.6	Open to hiking and horseback riding	
Sand Creek Trailhead	5.0	6.2	Access to northern campsites (permits required to camp)	
Monument/Preserve Boundary	5.4	5.8	There are 25 established campsites along the road between this boundary and Medano Pass	0.0
Medano Creek Crossing #2	5.6	5.6		0.4
Medano Creek Crossing #3	6.1	5.1	Bighorn sheep often found in meadows and on cliffs	0.9
Frenchman's Cabin	6.2	5.0	Ruins of Herard homestead, ca. 1875	1.0
Medano Creek Crossing #4	6.4	4.8		1.2
Medano Creek Crossing #5	6.8	4.4		1.6
Cliff to the north	6.9	4.3		1.7
Tight squeeze	7.5	3.7	Narrow roadway with large boulders alongside road	2.3
Medano Creek Crossing #6	7.6	3.6		2.4
Small creek crossing	7.7	3.5		2.5
Road splits around trees	7.8	3.4		2.6
Medano Creek Crossing #7	7.9	3.3		2.7
Small creek crossing	8.6	2.6		3.4
Beaver dams	8.8	2.4	Long meadows, marsh, and beaver dams	3.6
Three cabins	9.0	2.2	Ruins of 3 log cabins on the north side of the road	3.8
Medano Creek Crossing #8	9.6	1.6		4.4
Meadows	10.0	1.2		4.8
Medano Lake Trailhead	10.7	0.5	Continue 0.5 mile to north to start hike to Medano Lake, Mt. Herard; campsites available	5.5
Irrigation Ditch	11.0	0.2	Steep section to top of Pass	5.8
Medano Pass	11.2	0.0	Top of Pass (10,040')	6.0

Outwash area from Medano Creek

HIKES BY DESTINATION
(Mileages are "round-trip")

Destination	Starting Location	Mileage	Km	Feet	Meters	Difficulty	Duration
Carbonate Mountain (via Mosca Pass Tr.)	Mosca Pass	6.6	10.6	3,065	934.2	Moderate	Full Day
Carbonate Mountain (via Revelation Point Tr.)	Visitor Center	9.2	14.7	4,580	1,396.0	Difficult	Full Day
Castle Creek (via Sand Ramp Trail)	Point of No Return	2.2	3.5	130	39.6	Easy	2 Hours
Crystal Falls (via Rainbow Trail)	Music Pass Road/FSR 119	6.2	9.9	745	227.1	Moderate	Half Day
Dunes Overlook	Pinyon Flats CG	2.0	3.2	240	73.2	Easy	2 Hours
Dunes Overlook	Point of No Return	1.0	1.6	270	82.3	Easy	1 Hour
Escape Dunes/Ghost Forest	Dunes Parking Area	1.5	2.4	80	24.4	Easy	2 Hours
High Dune	Dunes Parking Area	2.0	3.2	650	198.1	Moderate	3 Hours
Little Baldy (a.k.a. Revelation Point)	Visitor's Center	4.0	6.4	1,335	406.9	Moderate	Half Day
Lower Sand Cr. Lake (via Music Pass Tr.)	Music Pass 4WD TH	6.4	10.2	2,060	627.9	Moderate	Full Day
Lower Sand Cr. Lake(via Music Pass Tr.)	Music Pass 2WD TH	11.5	18.4	3,420	1,042.4	Difficult	Full Day
Marble Cave/White Marble Hall Cave (via Rainbow/Marble Mountain Trails)	Music Pass Rd./FSR119	12.6	20.2	3,410	1,039.4	Difficult	Full Day
Marble Cave/White Marble Hall Cave (via Rainbow/Marble Mountain Trails)	FSR 120/2WD parking	12.5	20.0	4,065	1,239.0	Difficult	Full Day
Marble Mountain (via Rainbow/Marble Mountain Direct Trails)	FSR 120/4WD parking	6.4	10.2	3,680	1,121.7	Difficult	Full Day
Marble Mountain (via Rainbow/Marble Mountain Direct Trails)	FSR 120/2WD parking	10.4	16.6	4,750	1,447.8	Difficult	Full Day
Medano Lake	Medano Lake Trailhead	7.0	11.2	1,935	589.8	Moderate	Full Day
Montville Nature Trail	Montville Nature Trail Parking Area	0.5	0.8	150	45.7	Easy	1 Hour
Mosca Pass	Montville Nature Trail Parking Area	7.0	11.2	1,480	451.1	Moderate	Full Day
Mt. Herard (via Medano Lake Trail)	Medano Lake Trailhead	9.8	15.7	3,820	1,164.3	Difficult	Full Day
Point of No Return	Pinon Flats CG	1.0	1.6	270	82.3	Easy	1 Hour
Point of No Return	Amphitheater Parking Area	1.0	1.6	170	51.8	Easy	2 Hours
Sand Creek Trailhead (via Sand Ramp Tr.)	Point of No Return	6.8	10.9	455	138.7	Moderate	Half Day
Sand Pit Picnic Area	Point of No Return	1.0	1.6	100	30.5	Easy	1 Hour
South Zapata Lake	Zapata Falls Recreation Parking Area	9.0	14.4	3,490	1,063.8	Difficult	Full Day
Star Dune	High Dune	3.0	4.8	630	192.0	Moderate	Half Day
Star Dune	Dunes Parking Area	5.0	8.0	1,190	362.7	Moderate	Half Day
Upper Sand Cr. Lake (via Music Pass Tr.)	Music Pass 4WD TH	7.4	11.8	2,335	711.7	Moderate	Full Day
Upper Sand Cr. Lake(via Music Pass Tr.)	Music Pass 2WD TH	12.5	20.0	3,780	1,152.1	Difficult	Full Day
Wellington Ditch Trail	Pinon Flats Campground	2.0	3.2	130	39.6	Easy	2 Hours
Wellington Ditch Trail	Montville Nature Trail	2.0	3.2	130	39.6	Easy	2 Hours
Willow Lake	Willow Creek Trailhead	6.5	10.4	3,000	914.4	Moderate	Full Day
Zapata Falls	Zapata Falls Recreation Parking Area	0.5	0.8	200	61.0	Easy	1 Hour

Talus field on Marble Mountain Direct Trail

HIKES BY DIFFICULTY
(Mileages are "round-trip")

Difficulty	Destination	Starting Location	Mileage	Km	Feet	Meters	Duration
Easy	Wellington Ditch Trail	Pinon Flats Campground	2.0	3.2	130	39.6	2 Hours
Easy	Wellington Ditch Trail	Montville Nature Trail	2.0	3.2	130	39.6	2 Hours
Easy	Sand Pit Picnic Area	Point of No Return Parking Area	1.0	1.6	100	30.5	1 Hour
Easy	Point of No Return	Amphitheater Parking Area	1.0	1.6	170	51.8	2 Hours
Easy	Montville Nature Trail	Montville Nature Trail Parking Area	0.5	0.8	150	45.7	1 Hour
Easy	Zapata Falls	Zapata Falls Recreation Parking Area	0.5	0.8	200	61.0	1 Hour
Easy	Escape Dunes/Ghost Forest	Dunes Parking Area	1.5	2.4	80	24.4	2 Hours
Easy	Dunes Overlook	Pinyon Flats Campground	2.0	3.2	240	73.2	2 Hours
Easy	Castle Creek (via Sand Ramp Trail)	Point of No Return	2.2	3.5	130	39.6	2 Hours
Easy	Point of No Return	Pinon Flats Campground	1.0	1.6	270	82.3	1 Hour
Easy	Dunes Overlook	Point of No Return	1.0	1.6	270	82.3	1 Hour
Moderate	Lower Sand Cr. Lake (via Music Pass Tr.)	Music Pass 4WD TH	6.4	10.2	2,060	627.9	Full Day
Moderate	High Dune	Dunes Parking Area	2.0	3.2	650	198.1	3 Hours
Moderate	Willow Lake	Willow Creek Trailhead	6.5	10.4	3,000	914.4	Full Day
Moderate	Mosca Pass	Montville Nature Trail Parking Area	7.0	11.2	1,480	451.1	Full Day
Moderate	Sand Creek TH (via Sand Ramp Trail)	Point of No Return	6.8	10.9	455	138.7	Half Day
Moderate	Upper Sand Cr. Lake (via Music Pass Tr.)	Music Pass 4WD TH	7.4	11.8	2,335	711.7	Full Day
Moderate	Carbonate Mountain (via Mosca Pass Trail)	Mosca Pass	6.6	10.6	3,065	934.2	Full Day
Moderate	Medano Lake	Medano Lake Trailhead	7.0	11.2	1,935	589.8	Full Day
Moderate	Crystal Falls (via Rainbow Trail)	Music Pass Road/FSR 119	6.2	9.9	745	227.1	Half Day
Moderate	Star Dune	High Dune	3.0	4.8	630	192.0	Half Day
Moderate	Star Dune	Dunes Parking Area	5.0	8.0	1,190	362.7	Half Day
Moderate	Revelation Point (a.k.a. Little Baldy)	Visitor Center	4.0	6.4	1,335	406.9	Half Day
Difficult	Marble Cave/White Marble Hall Cave (via Rainbow/Marble Mountain Trails)	FSR 120/2WD parking	12.5	20.0	4,065	1,239.0	Full Day
Difficult	Marble Mountain (via Rainbow/Marble Mountain Direct Trails)	FSR 120/2WD Parking Area	10.4	16.6	4,750	1,447.8	Full Day
Difficult	Upper Sand Cr. Lake (via Music Pass Tr.)	Music Pass 2WD TH	12.5	20.0	3,780	1,152.1	Full Day
Difficult	Lower Sand Cr. Lake (via Music Pass Tr.)	Music Pass 2WD TH	11.5	18.4	3,420	1,042.4	Full Day
Difficult	South Zapata Lake	Zapata Falls Recreation Parking Area	9.0	14.4	3,490	1,063.8	Full Day
Difficult	Marble Mountain (via Rainbow/Marble Mountain Direct Trails)	FSR120/4WD Parking Area	6.4	10.2	3,680	1,121.7	Full Day
Difficult	Marble Cave/White Marble Hall Cave (via Rainbow /Marble Mountain Trails)	Music Pass Rd./FSR 119	12.6	20.2	3,410	1,039.4	Full Day
Difficult	Mt. Herard (via Medano Lake Trail)	Medano Lake Trailhead	9.8	15.7	3,820	1,164.3	Full Day
Difficult	Carbonate Mountain (via Revelation Point Tr.)	Visitor Center	9.2	14.7	4,580	1,396.0	Full Day

Cabin and meadow on Carbonate Mtn. Trail

HIKES BY DISTANCE
(Mileages are "round-trip")

Mileage	Destination	Starting Location	Km	Feet	Meters	Difficulty	Duration
0.5	Montville Nature Trail	Montville Nature Trail Parking Area	0.8	150	45.7	Easy	1 Hour
0.5	Zapata Falls	Zapata Falls Recreation Parking Area	0.8	200	61.0	Easy	1 Hour
1.0	Dunes Overlook	Point of No Return	1.6	270	82.3	Easy	1 Hour
1.0	Point of No Return	Pinon Flats Campground	1.6	270	82.3	Easy	1 Hour
1.0	Sand Pit Picnic Area	Point of No Return Parking Area	1.6	100	30.5	Easy	1 Hour
1.0	Point of No Return	Amphitheater Parking Area	1.6	170	51.8	Easy	2 Hours
1.5	Escape Dunes/Ghost Forest	Dunes Parking Area	2.4	80	24.4	Easy	2 Hours
2.0	Dunes Overlook	Pinon Flats Campground	3.2	240	73.2	Easy	2 Hours
2.0	Wellington Ditch Trail	Pinon Flats Campground	3.2	130	39.6	Easy	2 Hours
2.0	High Dune	Dunes Parking Area	3.2	650	198.1	Moderate	3 Hours
2.0	Wellington Ditch Trail	Montville Nature Trail	3.2	130	39.6	Easy	2 Hours
2.2	Castle Creek (via Sand Ramp Trail)	Point of No Return	3.5	130	39.6	Easy	2 Hours
3.0	Star Dune	High Dune	4.8	630	192.0	Moderate	Half Day
4.0	Revelation Point (a.k.a. Little Baldy)	Visitor Center	6.4	1,335	406.9	Moderate	Half Day
5.0	Star Dune	Dunes Parking Area	8.0	1,190	362.7	Moderate	Half Day
6.2	Crystal Falls (via Rainbow Trail)	Music Pass Road/FSR 119	9.9	745	227.1	Moderate	Half Day
6.4	Lower Sand Cr. Lake (via Music Pass Tr.)	Music Pass 4WD TH	10.2	2,060	627.9	Moderate	Full Day
6.4	Marble Mountain	FSR 120 /4WD Parking	10.2	3,680	1,121.7	Difficult	Full Day
	(via Rainbow/Marble Mountain Direct Trails)						
6.5	Willow Lake	Willow Creek Trailhead	10.4	3,000	914.4	Moderate	Full Day
6.6	Carbonate Mountain (via Mosca Pass Trail)	Mosca Pass	10.6	3,065	934.2	Moderate	Full Day
6.8	Sand Creek Trailhead(via Sand Ramp Tr.)	Point of No Return	10.9	455	138.7	Moderate	Half Day
7.0	Medano Lake	Medano Lake Trailhead	11.2	1,935	589.8	Moderate	Full Day
7.0	Mosca Pass	Montville Nature Trail Parking Area	11.2	1,480	451.1	Moderate	Full Day
7.4	Upper Sand Cr. Lake(via Music Pass Tr.)	Music Pass 4WD TH	11.8	2,335	711.7	Moderate	Full Day
9.0	South Zapata Lake	Zapata Falls Recreation Parking Area	14.4	3,490	1,063.8	Difficult	Full Day
9.2	Carbonate Mountain(via Revelation Point Trail)	Visitor Center	14.7	4,580	1,396.0	Difficult	Full Day
9.8	Mt. Herard(via Medano Lake Trail)	Medano Lake Trailhead	15.7	3,820	1,164.3	Difficult	Full Day
10.4	Marble Mountain	FSR 120 /2WD Parking	16.6	4,750	1,447.8	Difficult	Full Day
	(via Rainbow/Marble Mountain Direct Trails)						
11.5	Lower Sand Cr. Lake (via Music Pass Tr.)	Music Pass 2WD TH	18.4	3,420	1,042.4	Difficult	Full Day
12.5	Upper Sand Cr. Lake (via Music Pass Tr.)	Music Pass 2WD TH	20.0	3,780	1,152.1	Difficult	Full Day
12.5	Marble Cave/White Marble Hall Cave	FSR 120/2WD parking	20.0	4,065	1,239.0	Difficult	Full Day
	(via Rainbow/Marble Mountain Trails)						
12.6	Marble Cave/White Marble Hall Cave	FSR119	20.2	3,410	1,039.4	Difficult	Full Day
	(via Rainbow /Marble Mountain Trails)						

Hiking up summit ridge of Mount Herard

HIKES BY DURATION
(Mileages are "round-trip")

Duration	Destination	Starting Location	Mileage	Km	Feet	Meters	Difficulty
1 Hour	Sand Pit Picnic Area	Point of No Return Parking Area	1	1.6	100	30.5	Easy
1 Hour	Montville Nature Trail	Montville Nature Trail Parking Area	0.5	0.8	150	45.7	Easy
1 Hour	Zapata Falls	Zapata Falls Recreation Parking Area	0.5	0.8	200	61.0	Easy
1 Hour	Point of No Return	Pinon Flats Campground	1	1.6	270	82.3	Easy
1 Hour	Dunes Overlook	Point of No Return	1	1.6	270	82.3	Easy
2 Hours	Point of No Return (PONR)	Amphitheater Parking Area	1	1.6	170	51.8	Easy
2 Hours	Dunes Overlook	Pinyon Flats Campground	2	3.2	240	73.2	Easy
2 Hours	Castle Creek (via Sand Ramp Trail)	Point of No Return	2.2	3.5	130	39.6	Easy
2 Hours	Wellington Ditch Trail	Pinon Flats Campground	2	3.2	130	39.6	Easy
2 Hours	Escape Dunes/Ghost Forest	Dunes Parking Area	1.5	2.4	80	24.4	Easy
2 Hours	Wellington Ditch Trail	Montville Nature Trail	2	3.2	130	39.6	Easy
3 Hours	High Dune	Dunes Parking Area	2	3.2	650	198.1	Moderate
Full Day	Marble Cave/White Marble Hall Cave (via Rainbow /Marble Mountain Trails)	FSR 119	12.6	20.2	3,410	1,039.4	Difficult
Full Day	Upper Sand Cr. Lake (via Music Pass Tr.)	Music Pass 4WD TH	7.4	11.8	2,335	711.7	Moderate
Full Day	Medano Lake	Medano Lake Trailhead	7	11.2	1,935	589.8	Moderate
Full Day	Mosca Pass	Montville Nature Trail Parking Area	7	11.2	1,480	451.1	Moderate
Full Day	Carbonate Mountain (via Mosca Pass Trail)	Mosca Pass	6.6	10.6	3,065	934.2	Moderate
Full Day	Lower Sand Cr. Lake (via Music Pass Tr.)	Music Pass 4WD TH	6.4	10.2	2,060	627.9	Moderate
Full Day	Mt. Herard (via Medano Lake Trail)	Medano Lake Trailhead	9.8	15.7	3,820	1,164.3	Difficult
Full Day	Marble Mountain (via Rainbow/Marble Mountain Direct Trails)	FSR 120/2WD Parking	10.4	16.6	4,750	1,447.8	Difficult
Full Day	Carbonate Mountain (via Revelation Point Trail)	Visitor Center	9.2	14.7	4,580	1,396.0	Difficult
Full Day	Lower Sand Cr. Lake (via Music Pass Tr.)	Music Pass 2WD TH	11.5	18.4	3,420	1,042.4	Difficult
Full Day	Upper Sand Cr. Lake (via Music Pass Tr.)	Music Pass 2WD TH	12.5	20.0	3,780	1,152.1	Difficult
Full Day	Marble Mountain (via Rainbow/Marble Mountain Direct Trails)	FSR 120/4WD Parking Area	6.4	10.2	3,680	1,121.7	Difficult
Full Day	Marble Cave/White Marble Hall Cave (via Rainbow/Marble Mountain Trails)	FSR 120/2WD parking	12.5	20.0	4,065	1,239.0	Difficult
Full Day	South Zapata Lake	Zapata Falls Recreation Parking Area	9	14.4	3,490	1,063.8	Difficult
Full Day	Willow Lake	Willow Creek Trailhead	6.5	10.4	3,000	914.4	Moderate
Half Day	Star Dune	High Dune	3	4.8	630	192.0	Moderate
Half Day	Star Dune	Dunes Parking Area	5	8.0	1,190	362.7	Moderate
Half Day	Crystal Falls (via Rainbow Trail)	FSR 119	6.2	9.9	745	227.1	Moderate
Half Day	Sand Creek Trailhead (via Sand Ramp Trail)	Point of No Return	6.8	10.9	455	138.7	Moderate
Half Day	Revelation Point (a.k.a. Little Baldy)	Visitor's Center	4	6.4	1,335	406.9	Moderate

ADDITIONAL READING

NATURAL HISTORY

Colorado Division of Wildlife. Web site: http://wildlife.state.co.us/view.

Desert Guide - Army Corp of Engineers.
Web site: http://www.tec.army.mil/terrain/desert/lguide.htm.

Geology of Great Sand Dunes National Monument.
Web site: http://www2.nature.nps.gov/grd/parks/grsa/.

Great Sand Dunes National Park and Preserve.
Web site: http://www.nps.gov/grsa/.

National Parks Conservation Association - Great Sand Dunes. Web site: http://www.npca.org/explore_the_parks/new_parks/greatsanddunes.asp.

Pineda, Phyllis M. *Natural History of The Great Sand Dunes Tiger Beetle, Cicindela Theatina Rotger (Coleoptera: Carabidae), and Invertebrate Inventory of Indian Spring Natural Area, at Great Sand Dunes, Colorado.* Department of Bioagricultural Sciences and Pest Management, Colorado State University (Masters thesis.)

Trimble, Stephen A. *Great Sand Dunes, The Shape of the Wind.* Southwest Parks and Monuments Association, Globe, Arizona, 2001.

CULTURAL HISTORY

Bean, Luther E. "Land of the Blue Sky People, A Story of the San Luis Valley," *The Monte Vista Journal.* 1962.

Best, Allen. "Kit Carson: the Mountain and the Man," *Colorado Central Magazine - No. 80.* Central Colorado Publishing Company, October 2000.

Cumbres & Toltec Scenic Railroad. Website: http://www.cumbrestoltec.com/, 2001.

Great Sand Dunes National Monument. Website: http://www.alamosa.org/, 2001.

Jackson, Donald. *The Journals of Zebulon Montgomery Pike.* University of Oklahoma Press, Norman, Oklahoma, 1966.

Kantner, John. *Sipapu - The Anasazi's Ancestors from 10,000 to 8,000 B.C.* Website: http://sipapu.gsu.edu/timeline/, 2001.

Landreth, Libbie, Stuart Schneider and the staff of Great Sand Dunes National Monument. *Montville Nature Trail - A Step Into the Past.* Western National Parks Association, Tucson, Arizona, 1996.

Martorano, Marilyn A. "Culturally Peeled Ponderosa Pine Trees - Great Sand Dunes National Monument," *Great Sand Dunes National Monument - Stories of the Past*. The San Luis Valley Historical Society, Inc., 1990.

Martorano, Marilyn A. "So Hungry They Ate The Bark Off A Tree..." *Canyon Legacy - Vol. 1 Number 1*. Spring 1989.

Quillen, Ed. "Poncha: The Pass between the Rockies," *Colorado Central Magazine - No. 17*. Central Colorado Publishing Company, July 1995.

The San Luis Valley Historian, Volume XXII, Number 3. 1990.

Tushar, Olibama López. *The People of El Valle*. El Escritorio, 1992.

Williams, Jack R. *Ute Culture Trees - Living History*. Pikes Peak Research Station, Colorado Outdoor Education Center, Florissant, Colorado, 2001.

HIKING

Jacobs, Randy, Robert M. Ormes. *Guide to the Colorado Mountains*. Colorado Mountain Club Press, Golden, Colorado, 2000

Landreth, Libbie. *Exploring The Dunes*. Western National Parks Association, Tucson, Arizona.

O'Hanlon, Michael. *The Colorado Sangre de Cristo: A Complete Trail Guide*. Hungry Gulch Press.

CLIMBING

Borneman, Walter R., and Lyndon J. Lampert. *A Climbing Guide to Colorado's Fourteeners*. Pruett Publishing Company, Boulder, Colorado, 1978, 1989, 1998.

Dawson, Loius W. II. *Dawson's Guide To Colorado's Fourteeners, Volume 2 - The Southern Peaks*. Blue Clover Press, Monument, Colorado, 1999.

Roach, Gerry. *Colorado's Fourteeners - From Hikes to Climbs*. Fulcrum Publishing, Golden, Colorado, 1999.

MOUNTAIN BIKING

Alley, Sarah Bennett. *Bicycling America's National Parks: Utah and Colorado*. Countryman Press, 2000.

CAVING

Rhinehart, Richard J. *Colorado Caves: Hidden Worlds Beneath the Peaks*. Westcliffe Publishers, Engelwood, Colorado, 2001.

MAPS

Sangre de Cristo Wilderness and Great Sand Dunes National Park. Sky Terrain, Boulder, Colorado, 2001.

Sangre de Cristo Mountains #138. National Geographic/Trails Illustrated, Evergreen, Colorado, 2002.

ORGANIZATIONS

American Alpine Club
710 10th Street #100
Golden, CO 80401
(303) 384-0110
(303) 384-0111 Fax
www.americanalpineclub.org
A climbers' organization devoted to exploration of high mountain elevations, dissemination of information about mountaineering, conservation and preservation of mountain regions.

American Hiking Society
1422 Fenwick Lane
Silver Spring, MD 20910
(301) 565-6704
(301) 565-6714 Fax
www.americanhiking.org
A national organization dedicated to promoting hiking and to establishing, protecting and maintaining foot trails throughout the United States.

The Colorado Fourteeners Initiative
710 Tenth Street, Suite 220
Golden, Colorado 80401
(303) 278-7525
(303) 279-9690 Fax
www.coloradofourteeners.org
An organization to protect and preserve the natural integrity of Colorado's Fourteeners and the quality of the recreational opportunities they provide.

Colorado Mountain Club
710 10th Street #200
Golden, CO 80401
(303) 279-3080
(303) 279-9690 Fax
www.cmc.org
The largest hiking/climbing club in the Rocky Mountain Region. The club organizes over 2,000 hikes, ski trips, backpacking trips, bike trips, and other outdoor activities annually, and offers numerous classes in mountain-related activities.

Colorado Outward Bound School
910 Jackson Street
Golden, CO 80401
(720) 497-2400
(720) 497-2401 Fax
www.cobs.org
An educational institution dedicated to teaching wilderness-oriented skills and leadership, including backpacking and mountaineering courses.

Friends of the Dunes, Inc.
11500 Highway 150
Mosca, CO 81146
(719) 378-2312 Ext. 227
www.greatsanddunes.org
A non-profit citizen's support group for Great Sand Dunes National Park and Preserve that works in cooperation with the National Park Service, providing citizen involvement in planning decisions, and volunteer and financial aid for projects.

Leave No Trace, Inc.
P.O. Box 997
Boulder, CO 80306
(800) 332-4100
(303) 442-8217 Fax
www.lnt.org
An organization whose mission is to promote and inspire responsible outdoor recreation through education and partnerships.

The Mountaineers
300 Third Ave West
Seattle, Wa 98119
(206) 284-6310
(206) 284-4977 Fax
www.mountaineers.org
The largest outdoor recreation and conservation club in the Puget Sound region with an extensive outing and outdoor education program.

National Outdoor Leadership School
284 Lincoln Street
Lander, WY 82520-2848
(307) 332-5300
(307) 332-1220 Fax
www.nols.edu
An educational institution dedicated to teaching wilderness-oriented skills and leadership, including backpacking and mountaineering courses.

EQUIPMENT LIST

THE 10 ESSENTIALS

Food
Water
Emergency shelter
Extra clothing
First aid kit
Flashlight
Map and compass
Matches/fire starter
Pocket knife
Sunglasses/sunscreen

When preparing for a hike, always start with the *Ten Essentials* as your foundation. Boots should be light but sturdy (no tennis shoes). Backpackers will want heavier, stiffer boots for good support. For clothing, modern synthetics, like polypropylene and pile, are light, insulate well and dry quickly. But traditional wool clothing is still effective, even when damp. Avoid cotton entirely, as it loses all insulating ability when wet. Effective, good-quality clothing and other gear will often determine the difference between a safe, enjoyable day in the mountains and an unpleasant, or even potentially disastrous, experience.

FOR DAY HIKING

- ❏ Day-pack:1500 to 3000 cubic inches
- ❏ Insulating layer: poly tops and bottoms
- ❏ Shirt or sweater: poly or wool
- ❏ Pants: poly or wool
- ❏ Parka shell: waterproof, windproof
- ❏ Pants shell: waterproof, windproof
- ❏ Hat
- ❏ Gloves: poly or wool
- ❏ Extra socks

Backpackers

- ❏ Backpack: 3500 cubic in. or more
- ❏ Pack cover: waterproof
- ❏ Sleeping bag
- ❏ Sleeping pad
- ❏ Extra clothing
- ❏ Stove and fuel
- ❏ Cooking gear
- ❏ Eating utensils
- ❏ Food and food bags
- ❏ Tent or bivy sack
- ❏ Groundcloth: waterproof
- ❏ Personal toiletries
- ❏ Camp shoes
- ❏ Headlamp
- ❏ Repair kit and sewing kit

FOR BACKPACKING

- ❏ Water filter and/or iodine tablets
- ❏ Plastic trowel: for catholes
- ❏ Plastic bags: for garbage
- ❏ Rope or cord

Optional Gear:
Pillow
Camera gear and film
Reading material and/or journal
Fishing gear
Binoculars
Camp chair
Radio and cell phone
Walking stick

GPS USE

Hiking through fog on the dunes

Every point on the earth can be referenced using the **UTM grid system**. Thankfully for our purposes, we need only be concerned with the Great Sand Dunes National Park & Preserve.

The UTM grid system consists of two sets of straight, parallel lines, uniformly spaced, one set perpendicular to the other. This pattern resembles a giant *tic-tac-toe* grid. Each set of north-south parallel lines is referred to as a "zone". There are 60 zones covering the globe. The lower 48 states are represented by zone 10 on the West Coast, continuing consecutively through zone 19 on the East Coast. The Great Sand Dunes National Park & Preserve is all within zone 13.

Within each zone, UTM coordinates are measured from the north and from the east in meters, with each zone representing 1,000 meters or 3,281 feet. The "northing" values are measured consecutively from zero at the Equator in a northerly direction; hence, the name **northing**. Conversely, **easting** values are measured consecutively east from Zone 1, starting at the International Date Line.

All 7.5 minute USGS quadrangle maps have either UTM grid "ticks" (blue tick marks on the margin) or have the UTM grid printed on the body of the map itself. The value of each grid line or tick mark is shown below the point of reference. For example, Carbonate Mountain is located at *471756mN* (of the Equator) and *457632mE* (of the International Date Line). You can locate any point by taking a yardstick and drawing two intersecting lines (top to bottom and left to right) through your point of interest, connecting the matching tick mark values. Then read the UTM coordinates which locate your point of interest.

When you turn on your **Global Positioning System** (GPS) receiver, it will begin to communicate with a series of 12 GPS satellites which constantly circle the earth, transmitting signals back. This information is displayed in the form of northing (north-south) and easting (east-west) UTM coordinates. So if you know where you want to go, expressed in UTM coordinates, you can enter that information into your GPS receiver. Press the *Go To* button, and a line will be drawn from where you are currently standing to your destination (some GPS models may require a few extra steps before displaying this line.)

The line from where you are currently standing, to where you wish to go, is *as the crow flies*. There may be rivers, canyons, ridges, etc. between you and your destination. It is usually necessary to sit down with your map and plot a route, consisting of **waypoints** or "landmarks". Routes are created by recording specific UTM coordinates of features, such as lakes, trail branches and sub-peaks, along your planned route, and then entering these into the GPS receiver. You now have the means to get to your destination, regardless of fog or poor visibility. Note that some GPS receivers have the capability to download map information for display on the unit.

As you walk along your route, a line will appear on the GPS display showing where you have been, where you currently are, and optionally, where your next landmark is located. Think of this line as nothing more than a *trail of bread crumbs* which you can follow back to your point of origin. *Pretty slick, eh!* Who says you can't teach an old dog new tricks?

TRAIL SNACKS

What do the authors eat and drink for snacks while hiking? Unlike the late, health food guru **Ewell Gibbons**, we don't ascribe to the doctrine that "many parts of a pine tree are edible," nor do we drink *snake oil* to boast our energy levels.

The following list of goodies will probably drive nutritionists crazy, and it isn't for everyone, but it seems to work for us. We usually take a mixture of these, to make sure we're snacking, and enjoying it, as we walk. We don't take a lunch, *per se,* as we feel that it isn't a good idea to eat a large amount of food at one sitting and then try to hike. So, here it is:

- ❏ Apples (pre-cut & cored)
- ❏ Nabisco Fig Newtons®
- ❏ Nabisco Ritz® Cheese Crackers
- ❏ Cliff® Luna bars™ (*Lime & Orange* are great!)
- ❏ Kellogg's® Nutri-Grain® Yogurt bars
- ❏ Nabisco Ritz snack mixers® (*Cheddar* flavor)
- ❏ Power Bar® Protein Plus bars
- ❏ Power Bar® Dipped Harvest bars
- ❏ Dove® Chocolate Bar (This can become rather messy in hot weather, but it's worth it!)
- ❏ Lemon drops
- ❏ Home-made GORP (Good Old Raisins and Peanuts; but we add other nuts and dried fruits, plus M&Ms and perhaps some granola.)
- ❏ Bagel with cheese or peanut butter

For drinks, we usually take plain water, with a squeeze of lemon or lime juice, in a CamelBack™ hydration system. We also like to mix water 50/50 with Gatoraide® *High Tide* flavor and carry it in separate quart or liter bottles. The flavored water helps us consume an adequate amount of liquid while hiking.

We're always interested in learning about new ideas, so send us your snack/drink list and we'll try them out. Maybe they'll be in the next edition!

Scrambling up the dunes takes a lot of energy!

INDEX

Amphitheater 109, 115, 208

A

acknowledgments 6
Acute Mountain Sickness 27
age-predicted maximum heart rate 27
air station 103
Alamosa 22, 35, 63, 74, 78-79, 81, 83, 86-87, 204, 209-211, 213
Alamosa Economy Campground 81
Alamosa KOA 81
Alamosa National Wildlife Refuge 54, 101, 204
Alamosa Train Day 210
Alamosa Visitor Information Center 79, 199
Alashan Plateau 40
alligator 205, 209, 211
alpine forget-me-not 50
alpine sunflower 50
amphitheater 109, 115, 208
Ancestral Puebloans 58
animal tracks 52, 119
animals 22, 52-55
annual precipitation 36
antidune 38, 46
archaeological sites 57
archaeology 58
Arrastre Canyon 65
aspen 17, 50, 96, 124, 150, 157
Aspen Campsite 96, 109, 146
atlatl 57
avocet 17, 54

B

B&Ds Laundromat 79
Baca Grande Stables 207
Baca Grande Subdivision 172
Baca Ranch 68
backcountry camping 92-99

backpacking 98
bald eagle 53
barchan dune 42
Basin Houses 57
beaver dam 124
Beck Mountain 160
Best Western Alamosa Inn 83
bighorn sheep 16, 53, 106, 118, 161
birds 53-54, 100-102
birdwatching 100-102
bison 53, 118, 156, 202
black bear 17, 29, 53, 104, 118, 128, 180
black swift 100, 176
Blanca 78, 81, 84, 88, 206
Blanca massif 58, 182, 188-191
Blanca Peak 58, 132, 182, 188-189
Blanca RV Park & Store 81
blowout grass 49, 140, 143
blue grouse 100, 118
Blue Lakes 189
blue spruce 50
bobcat 52
bog iron 44
bristlecone pine 50, 153, 160
broad-tailed hummingbird 53, 100
buffalo soldiers 62, 206
bull snake 52
Bunch, Fred (NPS Ranger) 56

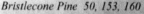

Bristlecone Pine 50, 153, 160

C

campfire programs 91
canada geese 54
Carbonate Mountain 126-127, 129, 148, 151-153, 155
Carbonate Mountain Trail 152-153
Carson, Kit 62, 63
Castle Creek 133, 142
Castle Creek Picnic Area 75, 104
Castles, Kites & Concert 32, 210
Cattails Golf Course 203
Challenger Golf Club 207
Challenger Point 176, 182, 192
Chaney, Steve (NPS Superintendent) 67
Chinese Wall 41
Chocolate Pantry & Gallery 203
Christmas bird count 102
circus beetle 55, 119
City Market 87
clarks nutcracker 53
clasts 44
Cleveland Peak 187
climate 36

Clovis people 57
clown beetle 55
Cold Creek 147
Cold Creek Campsite 97, 109, 174
Colfax Lane 114, 159, 163, 170
Colorado Alligator Farm 205, 209, 211, 212
Colorado Division of Wildlife 111
Comfort Inn of Alamosa 83
common loon 102

common nighthawk 100
common snipe 54
Como Lake Road 189
Cottonwood Creek 172, 173, 175
Cottonwood Creek Trail 162, 172-173, 191
Cottonwood Creek Trailhead 172
Cottonwood Inn Bed & Breakfast 83
Cottonwood Lake Trail 172-173, 191
Cottonwood Pass (Beer Pass) 98, 162, 173, 175
cottonwood trees 17, 43, 50, 97
cowboy gate 164, 166
coyote 17, 52, 118
Crater Lake 189
Crestone 84, 89, 172, 192, 207, 212-213
crestone conglomerate 44, 157, 184, 195
Crestone Music Festival 212
Crestone Peak 63, 132, 169, 171, 182, 190-191
Crestone Store 89
cross-country skiing 107
Crystal Falls 164-165
Crystal Falls Creek 164-166
Culebra Peak 68
cultural history 56-69
culturally peeled trees 59, 95, 144
Cumbres & Toltec Railroad 63

Culturally peeled tree 59, 95, 144

D

Days Inn 83
Del's Diner 88
Desert Sage Restaurant 89
designated primitive backcountry sites 92, 94
Dixon, Hobey (retired biologist) 57, 165
dogs 18, 29
Don Juan de Oñate 60
douglas fir 50
Down Home Adventure Days 211
dune field 40, 41, 131
Dunes Overlook 136
Dunes Overlook Trail 108, 137
Dunes Parking Lot 72, 130, 133, 135-136
Dunes/Piñon Flats Trail 130, 136

E

Early Iron Festival 212
earthquake 125
egret 16
elk 16, 53, 118
Ellingwood Point 181-182, 189
emergencies 77
engleman spruce 50
entrance station 71
Eolian Geology 39
escape dune 38, 43, 95, 133, 142
Escape Dunes Campsite 94, 142
eye protection 26

F

fairyslipper orchid 17, 50
falcon 53
fire 51, 122, 148, 161
Firefighters' Halloween Ball 213
fish 54
fishing 111
flower beetle 55
Folsom people 57
foot washes 74, 132
Forest Tango Art Works 206
Fort Garland 25, 62, 78, 84, 88, 206, 212-213
Fort Garland Motor Inn 84
Fort Garland Museum 206, 210
Fremont, John C. 63
Frenchman's Cabin 106
Friends of the Dunes 32-33, 57, 66, 91, 102, 165, 208
fulgurite 45

Foot washes 74, 132

G

Gardner 155
garter snake 150
gasoline 85
ghost forest 38, 43, 133, 142
giant sand treader camel cricket 55
Giardia 28, 92
gold 64
Golden Access Permit 71
Golden Age Permit 71
golden eagle 17, 53, 102
Grape Creek Trailhead, 163
Greasewood 202
Great Sand Dunes Lodge 82
Great Sand Dunes National Monument 66
Great Sand Dunes National Park and Preserve (location) 35
Great Sand Dunes National Park and Preserve Act 67

Great Sand Dunes Oasis Store 74, 80, 82, 85, 199
great sand dunes tiger beetle 17-19, 55
greater sandhill cranes 101
Grizzly Inn 83
Grizzly Inn Restaurant & Pub 86
Gunnison, John W. 63

Heavenly Valley 96, 146

H

Hastings, Frank 64
Head Lake 200
heat exhaustion 26
heat stroke 26
Heavenly Valley 96, 146
Herard, Ulysses 65
heron 54
High Dune 19, 43, 131-132
Holiday Inn of Alamosa 83
Hooper 78, 81, 207
Hoover, Herbert (President) 66
Horse Canyon 143
horseback riding 108
hot springs 207
Hudson Creek 166
Humboldt Peak 169, 171, 182
Hunan Chinese Restaurant 86
hunting 111

I

Iktomi's Kitchen 89
Indian Grove Campsite 95, 143
indian rice grass 49
insects 55

J

jeeping 22
Junior Park Ranger 115
juniper 50, 125

K

kangaroo rat 16, 52
kinnikinnick 50
Kit Carson Peak 68, 182, 192-197
Kit Carson Peak, The Prow 195-197

L

La Veta 69
Lake Como 188-189
Leave No Trace 30, 74
lesser sandhill crane 101
Liberty 174
lightning 27, 37, 45

Little Baldy 124, 126-129, 152
Little Bear Peak 132, 188-189
Little Medano Campsite 96, 109, 145
Little Medano Creek 144-146
Little Sand Creek Lakes 175
Little Sand Creek Lakes Trail 161, 174-175
lodgepole pine 50
Los Caminos Antiguos 60, 209
Louisiana Purchase 61
Lower Sand Creek Lake 161, 175
Lower Sand Creek Lake Trail 161
Lu's Mainstreet Cafe 78, 88
Luis Maria Baca Grant 62, 68, 172
Luther E. Bean Museum 203

M

magnetite 44, 64
magpie 53, 100
mammoth 57
Marble Cave 165-169
Marble Mountain 163-171
Marble Mountain Direct Trail 170-171
Marble Mountain Trail 164, 166, 169-170
Marble Mountain Trailhead 163
marmot 16, 53, 118
Medano Creek 16, 46, 104, 109, 126, 133, 156
Medano Lake 98, 106, 156-158
Medano Lake Trail 157
Medano Lake Trailhead 106, 113
Medano Pass 41, 60, 69, 113, 154, 156
Medano Pass Primitive Road 22, 65, 75, 99, 103-106
Medano-Zapata Ranch 53, 200, 202, 208
Milagros Coffeehouse 86
Milwaukee Peak 160, 162, 169, 171-172, 175, 185
Moffat 84, 172, 207
monsoon season 36
Monte Vista National Wildlife Refuge 54, 101
Montville Nature Trail 108, 123, 148-149, 150, 155
Montville Toll Road 64
Montville-Visitor Center Trail 148
Morris Gulch 125
Mosca 35, 78, 205, 212
Mosca Campground 201
Mosca Creek 149-150
Mosca Creek Picnic Area 75, 131
Mosca Pass 41, 60, 63, 69, 129, 150-152, 154-155
Mosca Pass Road 151, 154
Mosca Pass Trail 100, 108, 148, 150-152, 154-155
Mount Herard 65, 69, 106, 132, 138, 143, 156-158
Mount Herard Trail 158

Mount Herard Trail 158

Music Pass 154, 159-162, 166, 172-175

Mount Zwischen 69
mountain ball cactus 128
mountain biking 23, 112, 176
mountain bluebird 17, 53, 100, 102
mountain chickadee 100
mountain lion 29, 53, 118
mountain mahogany 50
mountain pine beetle 164
mourning dove 54
mule deer 52, 118
mullein 49-50
Music Pass 154, 159-162, 166, 172-175
Music Pass Creek 164
Music Pass Road 106, 154, 163, 170
Music Pass Trail 160, 175
Music Pass Trailhead 154, 159
Myers, Patrick (NPS Ranger) 16, 48, 151

N
Narrow-Gauge History Center 203
National Parks Annual Pass 71
Native Americans 50, 59
natural history 38
Nature Conservancy 49, 67, 202, 208-209
North Crestone Campground 81
North Fork Trail 180

O
Off-road vehicles 106
Old Fort Market 88
opuntia bug 49
Oscar's Restaurant 86

P
pack animals 108-110
parabolic dune 42
phlox 50
photography 116, 200
Pico Asilado 160, 169, 171, 173, 185
pika 16, 53
Pike, Zebulon 60-61
Pikes Peak 60, 69, 160
Pineda, Phyllis M. (NPS Resource Specialist) 55
Piñon Flats Campground 74, 76, 136, 141
piñon jay 53, 100
piñon pine 50-51, 76, 125, 139
plants 22, 48-50
playa 40
Point of No Return 75, 94, 104, 109, 136, 140-141
ponderosa pine 17, 50, 59, 125, 134, 138, 141

Ponderosa Point 113
Ponderosa Point Picnic Area 75, 104, 140
porch talks 115, 123
porcupine 53
prairie sunflower 49
prickly pear cactus 49, 125
pronghorn antelope 17, 53, 118
ptarmigan 17, 54, 118
Ptarmigan Peak 129

R

rabbit 52
rabbitbrush 49, 50
Rainbow Bed & Breakfast 84
Rainbow Trail 114, 159, 163-171
rainbow trout 162
ranger-led walks 115
rattle snake 52
Red Mountain Outfitters 110
Red Wing 102, 155
red-tailed hawk 100
red-winged blackbird 102
Revelation Point 124, 126-129, 152
reversing dune 41
Ride the Rockies 210
rio grande cutthroat trout 54, 162
Rio Grande River 61, 203
rio grande sucker 54
Riverwalk Nature Trail 204
roadrunner 53
robber fly 55
rough-legged hawk 54
Russell Lakes State Wildlife Area 54

S

sabkha 43, 49, 202
sage 49, 125
Saguache County 69
saltation 40
San Juan Mountains 19, 35, 40, 126, 132
San Luis Lake 200
San Luis Lakes State Park 25, 54, 80, 102, 113, 200-201
San Luis Valley 35, 39, 46, 58, 62, 102, 126, 138, 178, 199, 209
San Luis Valley History Center & Museum 203
Sand Creek 16, 147, 161, 174
Sand Creek Campsite 97, 109, 145, 147, 174
Sand Creek Trail 147, 161-162, 173-175
Sand Creek Trailhead 96, 104, 144-145
Sand Dunes Swimming Pool 207
Sand Pit Picnic Area 75, 140

Porch talk 115,123

Sand Pit Trail 135, 140
Sand Ramp Trail 95, 104, 108, 136, 141-147, 174
sand sheet 43, 123
sandhill crane 17, 54
Sangre de Cristo Mountains 17, 19, 35, 39, 60-61, 118, 126, 150, 154
Sangre de Cristo Wilderness Area 166, 172, 178, 190
Sawmill Canyon Campsite 94
scurf pea 49
Shockey's Crossing 104
Silver Star Bed & Breakfast 84
slender spider flower 49
slipface 41, 135

snow avalanche 180
snowboarding 19, 23, 107
snowy egret 54
South Colony Road 166, 170
South Crestone Trailhead 192
South Zapata Creek 179
South Zapata Lake 178, 181
South Zapata Lake Trail 177-181
spanish conquistadors 60
Spanish Creek 172, 195
Spanish Gully 166-167
Splashland Hot Springs 207
Star Dune 19, 27, 42, 97, 131-132
Steller's jay 53, 100
stilting 55
Sunday Concert Series 208
Sunshine Laundry 79
surface creep 40
surge flow 46-47

Surge flow 46-47

T

Table of Contents 7-13
Teddy Bear Parade 213
Thunder Valley Speedway 209
Tijeras Peak 161, 169, 171, 187
trail etiquette 109
transverse dune 41
tundra 16, 50
turkey vulture 102

U

UFO Watchtower & Campground 81, 210
ultraviolet rays 26
Upper Sand Creek Lake 162, 175
Upper Sand Creek Lake Trail 162
Ute Café 88
Ute Creek RV Park 81
Ute people 58, 60, 65, 143

V

Valdez, Andrew (geologist) 40, 43
Valley Farmers' Market 209, 213
Visitor Center 72, 74
Visitor Center Interpretative Trail 120, 122, 130
Volunteer-in-Park (VIP) Program 33, 57

W

water 28, 46- 47, 145
water bar 125
weather 36
Wellington cabin 149
Wellington Ditch 64
Wellington Ditch Trail 64, 148-149
Wellington, Frank 149
Westcliffe 155, 159, 163
western meadowlark 102
Wet Mountain Range 160, 169, 171
Wet Mountain Valley 154, 163, 169
White Eagle Village 84
white fir 50
White Marble Halls Cave 165-168
whooping crane 54, 101
wickiup 59
wild rose 50
Willow Lakes 192
Willow Lakes Trail 192
Willow Spring B&B 84
winter hike 171
winter-fat 49, 50, 125
Wolf Springs Ranch 156
woodpecker 54

Visitor Center 72, 74

Y

yarrow 49-50
yucca 49, 125

Z

Zapata Creek 177
Zapata Falls 69, 176-177
Zapata Falls Recreation Area 100, 113, 176-181
Zapata Falls Trail 177
Zapata Ranch 69
Zapata River 69

MEET THE AUTHORS

Charlie Winger began hiking and climbing in the mid-seventies when he moved to Colorado. Over the past 25+ years, he has developed strong mountaineering skills. Charlie has climbed and hiked extensively, including the 200 highest peaks in Colorado, the 100 highest peaks in the lower 48 states, and the 50 State highpoints of the United States.

Charlie has also climbed technical peaks in many parts of the world, including Alaska, Chile, Peru, Bolivia, Ecuador, Nepal, India, Switzerland, Iceland, Russia, Canada and Mexico. His favorite outdoor activity is ice climbing — ascending frozen waterfalls using ice tools (special ice axes) and crampons. A sport designed for lunatics!

Diane Winger didn't begin hiking until the late 1980s, although she has lived in Colorado all her life. She also became interested in technical rock climbing, and has enjoyed climbing at local areas, such as Eldorado Canyon near Boulder, Colorado, as well as numerous visits to her favorite out-of-state climbing area, Joshua Tree National Park in California. Most of her hiking has been in Colorado, although her favorite outdoor activity is trekking — she and Charlie have enjoyed 4-day walks along the Milford and Keppler Tracks in New Zealand and along the Inca Trail to Machu Picchu in Peru.

The Wingers live within 50 miles of the Great Sand Dunes near Beulah, Colorado and are the authors of *Highpoint Adventures: The Complete Guide to the 50 State Highpoints* (Colorado Mountain Club Press: 2002).

PHOTO AND ARTWORK CREDITS

All photography by **Charlie** and **Diane Winger**, except as noted below. All copyrights are the property of the individual.

Aaron Locander: title page, pgs. 6, 18 (back), 20 (back), 38, 40, 61, 216 (back), 226

Courtesy of The **Colorado Mountain Club**: page 60, 239

David Anschicks: pgs. 186, 187

Nelson Chenkin: pgs. 29, 36, 66 (lower), 71, 104 (upper)

Kris Illenberger: pgs. 4-5, 116 (lower)

Courtesy of the **National Park Service:** pgs. 34 (back), 44 (upper), 45 (lower), 49 (first and third from top), 50 (first and third from top), 51 (lower), 53 (all), 56 (upper), 92, 94, 100 (upper), 115 (upper), 116 (upper), 200

Mike Endres: page 239

Phyllis M. Pineda: title page (tiger beetle), pg. 55 (tiger beetle)

Terry Root: pgs. 54 (all), 100 (lower), 102 (all), 118 (second and third from top), 128 (upper), 189, 191

Artwork: *Sandy the Tiger Beetle* by **Lisa Gardiner**

ABOUT THE COLORADO MOUNTAIN CLUB

The Colorado Mountain Club is a non-profit outdoor recreation, education and conservation organization founded in 1912. Today with over 10,000 members, 14 branches in-state, and one branch for out-of-state members, the CMC is the largest organization of its kind in the Rocky Mountains. *Membership opens the door to:*

Outdoor Recreation: *Over 3100 trips and outings led annually.* Hike, ski, climb, backpack, snowshoe, bicycle, ice skate, travel the world and build firendships that will last a lifetime.

Conservation: *Supporting a mission which treasures our natural environment.* Committed to environmental education, a strong voice on public lands management, trail building and rehabilitation projects.

Outdoor Education: *Schools, seminars, and courses that teach outdoor skills through hands-on activities.* Wilderness trekking, rock climbing, high altitude mountaineering, telemark skiing, backpacking and much more — plus the Mountain Discovery Program designed to inspire lifelong stewardship in children and young adults.

Publications: *A wide range of outdoor publications to benefit and inform members.* Trail and Timberline Magazine, twice-a-year Activity Schedule, monthly group newsletters, and 20% discount on titles from CMC Press.

The American Mountaineering Center: *A world-class facility in Golden, Colorado.* Featuring the largest mountaineering library in the western hemisphere, a mountaineering museum, a 300-seat, state-of-the-art auditorium, a conference center, free monthly program nights and a technical climbing wall.

Visit us at the beautiful American Mountaineering Center!

JOINING IS EASY!

Membership opens the door to:
ADVENTURE!

The Colorado Mountain Club
710 10th St. #200 Golden, CO 80401
(303) 279-3080 1(800) 633-4417
FAX (303) 279-9690
Email: cmcoffice@cmc.org
Website: www.cmc.org

CPSIA information can be obtained at www.ICGtesting.com
Printed in the USA
LVOW030416270911

247892LV00003B/2/P